# Breaking
## the
### Silence

# Breaking
## the
### Silence

Little Rock's
Women's Emergency Committee
to Open Our Schools, 1958–1963

By Sara Alderman Murphy
Edited by Patrick C. Murphy II

The University of Arkansas Press
Fayetteville / 1997

01  00  99  98  97    5  4  3  2  1
First paperback printing 1997

*Designed by Liz Lester*

☉  The paper used in this publication meets the minimum requirements of the American National Standard for Permanence of Paper for Printed Library Materials Z39.48-1984.

*Library of Congress Cataloging-in-Publication Data*

Murphy, Sara Alderman, 1924–1995.
    Breaking the silence : Little Rock's Women's Emergency Committee to Open Our Schools, 1958–1963 / by Sara Alderman Murphy ; edited by Patrick C. Murphy, II.
        p.    cm.
    Includes bibliographical references (p. ) and index.
    ISBN 1-55728-456-3 (cloth: alk. paper)
    ISBN 1-55728-515-2 (paper: alk. paper)
    1. Segregation in education—Arkansas—Little Rock—History—20th century.    2. Women's Emergency Committee to Open Our Schools (Little Rock, Ark.)—History.    3. White women—Arkansas—Little Rock—Political activity—History—20th century.    4. Little Rock (Ark.)—Race relations.
    I. Murphy, Patrick C., 1952–    .  II. Title.
    LC212.523.L58M87    1997
    379.2'63'0976773—dc21                            97–2344
                                                     CIP

*This project is supported in part by a grant from the Arkansas Humanities Council and the National Endowment for the Humanities.*

For Sean, Ryan, Emily, and Robert . . .
Much love, Shoo Shoo

# Contents

# Illustrations

The following illustrations appear
after page 134.

# Preface

Sara Alderman Murphy, my mother, passed away on April 15, 1995, after battling cancer the last sixteen months of her life. Although she courageously continued to work on this manuscript through radiation treatments and chemotherapy as late as January of that year, her illness ultimately prevented her from completing the book as she had hoped.

Her ongoing commitment and support of early childhood education, her advocacy on issues affecting women, and her work with Betty Bumpers in Peace Links were natural extensions of her involvement with the Women's Emergency Committee to Open Our Schools and as a woman in the civil rights movement. I was privileged to have had the opportunity to work side by side with my mother on a number of research projects after she retired, and I am proud to have had some small role in helping complete this work. I also want to thank Victor Ray, who is part of this story, for his invaluable assistance and advice with the final editing.

I am extremely grateful to the many people who agreed to be interviewed for this book. My mother once commented that it is interesting how everyone's version puts themself at the center of the stage—but the stage is big enough for everyone. The important thing is for people to know that *women* were the leaders in getting the schools reopened and in changing attitudes. Certainly by standing up and letting themselves be heard, they were able to change the course of history.

History is a delicately woven fabric. What one person does hangs together only because of what others move in and do. It does not take away from the original design, but enriches and enlarges it and gives it more meaning. It is important for people to see that what they do at one stage opens the way for yet another phase, which builds on the sturdy foundation of what has gone before. My mother liked to quote Betty Bumpers's observation that once women started pursuing matters they felt strongly about, "it felt so good they never wanted to sit down again." Sara Murphy found her calling in Little Rock in 1958, and truly she never wanted to sit down again. I am proud of her and of the legacy she left for all of us.

Patrick C. Murphy II

# Foreword

This excerpt from the end of Lillian Smith's *Killers of the Dream* was read at Sara Murphy's funeral service at her request. She had read this passage at her friend Esther Brown's funeral in Kansas City some twenty-five years earlier:

> So it goes: violence and nonviolence; factual arguments and gobbledygook; quiet protest and noisy mob. Terrorism flares up in one town while the neighboring town is developing a courageous concern; sudden insights light up public opinion, foul words blur the situation, one act of heroism stirs the heart, one cruel incident pierces the conscience—then apathy creeps back, until another incident occurs.
>
> If only we could afford this zigzagging walk into the future! But each day the slowness becomes more dangerous. What will quicken us? What will illumine our minds? What can be said or done that will compel us to slough off inertia and complacency and take our stand for the human being against his unnumbered enemies? If only we could see the brokenness in each of us and the necessity for relationships; if we could rise up against the killers of the dream. But, sometimes, that killer of dreams is in us and we do not know how to rid ourselves of it.
>
> Once, long ago, a little crazy hypothesis was thrown across a dark sky and left there. And people could never forget it. Religions were built by its light, poets' minds shone in its brightness, political systems used its warmth to draw men closer together, and science examined it cautiously and "proved" it to be the essence of sanity, the seed of human growth. It may be only a bedtime story that men told themselves in their loneliness; it may be a lie; this sanctity of the human being, this importance of man the individual, this right of the child to grow, but when it is proved so, there will no longer be an earth to witness the lie's triumph and no men here to mourn the loss of their dream.

So we stand: tied to the past and clutching at the stars! Only by an agonizing pull of our dream can we wrench ourselves from such fixating stuff and climb into the unknown. But we have always done it and we can do it again. We have the means, the technics, we have the knowledge and insight and courage. All have synchronized for the first time in history. Do we have the desire? That is a question that each of us must answer for himself.

# Introduction

White women in the South have always been a little subversive. Perched on the pedestals where men placed them as long as they performed well in their half-person roles, they had a commanding view of the social landscape. It was not a pretty picture.

As Lillian Smith wrote in 1949, Southern white women saw bargains struck by their husbands to keep themselves at the top of a structure that condoned lynchings, while Jim Crow laws and segregated schools kept blacks in the cotton fields and the kitchens. Alliances were built with hate-mongering politicians and fundamentalist preachers to keep poor whites blaming blacks and other minorities for their own low status. And the wives of the men in power were treated like children who were too retarded to keep their own checkbooks or to be heard. Many of them were often put down and occasionally abused.

World War II brought a rising awareness of both the capacity of women to be more than housewives and of the rights of blacks to be more than second-class citizens. The Swedish author Gunnar Myrdal tied together the denial of rights to blacks and the earlier legal treatment of women and children as chattel. In his 1944 book *An American Dilemma,* which influenced the *Brown* decision a decade later, Myrdal wrote that "When a legal status had to be found for the imported Negro servants in the seventeenth century, the nearest and most natural analogy was the status of women and children." The earlier common law, which could invoke the Ninth Commandment in linking together women, servants, mules, and other property, provided the underpinning for the preindustrial paternalism that denied rights first to women and later to blacks. Myrdal predicted, citing a study done by his wife, Alva, that while barriers for blacks were much stronger than those for women, these would give way before a change came in the barriers for women, which he claimed were more "eternally inexorable."[1]

By the late 1940s, Lillian Smith gave shape and substance to the idea that segregation distorted and warped relationships between men and women as well as between blacks and whites in the South. Smith declared that many white women knew they were being used to prop up a system badly in need of dismantling when men placed them on pedestals of "sacred womanhood." However, a pedestal is a cold and lonely place, and Smith observed that the women "left it when no one was looking and explored a bit," adding that this was happening as far back as in her mother's day.

> These ladies went forth to commit a treason against a southern tradition set up by men who had betrayed their mothers, sometimes themselves, and many of the South's children white and mixed, for three long centuries. It was truly a subversive affair. . . . Shyly, these first women sneaked down from their chilly places, did their little sabotage and sneaked up again, wrapping innocence around them like a lace shawl. They set secret time bombs and went back to their needlework, serenely awaiting the blast.

Meanwhile, the men "whipped up lynchings, organized Klans, burned crosses, aroused the poor and ignorant to wild excitement by an obscene, perverse imagery describing the 'menace' of Negro men . . . waiting to rape our women," Smith wrote. "And not once did they dream their women did not believe their lies."[2]

Smith said that the Association of Southern Women for the Prevention of Lynching (ASWPL) in the 1930s finally brought the insurrectionists together as church women, "but churches were forgotten when the women spoke their revolutionary words."

> They said calmly that they were not afraid of being raped; as for their sacredness, they could take care of it themselves; they did not need the chivalry of a lynching to protect them and did not want it. Not only that . . . , but they would do everything in their power to keep any Negro from being lynched.

With this brave declaration "they aroused the conscience of the South and whole country about lynching and they tore a big piece of this evil out of southern tradition."[3]

Smith maintained that segregation was symbolic of the "tensions within and between human beings and of the walls that separate them from each other and from new ideas and experiences." Her passionate insistence that it should be abolished altogether, so that both blacks and whites could "grow into wholeness," put her at odds with some of the more moderate but highly respected writers in the white South (such as Hodding Carter, who called her a "strident old maid").[4] But her book provided a conceptual base that rang true for many Southern women. It encouraged them, including some in Little Rock, to trust their own instincts and experiences in challenging those who were willing to shut down institutions rather than integrate them.

■   ■   ■

My entry into the civil rights movement began in 1958. The year before, federal troops, and later a federalized National Guard, protected nine black children attending classes at Little Rock's Central High School. But in 1958, Gov. Orval Faubus closed the city's high schools to prevent further integration (during a special session of the state legislature in August 1956, he had been given the power to do just that). Mrs. D. D. Terry, the wife of a former congressman, called together a group of women who formed the Women's Emergency Committee to Open Our Schools (WEC). During the following year, we organized some fifteen hundred women who began to exert their collective power to oppose the segregationist control of the state and the school system. Many wanted to remain anonymous because they feared that their husbands' jobs would be lost. We were harassed by the White Citizens Council and were held in contempt by our own friends. We worked to prod the men into opposing what was happening. An American Association of University Women (AAUW) survey of business showed that the community was suffering from the economic impact of the school closings.

Our big chance came later in the year when segregationist members of the school board tried to purge a group of teachers for various reasons from the schools. A group of businessmen, egged on by the women, decided to recall the segregationist members of the board and, with the WEC doing the organizational work, put together a group called Stop This Outrageous Purge (STOP). The opposition organized its own group, the Committee to Retain Our Segregated Schools (CROSS), and worked to recall our three members of the school board. STOP won that battle, and the schools were reopened the following year.

Three years later in 1962, I ran for the Little Rock School Board as the first woman integrationist candidate. The opposition, a moderate segregationist whom we had backed in an earlier campaign, called me a Communist and a "fire that had to be put out." I received weird telephone calls, and there were some unpleasant incidents. I also lost the election.

But I was convinced that we could not go through the motions of school desegregation while at the same time trying to avoid it, that what we needed was a massive community reeducation effort. So in 1963 I organized a group called the Little Rock Panel of American Women; I consider this effort to be the most important thing I have done.

The panel was my chief outlet for staying involved. It consisted of about thirty women who represented different religious and racial groups in the community. The panel, a force in its time because it was so different from anything else, was made up of young mothers and housewives (not many of us had careers then) who talked informally about how prejudice had affected their lives and the lives of their children. Each group had a Catholic, a Jew, a black, sometimes another minority, and a white Protestant, who each spoke briefly, using personal anecdotes, and then answered questions from the audience. They asked all kinds of things from "Do you want your daughter to marry one?" to "Why don't the Jews believe in Jesus?" We became very good at fielding questions.

The women spoke in churches and schools and before civic groups and helped them understand what the civil rights movement was all about. We learned a lot ourselves and helped to open up restaurants and communities where blacks had never before crossed over certain lines. It caused us to become more involved in political and community affairs. We elected people to the school board,

we started educational reform groups, and we worked in guberna-
torial races.

From one of the black panelists, Gwen Riley, who was honest, witty, and together, I learned what it was really like as a young
black mother. Her husband, Rev. Negail Riley, served as campus
minister at Wesley Chapel at Philander Smith College, and he helped
black college students get involved in the civil rights movement. I
sat in Gwen's kitchen and listened to some of the leaders in the civil
rights movement from across the South and heard the strategy
planned for integrating the lunch counters at Woolworth's in downtown Little Rock.

■   ■   ■

I have made notes on this story for years, and I eventually nar-
rowed the time frame for this book to the years surrounding the formation of the WEC in 1958 through the development of the Panel of
American Women in the early 1960s. This story is about working for
change as an ordinary woman. My premise is that ordinary women
are most effective when they "bloom where they are planted." They
also increase their power when they band together and support each
other. I think the organizing became a personal crusade for women.
They had been kept silent, held down, put into stereotypes, and not
listened to for so long that by the 1960s they were heady with their
own power.

Most of the work I have done was with white middle-class
women like myself. I understood where they were coming from,
what their anxieties were, what the emptiness of their lives could
be, and their enormous potential. This story about my involvement
in two important movements is my own effort to share the piece of
truth I know. Other women were more committed and brave than
I, others were more out front and participated on a grander scale; but
if I tried to tell their stories I would have to embellish on them,
because I do not know what went on inside them as they made their
stands. These women are a part of my story because of my profound
admiration for them (and, occasionally, irritation and impatience
with a few) as we worked together. My portraits of them will be as

I knew them. They were a remarkable bunch, all of them. For a small city, Little Rock had an incredible number of gifted, tough, courageous women at a time when there were few men who could meet that description. We were indeed bereft of male leadership. Governor Faubus could hardly be called a knight in shining armor, and there was a strangely silent white male-power structure for more than a year.

■　■　■

When I attended the first Women's Emergency Committee to Open Our Schools meeting, I knew little about the history of the Terry mansion. Because it was no ordinary place, the house held a kind of mythic or symbolic power over me. As I walked up the front brick steps, across the spacious columned veranda, and through the front door, I sensed that the house itself was inextricably linked to the mission we were setting about.

The sadness of all our Southern pasts hung suspended like cobwebs in its rooms. By coming together as women, we could perhaps sweep them out of our lives and out of the life of our community. No one was more aware of the need to do that than was Adolphine Fletcher Terry, who because she lived there, was profoundly shaped by the house's past but recognized the need for the house—and all of Little Rock—to move toward a new era when it would symbolize something better. I felt fortunate to know these women, some of whom became my mentors as well as my friends, from all of whom I learned much more than I was able to teach. Their story needs to be told, and I can only tell it accurately by telling my own. The change for me was greater than for any we attempted to change.

# ■ 1 ■

# Adolphine Fletcher Terry

In the summer of 1889, when she was seven years old, Adolphine Fletcher moved into the legendary white-columned Little Rock house that was to be her home until she died. It was the "state's grandest mansion," built in 1840 by Albert Pike, a man of great intellect and unbridled temperament, who wrote both poetry and prose, fought in duels and in two wars, practiced law, and edited a Whig newspaper.

John Gould Fletcher Jr., Adolphine's younger brother and a Pulitzer Prize–winning poet, described Pike as Arkansas's "most eminent man," with accomplishments that qualified him as a "Southern gentleman of the old school." He emerged from the Civil War as a Confederate general and rose to be a national figure in the world of Free Masonry.[1]

Pike was less highly thought of north of the Mason-Dixon line, where stories circulated about atrocities, including the scalping of Federal soldiers by Indian troops under his command. In fact, after the war, he was so unwelcome in New York (where he was called an uncivilized butcher) that he fled to Canada and later settled in Washington, D.C.[2]

Young John, however, was caught up in the wonder and romanticism of growing up in the mansion Pike had built: "It was from this house, with its ten lofty rooms, its wide hall with great folding doors, its six white columns, its green wooden-shuttered windows, its broad lawn dotted with oaks two hundred years old, vast locust and magnolia trees, that I learned what it was to have been a southerner of the aristocratic sort in the days before the Civil War. The flavor of the old South hung about that house and hangs about it still."[3]

The splendor of her new home was somewhat offset for the imaginative and energetic Adolphine, however, by the fact that it was whispered around that the ghost of Mary Ann Hamilton Pike, the wife of the original owner, might still be roaming about. At bedtime, Adolphine, her brother John, and Cordelia, a black girl who lived with the family, would scamper cautiously together up the back stairway to an arched, curtained landing. From there, they raced in the dark, terrified, to their beds, hoping to avoid any encounters with the supernatural Mrs. Pike.[4] John also reported, "it was said that the old lady's ghost had been frequently seen in the library downstairs, rocking herself in a certain rocking chair."[5] Adolphine wrote later:

> Naturally neither Cordelia, John nor I ever talked over these things among ourselves nor with the adults. . . . Instinctively we felt that the terror would become more real if it were discussed— and even worse you might be laughed at. But we were all affected by it. As grown-ups Cordelia and I have faced the situation together and John, who became a poet, made a record of his emotions in *Ghosts of an Old House*.[6]

Adolphine, curious as she grew older to know the real story, learned that prior to her marriage, Mrs. Pike had lost her entire family in a boating accident on the Arkansas River. A frail, beautiful woman, Mary might have recovered from that tragedy had her marriage to the "witty, brilliant, [and] difficult" Albert Pike not been such a rocky one.[7]

"She had this house to cope with and she had a baby every year because nobody had ever heard of birth control," Adolphine wrote. Then she buried child after child—five of the eight boys and one of the two girls. Two died during what Adolphine called "the dreaded second summer, a period of life which, before the advent of modern methods for handling of milk, filled the cemeteries with infant graves." Another older child fell into a pile of burning leaves, one drowned in the Arkansas River, Indians killed another during the Civil War, and her oldest daughter took her own life.[8]

Mary Pike got little support from her famous husband, who spent much of his time away.[9] Even when he was home, their communication left much to be desired. One day (so one of the stories older neighbors told Adolphine went) Albert Pike sent word to Mary to prepare a light supper for friends he was bringing home that night. When they arrived, she ushered them into the dining room where they were greeted with candles blazing everywhere but nothing else.[10]

General Pike left Little Rock permanently after the Civil War, taking his two daughters but not his wife, whom he left alone in the huge Little Rock home. He became editor of the *Memphis Appeal* for two years before moving north and later settling in Washington.[11]

When her beloved daughter Isadore committed suicide in Memphis, Mary Pike was not notified. She read about it in the morning paper and screamed so loud that neighbors heard her several houses away. When her mind began to unravel toward the end of her life, one of the neighbors finally took her in.[12]

While extolling the accomplishments of her husband in his history of Arkansas, John Gould Fletcher dismissed Mary Pike as "a vivacious brunette . . . and, as it later developed, a woman of violent, ungovernable temper."[13] Both John and Adolphine recalled a childhood story of how an elderly Mrs. Pike once lashed out at a young black girl so strongly, the girl jumped out of an upstairs window and broke her leg.[14] But Adolphine suggests that some of Mary Pike's later irritability and inability to cope could have stemmed from both the loss of so many children and life with a "temperamental husband" who eventually left her.[15] Adolphine also observed in another context that "the failure of a marriage was blamed on the woman."[16]

Whatever the reason, Adolphine's childhood ghost had suffered more than her share of ordeals and was thought by the superstitious to have good reason to return to the scene of her earthly anguish. The ever-practical Adolphine felt compelled to explain that when the gas lights used in her childhood were replaced with electric lights that illuminated homes better, most ghosts, including that of Mary Pike, tended to disappear.[17]

The Pikes' surviving daughter, Lilian, first rented the family home to the Arkansas Female College in 1871, and then fifteen years later sold it to Adolphine's unmarried aunt, Loudovica Krause, who continued to run a school there for three more years. When the school went under financially in 1889, Adolphine's father bought the house from her Aunt Lou, who left the night they moved in and was never heard from again. Although the family later learned that Loudovica Krause was living in eastern Texas, her humiliation at the school's failure apparently accounted for both her dramatic departure and the severing of family ties.[18]

Adolphine's father, John G. Fletcher, and a friend, Peter Hotze, returned to Little Rock after serving in the Civil War together to open Fletcher and Hotze, a general store. They expanded their business interests in 1867—a bumper year for cotton in Arkansas—when they bought up all the cotton for miles around. When they attempted to send it down the river to market at New Orleans, they found all the boats already loaded with other people's cotton. It was six weeks before the Fletcher-Hotze cotton could be moved south and, as luck would have it, during that time the price of cotton in New Orleans spiraled upward. The two men made twenty thousand dollars, a postwar fortune large enough to establish them as men of means and prominence.

Fletcher was a well-to-do banker and the mayor of Little Rock (he had also been the first sheriff of Pulaski County) by the time he married Adolphine Krause in 1876. They lived for a while in the Krause family residence above two stores at Cherry and Main Streets. Six years later, baby Adolphine arrived (unfortunately acquiring her mother's unwieldy Germanic name, a feminized version of Simon Adolph, the child's great-grandfather).

The family then moved into more spacious quarters, renting Senator Garland's home at Fourteenth and Scott Streets. When they were unable to purchase the senator's home, they decided to buy the school from Loudovica and restore it to the stately residence it had once been.[19]

■   ▓   ■

Cordelia came to the Fletcher residence as a young child to live with her aunt, Mary Durham, in a small house in the backyard. When Durham became too ill to work and had to leave, Cordelia became a "member of the household," as Adolphine's mother later described her to a census taker. She moved into the big house where she did small chores and helped keep track of the Fletcher children. Adolphine, two years younger than Cordelia (whom she called "her black sister"), later surmised that her mother's fear that she and John might be kidnapped was at least one reason for Cordelia's presence.

Cordelia stayed until she finished both high school and college, after which time she became a missionary to Africa before returning to teach at Little Rock.[20] Her high interest in education was undoubtedly intensified by growing up in the Fletcher household, although both she and Adolphine gave much of the credit to an unusual teacher named Charlotte Stephens.

Stephens first taught Cordelia in the segregated black Arsenal School, located across the street from the white Sherman School, which Adolphine attended, just a block from the mansion. Both schools were drab, unpainted wooden buildings that looked alike on the outside. They served as stark reminders of the high cost exacted from white as well as black children for maintaining segregation in an impoverished post–Civil War South. Adolphine later wrote that "our school was as devoid of educational frills as theirs."[21]

Still, segregation itself was the caste system's way of attempting to etch a sense of inferiority on black children's minds. Charlotte Stephens, Little Rock's first black school teacher, was a strong, confident person who worked to dispel that kind of feeling in her students. She encouraged Cordelia to become a teacher by telling her stories of how some blacks, including her own father, had helped other blacks overcome almost insurmountable difficulties in getting an education. The story about Charlotte's father, Wallace Andrews, who was born a slave, was included in the two books Adolphine later wrote, *Cordelia: Member of the Household* and *Charlotte Stephens: Little Rock's First Black Teacher*.

According to Adolphine's accounts, prior to the Civil War, many Southern states had laws prohibiting the education of black slaves. In Arkansas, although there was no law against it, slaves could be severely punished if caught attempting to read and write. Wallace Andrews was taught as a child to read by his mistress, Mrs. Chester

Ashley, who, because she was white, was able to ignore the unwritten ban.

Andrews, as one of the few light-skinned, literate slaves around, rose to be butler in the Ashley household. He spent his off hours reading the Bible and preaching to other slaves in the evenings, activities heartily endorsed by the whites. They were not aware, however, that when Andrews held prayer meetings in his house, he also discussed with his fellow worshippers their potential for learning to read and write. "You cannot serve the Lord better than by using your mind," he would tell them. Resistance to slavery was growing, he said, and their lives would change when they were free. Some were afraid to listen to him and left, but he placed books on the chair seats for those who remained. He then told them to kneel before the chairs because nobody would stop them from praying. During prayer meeting he taught them to decipher the words on the printed pages in front of their lowered heads until they were reading on their own.[22]

The Pike mansion was only a few blocks away from the Ashley home, and both Albert Pike and Adolphine's father had been slave owners before the Civil War. Her mother, however, was an artistic and well-read person who maintained an attitude of openness toward blacks and an interest in helping them do well. Her mother's early teachings, combined with the closeness she felt toward Cordelia, caused young Adolphine to question some of the prevailing white beliefs about blacks.

Adolphine recalled in her memoirs a visit that Molly, an older cousin who lived on a nearby plantation, made to their home when Adolphine was ten years old. Molly appeared at breakfast one morning visibly upset.

"We must call the police at once," Adolphine reported Molly as saying. "My diamond ring has been stolen off the night stand where I left it. I'm sure it must have been Fred who took it."

Fred was a trusted black teenager who worked for the Fletchers, and Mrs. Fletcher brushed aside Molly's assumption. "Fred would not have done something like that," she said. "Why don't you and Adolphine go look for it out in the part of the yard where you were yesterday?" Molly unhappily followed her younger cousin outside to hunt for the ring. Suddenly Molly spotted it caught in a flounce on her full-skirted dress and shouted, "My ring—it's here on my dress!" She conveniently forgot she had minutes before accused Fred of taking it, but Adolphine remembered. Years later she was to write:

> I had already come to recognize the fact that black people had very little chance to hold their own in an argument with a white person. I visualized what it would have done to Fred, a decent 17-year-old . . . if he had been taken off to jail . . . while we continued to search for the ring and perhaps never found it. . . . In all my life, I think I have never accused anybody of taking anything. I would rather lose a material thing, even if it had some financial value, than take the risk of accusing a person unjustly.[23]

Adolphine, however, still clung to her share of the notions passed down through a segregated society when she enrolled as a student at Vassar College in 1898. She traveled by train with her father to Poughkeepsie, New York, and upon her arrival was overcome with homesickness, dissolving into tears when she saw the college. As only the second person from Arkansas to go to Vassar (the first, Blanche Martin, who was to become her best friend, helped tutor her for the entrance examination), she felt out of place and estranged. One evening in a heated dormitory discussion about lynching, Adolphine reverted to a Southern saying she had heard all her life, although, she carefully pointed out, not from her family.

"If a black man rapes a white woman, he deserves to be lynched," Adolphine exclaimed. A fellow student, Lucy Burns from Brooklyn, gave her a shocked look. "You don't really believe that revenge on one poor black wretch is more important than maintaining a system of law and order for the whole community, do you?" Burns asked. Adolphine wished she had been less quick to speak.

> I knew she was right and it really has affected my entire life. It gave me an entirely different look, an adult look, at the situation which we faced here in the South. . . . I think that was

the beginning of my spiritual education and the beginning of wisdom, and learning not to accept a thing because everybody in the community was saying it.[24]

Her homesickness soon dissolved, and she stayed at Vassar until she graduated, returning to Little Rock and the big house with broadened ideas and determination. "She came out of Vassar in 1902 ready to change the world and she kept trying until her dying day to do it," an old friend and fellow conspirator, Judge Edwin Dunaway, declared.[25] Adolphine did not, however, avoid the social whirl during or after college when she returned to Little Rock. She became a debutante and served as a bridesmaid in at least ten of her friends' weddings. She recalled her cousin's wedding the summer before she finished Vassar at which she wore a white dress with pink ribbons and carried pink sweet peas. She was hanging greenery just before that wedding when she met her first boyfriend, whom she circumspectly referred to as Mr. Abbot, adding that he spoke French. Although she claimed not to be in love with him, Mr. Abbot did cause her to enroll in French at Vassar, which she flunked and had to make up. Adolphine left this advice for other inexperienced young women:

> The experience of having a beau was a valuable thing. I began to learn a secret that all girls should learn early, and that is the secret of carrying on a conversation with a man, any man. Men love to talk about themselves. A girl may think they are interested in her, and perhaps they are to a certain extent, but they are much more interested in themselves. All a girl has to do is listen to any man, just turn him on and let him talk and he will have an enjoyable time.[26]

Having mastered this lesson with Mr. Abbot, she parted company with him. The following year she put her energy into a two-woman campaign that she and her Vassar friend, Blanche Martin, were conducting to promote school consolidation in Arkansas. They wrote articles for small-town newspapers, made speeches, and lobbied. The two succeeded in getting consolidation on the state's legislative agenda at a time when the state had five thousand school districts (consisting mostly of one-room schools that went through the eighth grade) and only thirty high schools.[27]

When her father died in 1906, Adolphine inherited a large portion of downtown real estate, which made her a financially independent and powerful woman. She became engaged shortly before her father's death to David D. Terry, an affable, easygoing lawyer who was able to listen to her as well as to talk about himself. The blond, curly-haired Dave, whom she did not refer to as "Mr. Terry," took a year and a half of further graduate study at the University of Chicago. That and her mother's illness caused the engagement to be extended for four years. Her mother, who had developed cancer, insisted they not marry until after she died because she wanted Adolphine close by after John, on whom she doted, had upset her by dropping out of Harvard and going off to live in Europe. Also, she had postponed her own marriage to John Fletcher until her mother's death.

Six weeks after her mother died in 1909, Adolphine and Dave finally were married in the front parlor of the mansion. Only a handful of friends, relatives, and black servants who had previously worked for the family were present. Adolphine told younger family members later "there were more blacks than whites at my wedding."[28]

She settled with her new husband in the mansion that had been her childhood home and somewhat reluctantly followed the custom of wearing black for a year to mourn the loss of her mother. She implied later that wearing brighter colors would have better reflected her own mood at the time. "Dave and I hit it off very well indeed," she wrote. "We really loved each other and in addition, we thought the same things were amusing."

Shortly after the birth of her first son, David, Adolphine Terry was recruited to chair a newly established juvenile court board. She became personally involved with the problem children she met, taking one of them, a girl whose sister worked in the city's red-light district, into her home for a while. She helped start an industrial school for girl juvenile offenders (one was already available for boys) and lured her friend Blanche Martin for the role of head administrator. When Martin resigned because of political appointments made to her staff by a governor neither of them liked, Terry also resigned as chair of the industrial school board. She continued, however, to chair the juvenile court board for nineteen years.[29]

Two years later, her joy in the arrival of a daughter, whom she named Mary after her younger sister, was short lived. When the baby was a few days old Adolphine discovered that both of the child's legs had been broken before birth and that she suffered from a fragile bone structure that would continue to cause frequent and painful fractures. (Her sister later told younger family members that Adolphine cried for two years after Mary was born.) Terry took her daughter to several specialists over the country for ten years while Mary's bones continued to crack and she gradually became more crippled.

From her wheelchair, Mary became, like her mother, a strong, independent thinker and an ardent supporter of her mother's causes, but Adolphine struggled for a long while with the grief she felt over her daughter's imperfect physical condition. By writing a book, *Courage,* under the assumed name of Mary Lindsey, she was finally able to talk about it. After telling about the setbacks and accomplishments of her daughter, called "Anne" in the book, Terry wrote:

> The peace which has come to me is, I think, partly the result of decisions I made long ago. When I resolved that I would accept Anne as she actually was, and give way to no more sorrowful day-dreaming about her, I pulled down a shade over what she might have been. Now if I should look behind the shade, the place would be empty. . . . I can see her as she is, and rejoice in her attainments without regret over the fact that she is, in certain ways, less well favored than other people.[30]

When women were struggling to get the vote, Adolphine's sister, Mary, who was still single, served as president of the local suffragist group. Although limited in her activities by the attention her daughter required, Adolphine marched in more than one of the equal rights parades held in downtown Little Rock.[31]

Terry also held a "home meeting" for a White House "picketer," Jane Pincus, who was in Little Rock to address an "open air meeting" downtown on November 10, 1917. Pincus, who was to speak from an automobile decorated in National Women's Party banners, said in an interview: "The White House pickets merely walked up and down with such banners as will be shown on our car. . . . It was the onlookers who blocked traffic. There was no disturbance except when the pickets were arrested. The arrests were illegal."[32]

Terry recalled much later that, despite the disclaimers Pincus made, suffragists "acted like complete hellions to get the vote. We of the 'lady' class had always been on a pedestal, . . . beauteous womanhood, all that kind of junk. The men had looked up to us, idolized us. They changed their attitude when we tied ourselves to telephone poles and did the most unseemly and unladylike things to attract attention to our cause."[33]

In the meantime, black women in Little Rock, while not a part of the local suffragist movement, were making a name for themselves as leaders in a different venture. A group of them had run such a highly successful hospitality program for black soldiers during World War I that the national Young Women's Christian Association gave them forty thousand dollars in the early 1920s to start their own YWCA. Terry said that because the local white "Y" would not "touch it with a forty-foot pole," three white women, of which she was one, were added as advisers. She agreed to serve, although she felt their appointments might be an affront to the black women, whom she considered capable of running their own program. It turned into a real learning experience for the white advisers. As a member of the newly formed Phyllis Wheatley YWCA board, Terry got to know black women who were "well educated and leaders in the community with plenty of ideas of their own."

> We got more out of the experience than we gave, because we made friends among these black women who since the Civil War had never been thought of as possible friends of ours, and who had lived in a world apart. They were the wives of professional men, and they provided us with an education. We, the daughters of Confederate veterans who had heard a great deal about the white side of the war, now learned of the suffering of the black population, before, during and after the war, and of all the lacks from which they still suffered.[34]

Terry was concerned when a lynching whipped up a new wave of hatred of blacks at Little Rock in the spring of 1927, but she downplayed its importance. She considered the whites who participated as a fringe element living in a world far removed from her own and felt Little Rock otherwise had made good progress in race relations.

Still, the lynching exposed a festering sore that was always just beneath the surface in the seemingly civilized way the segregated life of the city was ordered. And black leaders knew well that lynching was the acting out by a few of the broad and deep animosity many other whites felt. Most shocking and ominous to them was the fact that the burning of the lynching victim took place in the center of town, near a major black church, and that neither the police nor the sheriff's office tried to stop the lynchers.

The trouble began when the body of a white twelve-year-old girl, Floella McDonald, was found in the belfry of Little Rock's First Presbyterian Church, just two blocks from the Terry home. The black sexton was first jailed as the likeliest suspect, and then his fifteen-year-old son, Lonnie Dixon, was accused and confessed. A mob of several thousand stormed first the city jail and then the state penitentiary, demanding that the boy and his father, who was still being held, be turned over to them. Law enforcement officers, however, whisked them out of town. The mayor promised even before Lonnie was tried that he would be executed (he was executed on his sixteenth birthday). They had not, however, quelled the mob's thirst for a lynching.

Four days later, a second mob converged on a retarded black man, John Carter, who was accused of having climbed on a wagon in which two white women were riding just outside of town. Reports of the wagon incident were hazy (there was no charge of rape), but what subsequently happened was quite clear. In a savage display of pent-up hatred, a group of white men hunted down Carter, made him stand on a car with a noose around his neck, and drove the car out from under him. They riddled him with some two hundred bullets and dragged his body behind a car into town as part of a horn-blowing, shrieking caravan of lynchers. At the edge of the black business district at Ninth and Broadway, the mob, which had grown considerably larger and included women, placed Carter's body on the streetcar tracks and burned it. A black woman who was fifteen years old at the time recalled their "blood-curdling cries" and the fact that the mob chopped up the Bethel AME Church pews to build their fire. Another woman remembered "the flames leaping high into the sky; and the noise of the running, screaming mob."[35]

J. N. Heiskell, a lone voice of protest in the community, wrote in an *Arkansas Gazette* editorial that "the city of Little Rock suffered last night the shame of being delivered over to anarchy. Little Rock and Pulaski County must demand an accounting from the officers who have failed us."[36]

That was Little Rock's last lynching. From 1882 until 1930, 294 persons had been lynched in Arkansas, 230 of whom were black. During the 1920s, 13 lynchings occurred in the state, and during the 1930s, only 2 took place. The lynching figures fell throughout the South, from 260 for 1922–33 to 49 for 1934–37.[37]

Terry recalled that there had been only one other Little Rock lynching in the more than ninety years that she had lived in Little Rock. The first was in 1892 when she was ten years old. Of the 1927 event, she said, "A very small crowd took the man and all the people just fell back and the professional people, the police, the sheriff, nobody tried to save this Negro and he was lynched." Dave Terry's sister and her husband from Massachusetts were visiting Little Rock on their first trip south after their marriage when the 1927 lynching and burning occurred. The wild, sadistic noises from Ninth and Broadway and the flames reddening the sky could be heard and seen at Terry's home, only eight blocks away. Terry and her visitors from the north stood on the lawn—ironically under magnolia trees, those symbols of gracious Southern living—to watch from a distance the horrible aftermath of Little Rock's last lynching.[38]

Terry believed the lynching was a spontaneous action of hate and was disconnected with any organization. She told interviewer John Pagan that "I've never found a record or has any lawyer ever told me about there being an organized Ku Klux Klan in Little Rock after the war."

Actually, thousands had joined the Arkansas Ku Klux Klan when it was in its heyday during the early 1920s. Four years before the mob incident, a lawyer named James A. Comer, the Exalted

Cyclops of Little Rock Klan No. 1, had offered on behalf of the KKK to build a municipal auditorium for Little Rock if the Klan could hold its meetings there. The offer was declined. Edwin Dunaway recalled,

> At that time, they [the Klan] had planned parades on Main Street. They'd go down Main Street with torches and robes and riding on horses and I can remember what a sight it was. They controlled politics in this county and in some parts of the state.[39]

During the early 1920s, Dunaway's father, who was prosecuting attorney in Pulaski County, ran for Congress on an anti-KKK ticket and lost to Hartsell Ragon from Clarksville, the KKK candidate. Congressman Brooks Hays's father, Steele Hays, was also a losing candidate in that race.

Little Rock was the headquarters for the national Women's Klan, headed by Robbie Gill Comer, the wife of James Comer. Annie Griffey, a neighbor of Dunaway's family when they lived on Battery Street, was assistant superintendent of schools and belonged to the Women's Klan, whose headquarters was in a large home at Seventeenth and Main.[40]

Terry had two other children, Sally and Bill, and adopted still another one, Joe. Bill, like his older brother, was a healthy child, but Sally developed mental and emotional disabilities that were to cause distress to her parents as Mary's physical handicap had already done.

Joe joined the family after fourteen-year-old Mary became attached to him while spending time in a Boston hospital. Joe was a baby then, a ward of the hospital, and he was suffering from a bad case of eczema on his face. Mary insisted that she take him home with her, and her mother, who could not refuse Mary anything, relented. When Dave Terry came to pick them up at the train station, he found Mary in her wheelchair, their three other children, and Adolphine holding a baby whose face was smeared with black salve. Even the good-natured Dave was a bit taken back, but he agreed that the baby, Joe, would become their fifth child.[41]

■   ■   ■

Terry cut her teeth in politics when her father ran for governor three times, and the fact that he lost each time did not diminish her love for it. According to her son Bill, she, rather than her husband, was the politician in the family: "She probably was the one who suggested that [my father] go into politics." Dunaway said that Mr. Dave Terry was a "very fine man, a good solid citizen," but agreed that he did not have the burning interest in political races that Adolphine had. With her help, however, he won five terms in the U.S. House of Representatives, where his father before him had served for ten years.

Dave Terry's headquarters for his first congressional race in 1933 against Brooks Hays and Sam Rorex was in the old, run-down Southern Hotel, which Adolphine Terry and her sister, Mary Drennan, owned, at Markham and Main Streets. Dunaway recalled that he was there election night as the returns came in:

> Terry was trailing Brooks Hays considerably. Everybody gave up and said he was beat. . . . Sam Rorex was scheduled to carry Yell County, a machine county, [for Hays]. . . . This was before air conditioning [and] it was hotter than the dickens. Everybody had gone home. Mr. Dave had gone home and gone to bed. Miss Adolphine and I were sitting in some cane bottom chairs out on Markham Street to get a little air. The phone rang inside and I . . . answered it and they wanted her. She went to the phone. . . . [T]he message was that Sam couldn't make it and Mr. Terry . . . was going to get enough votes to be in the runoff with Brooks Hays. She called Mr. Dave and he put on his clothes, came back, started up the campaign again and won.[42]

Adolphine made the ultimate political concession to help her husband's second campaign for Congress by accepting the presidency of the local American Legion Auxiliary. In a humorous vein she wrote, "It was the last thing I wanted to do but I felt I would be repaid if I heard that the wife of one of Dave's opponents bit herself when she read the news in the morning paper and gave herself hydrophobia."

She also headed up the state American Legion Auxiliary's committee on Americanism, a word that she said "was not popular with me" until she learned that her duties included establishing libraries, something she did believe in. Arkansas had been identified as "the most bookless state in the Union" by the national Legion Auxiliary, and it fell Terry's lot, as Americanism chair, to attempt to rectify that. There were only three "feebly functioning" libraries then, with the rest closed down by the Depression. Terry succeeded in getting American Legions across the state to set up libraries in more than one hundred of their trim little brick legion huts. She begged and borrowed books from the libraries of well-to-do friends and their heirs to stock the legion libraries. Her efforts led the state legislature to enact a state library program.[43]

Few businesses were able to pay rent on time for the buildings she owned during the Depression, and despite the family wealth, Adolphine Terry suffered from a persistent lack of cash. Dunaway recalled that she came across the street to his mother's door bringing a dozen of her own Royal Doulton cups and saucers in a shoe box as a wedding present for his sister. All during the Depression, however, "her back door was a place where people came daily by the dozens for a handout and she never turned anybody away."[44]

Both Terrys were staunch Democrats and as such supported Pres. Franklin Roosevelt's New Deal legislation, which helped to alter the Depression-ridden landscape in Arkansas. Adolphine Terry, who became president of the Congressional Wives Club in Washington, also became acquainted with Eleanor Roosevelt, about whom she wrote:

> Eleanor was a wonderful woman. I think she had a great deal to do with his becoming president. . . . Before she became the first lady she had a strident, harsh voice; it was the worst radio voice I had ever heard. Her remarks usually ended up with a silly little nervous giggle, which was most distracting. I don't know what she did, probably she took speech lessons, . . . for by the time Dave went to Washington a year later, her voice was well modulated, she had dropped the nervous giggle and was a polished speaker.
>
> As the president's wife she dressed very well. She had style and beauty of a strange kind. . . . She was very tall and thin and erect and was always extremely well dressed in clothes that

were quite unusual. She spoke with assurance and great dignity, and to me it seemed, with great charm. I greatly admired her and it irritates me that all these years afterward some of their children have worked up stories that reflect badly on them.[45]

With the memory of Little Rock's last lynching still vivid in her mind, Terry gave her support in the late 1930s to the Association of Southern Women to Prevent Lynching (ASWPL). This organization set out to create a mindshift about lynching in communities across the South in 1930. By the end of the decade, it had attracted forty-four thousand mainstream Southern churchwomen to its ranks.[46] The ASWPL was not integrated, nor did it attack segregation as such. It became important, however, because it caused white church women to examine the moral teachings of their churches and synagogues and recognize how far afield from those were the atrocities and injustices against blacks they saw being committed around them.

As a congressman's wife, Terry lent credibility to the Arkansas chapter of the ASWPL by serving on the fifteen-member state council in 1937 along with Erle Chambers, the state's first woman legislator, and Mrs. W. P. McDermott, later president of the Little Rock School Board. The Arkansas council sought to get the ASWPL's word out to as many white women as possible by asking how they in good conscience could seek to convert the heathens overseas when brutal lynchings were taking place in their own backyard. The message hit home, for the state Methodist Woman's Missionary Societies and the Baptist Woman's Missionary Unions signed on, as did the Arkansas Federation of Women's Clubs, the Arkansas Democratic Women's Clubs, and the Little Rock branch of the American Association of University Women (AAUW), of which Terry was a founding member.[47] In the same year, Arkansas proudly announced that no lynchings had occurred and several had been prevented. The state council sent letters to sheriffs and other peace officers asking them to sign anti-lynching pledges and mailed notes of appreciation to them when they had a hand in averting lynchings.

"Our Arkansas officials are wide awake to their responsibilities and making every effort for a lynchless state," the Arkansas report declared. In one case, "a lynching was prevented by the sheriff, the prosecuting attorney and a quick court trial given."[48] "Legal" lynchings, in which innocent blacks were sentenced to death, could and did occur. Removing the process from the streets did not guarantee that justice would be rendered. It was a step, however, toward making the courts and legal system face up to, rather than avoid, dealing with the Ku Klux Klan brand of vigilante violence.

The ASWPL had been founded in 1930 by an energetic Texan named Jessie Daniel Ames, who worked in Atlanta for the Council for Interracial Cooperation (CIC), one of the first and most influential organizations for bringing groups of blacks and whites together in the South. The CIC was headed by the widely respected Dr. Will Alexander, who often found Ames to be a thorn in his side. Before Ames joined the CIC, she had been a leader in the suffragist movement in Texas, where she had founded the Texas League of Women Voters, worked on social reform issues, and had a penchant for action.

A black CIC leader named Nannie Burroughs challenged Ames in one of the CIC meetings to do something about lynching. Burroughs said lynching "was carried on for the protection of white women and when the white women got ready to stop lynching, they'd stop it and it wouldn't be done before." Ames had found her niche.[49]

She spent the next decade organizing Southern white church and club women to change attitudes about lynching from acceptance and silence to abhorrence and action. The ASWPL pledge that the women signed put them on record against "an indefensible crime, destructive of all principles of government, hateful and hostile to every ideal of religion and humanity, debasing and degrading to every person involved."[50]

Once, the Associated Press notified Ames that a black man had escaped to Tennessee and a mob was looking for him. Ames located the chair of the Tennessee ASWPL council, who was visiting in a town north of Memphis. "Funny how a woman could stir up things if she wanted to," Ames recalled. "And she [the state chair] kept it so stirred up that the Negro got over into Arkansas, and he was out of their reach."[51]

The Arkansas ASWPL's own call to arms against lynching had a curious turn to it. The statement read:

That the degradation of women is the doom of any race and that among the number of underlying causes of the present racial situation in America is the lack of respect and protection for Negro womanhood. Recognizing with sympathetic appreciation the high standards of virtue set by the best element of Negro women, we pledge ourselves to an effort to emphasize the single standard of morals for both men and women to the end that righteousness may prevail, and that racial integrity may be assured, not to one race, but to both.

"While black [CIC] participants shared these concerns, they could scarcely have assented to all the implications of the white women's words," Jacqueline Hall observed in *Revolt against Chivalry*. The Arkansas statement called for elevating the status of black women, but at the same time it pleaded for racial integrity, which, Hall said, "for blacks functioned as a code word for segregation. Indeed, a number of the original black members of the Interracial Woman's Committee were themselves products of interracial unions, and they were motivated more by outrage at sexual abuse and sexual mythology than by opposition to legitimate human relationships."[52]

The statement, however, was a beginning of the Arkansas white women's awareness that racial matters needed addressing and that, by banding together, they could be a force in eliminating lynchings. Terry was so struck by the collective impact the ASWPL women had that she was to use it as a model for the Women's Emergency Committee in 1958.

But entries in Terry's 1939 diary underscored her own ambivalence about the contorted realities of segregation. Traveling with Bruen, the family's black chauffeur, and two of her children from Washington to Little Rock in 1939, Terry found a tourist camp in Virginia to spend the night, the only place available for miles on that stretch of road. The owner offered to let Bruen stay in a little-used night watchman's room, but her son Joe and Bruen reported after inspecting it that it was "too dirty and smelly for anyone to use." "It is always hard to find a place for a colored man," Terry wrote a little defensively. "And Bruen slept in the car. Mary was more worried than I. If a person my age can sleep two nights in a day coach on a trip to Washington, as I frequently do, certainly a boy of 21 should be able to rest fairly well in a car."

Another night on that trip was spent at Scottsboro, Alabama, where in 1931 eight blacks were sentenced to the electric chair on an accusation, later repudiated, of rape. Strangely enough, "the only place, north or south, where our colored chauffeur was taken directly into a hotel and given one of the guest rooms along with the others, was in the deep South, in Scottsboro, Alabama," Terry reported, relieved to see right prevail in this case.[53]

■  ■  ■

In 1939, Adolphine Terry and nine others, including Erle Chambers and Edwin Dunaway, formed the Little Rock Housing Association. It was a forward-looking effort to get some of the federal funds created by the 1937 Housing Authority Act channeled into Little Rock to combat slum housing.

When the Terry group first attempted to get the city council to approve a local housing authority, Mayor J. V. Satterfield and Redding Stevenson, who headed the Little Rock Realtors Association, opposed them. Stevenson became chair of the new authority in 1940, and when he realized he would now have a hand in how the money was spent, he became an advocate of the housing program.[54] By 1945, Dunaway, then a state representative, was able to get enabling legislation for urban renewal through the state legislature, although federal funds for this were not made available until 1949.[55]

Terry and Dunaway also served on the board of the interracial Urban League, which was pushing for improvements for blacks "through evolution not revolution"; Amelia B. Ives, a black school principal, founded the local league branch in 1937.[56] One of the Urban League's early causes was to get better recreational facilities for blacks. Among other things, the league pushed to improve Gillam Park. It was an isolated piece of scrubby land, inaccessible except by a dirt road, but it was the only recreational area the city provided for blacks in the 1930s.[57] Not until February 1949 was a referendum held on whether the city should issue $359,000 in bonds to fund Gillam Park improvements. By then, other groups had joined the Urban

League in support of the project. The Mayor's Interracial Advisory Committee endorsed the suggestion of its only black member, I. S. McClinton, that the city put a bond issue before the people.[58] The bond issue barely squeaked through by 124 votes in a light voter turnout only after much public discussion about whether that much money should be used to fund park improvements for blacks. There was agreement that blacks needed parks since they were not allowed in the all-white ones, but the city wanted as little as possible spent on them.[59] Two years later, the Urban League's black director, Harry Bass, recalling the favorable vote and the league's role in it, was quoted as saying: "I've been in all the major cities of the South. And the race situation is better in Little Rock than anywhere else."[60]

These early efforts to provide parks and low-income housing for blacks prompted Little Rock to become one of the first cities in the country to apply for urban renewal funds soon after they became available in 1949. The Gillam Park bond issue suddenly became a potential bonanza instead of the extravagance its opponents had portrayed it as being. The $359,000 could be used as a match to bring millions in urban renewal funds, but city officials had to go back to the voters to get approval for accepting the new federal funds in 1950.[61] The fact that the city had a match did not make it any more palatable to those who had opposed it in the first place. This time a much fiercer fight ensued.

"The urban renewal referendum was the most bitter and divisive public issue to take place in Little Rock . . . between the end of the Second World War and the shattering conflicts of 1957," wrote Griffin Smith Jr., who was later to become editor of the *Arkansas Democrat-Gazette*.[62] Conservatives, including slum landlords and others opposed to public housing, labeled the proposed city ordinance "socialistic" and attacked it in a series of expensive ads. Some blacks in what were considered "blighted" areas and some white leaders who opposed using the park funds to get housing funds also protested.

Among urban renewal supporters were many businessmen in the city's white power structure, who trumpeted the sizable amount of money it would bring to the city. The *Arkansas Gazette*'s executive editor, Harry Ashmore, said that in Little Rock as in other cities:

Local authorities could get federal grants for so-called slum clearance and they could clean out an old slum, which in almost every case, of course, tended to be a black neighborhood. And then they were required, if they did that, to provide equivalent housing within presumably the reach of the income groups of the displaced. And they could then sell this land for any purpose. It didn't have to be for housing if they built equivalent housing somewhere else.[63]

The Committee for Progress, made up of prominent citizens, persuaded Adolphine Terry (Mrs. D. D. Terry, as she was identified in the press) to co-chair the group. Terry promptly organized an auxiliary committee of twenty-two women to present "the women's view" on radio programs and before community and civic groups, stressing the importance of slum clearance and low-rent housing as both "an exercise in responsible democracy and a solution to health problems among the poor."[64] The women envisioned safer and more sanitary homes for the three thousand poor families who were living in substandard housing. Mrs. Terry's Committee for Progress did not question the fact that the families would be moved out of their old neighborhoods and that the new housing provided for them would further segregate them by distance.

Terry and the Committee for Progress won the hard-fought urban renewal election on May 9, 1950, with heavy support from black voters except for those in a few precincts designated as blighted. Mrs. Terry's victory celebration was short-lived, however, for personal tragedy struck once again the next day: her famous brother, John Gould Fletcher, drowned himself in a pond near Johnswood, his home on the western edge of Little Rock.[65]

In 1951, the city completed work on Gillam Park, which included its own swimming pool, pavilions, a baseball diamond, and a small amusement area, but did not include the four lighted tennis courts that had been promised. Shortly thereafter, the over $3 million Booker Homes project, which provided four hundred houses for blacks and adjoined Gillam Park on the east side in the still-remote Granite Mountain area, was also completed. The smaller neighborhood parks that blacks had requested in the central part of the city never materialized, "although some comparable parks were constructed in the urban renewal areas."[66] The city also approved a golf course at Gillam Park in 1953, but it was never built. At about the same time, the 250 children in the new Booker Homes project discovered that they had no city schools to attend. They had to travel many miles into the county to attend overcrowded classrooms before a school near them was belatedly built.[67]

The Little Rock Housing Authority, in its first major slum clearance effort in 1952, sought to clear ten blocks of mostly black homes in the Dunbar High School section of the central city. Black homeowners there organized to stop that effort. The Housing Authority planned to use four blocks to build a community center and a new school, and they intended to use the other six blocks for private development of apartment buildings. Although the targeted area included a number of "shotgun" shacks owned by white landlords, it also included some of the most substantial black housing in the city.[68] A group of black women, who identified themselves as "housewives," protested having their homes taken by declaring in a statement:

> We have given almost everything we have except our very life blood over a long period of years to pay for these homes, improvements and educate our children. Now for the Housing Authority to come and say we must move away to a much less desirable, convenient and suitable location is far more than we can understand or submit to willingly. Is there a law anywhere in the United States that says one private property owner must sell what he has so another private owner can buy it to make a profit?[69]

Prior to that, one of these same women had written in a letter to the *Gazette* editor: "I feel that the choicest area of the Negro residential section has been selected for clearance."[70] Charles Bussey, who headed the black Veterans Good Government Committee, became the representative of the protesting Dunbar property owners. As he said later: "This was some of the best property we had with nice homes. There was no use bothering this property."[71]

A total of 118 property owners signed a petition against the clearance project. Four black property owners filed suit in chancery court to save their homes, but the clearance occurred on schedule.[72] The *State Press,* a black newspaper, editorialized in 1953: "We stated time after time that the Negroes who were working with the Little Rock Housing Authority to dispossess the Negroes of their homes, were not serving the best interests of Negroes. We told you the move was to centralize all Negroes in one area and forget about them while the city progresses in another direction."[73] Annie Abrams, a black leader who remembered the Dunbar project, said later it was the beginning of a "nomad pattern" that discouraged inner-city black families from putting down roots.[74]

The fact that Harry Bass sided with Redding Stevenson and the Housing Authority in the Dunbar dispute in 1952 did not endear him to certain other blacks, who circulated a petition to the Urban League expressing disapproval and asking that he be transferred. In 1954, Bass ran into trouble with the city for operating a lottery (which he claimed was to raise money for a new black hospital) and for soliciting white politicians for money to get black votes. The Urban League board asked for his resignation. When he refused to give it, most of the board, including Adolphine Terry, resigned.[75] Some of the other board members returned after Bass finally departed and a new director was hired. Terry, who had written a strong letter to the national Urban League complaining about its support of Bass, was not invited back.[76]

At the same time, two conservative white school board members, Foster Vineyard and Louise McLean, had almost blocked the Dunbar project at the last minute for a reason quite different from those put forth by the black housewives. The board members refused to accept the property for the school until a clause they found objectionable in the contract was removed. As a weak attempt to guarantee equality of treatment that would meet anti-discriminatory federal guidelines, the contract read, "The school board agrees not to restrict the sale or use of the property upon the basis of race, color or creed." Vineyard said the final clause rendered the contract illegal under the state's segregation law because it would not prohibit white children from attending classes there. McLean agreed and the clause was removed.[77]

■  ■  ■

In the 1940s, Congressman Terry left his House seat to run for the U.S. Senate but lost both that election and a later race for governor; Brooks Hays replaced Terry in the House in 1942. Adolphine Terry threw her own hat in the ring for the Arkansas State Senate in the early 1950s. She ran many ads and spoke on the radio attacking her opponent, incumbent Ellis Fagan, as representing the utilities and other special interests. She earned a respectable 11,610 votes, despite her gender and her liberal leanings, to 18,717 for her opponent. Surprisingly, Fagan later emerged as a strong ally in the fight for reopening the schools.[78]

In addition to her political ventures, Adolphine Terry constantly throughout her lifetime took on a wide range of nonpolitical, community and church chores; when she was seventy-five years old and in the middle of starting the Women's Emergency Committee to Open Our Schools, she agreed to teach a Sunday school class for seventh grade girls at Christ Episcopal Church.[79]

In 1966, when she was eighty-three years old, Terry was honored by the community at a fully integrated dinner at the Marion Hotel ballroom in Little Rock. In his speech at the dinner, Harry Ashmore, the courageous editor of the *Arkansas Gazette* (who had returned to Little Rock from Santa Barbara, California, where he headed the Center for the Study of Democratic Institutions), described Terry this way: "She simply set aside the spurious considerations of race and opened her heart to all those who lived around her. Her operating assumption is that most of us, black or white, are better than we usually have a chance to be. . . . Surely Adolphine Terry has earned the right to remind Southerners that, having done their worst, and failed, they may now find the way clear to do their best."[80]

Terry still had a foot in two worlds—one, her own segregated past in which she still functioned in a *noblesse oblige* manner, and the other, the new integrated future that she believed in and that she knew demanded inclusion and equality. She and the Little Rock women who shared her views were faced with their own painful changes during this period of transition, but they understood with great clarity the direction in which they intended to move. They were not doing it just for blacks. They were also doing it for themselves.

# ▪ 2 ▪

# Little Rock in the 1950s

Unlike Adolphine Terry, whom I did not meet until 1958, I was not a Little Rock native. When I moved to Arkansas in 1950, I often drove along highways where the evidence of poverty spilled out over the countryside. Ancient, battered pickups were parked in front of run-down houses with washing machines and old, discarded couches on the front porches and surrounded by rusting car bodies. In the little towns, the schools were often in need of paint and repair and had desolate playgrounds devoid of equipment. The black schools were always easily recognizable—they were in a worse state of disrepair than the white schools and stood alongside unpaved streets in the midst of shacks without even battered pickups or old furniture out front. Even World War II, which had produced jobs and affluence in other parts of the country, had not brought the state far out of the Depression of the 1930s. By most economic and educational indicators, such as per capita income, public school expenditures, and teacher salaries, Arkansas was last in the nation.

The Little Rock to which I came in 1950 was a pleasant city with wide, tree-lined streets and a sprinkling of black and white neighborhoods across the center of town. It was more like a southwestern city, but without the heavy, moss-hung closeness of narrow streets and the similarly narrow thinking of the town I had moved from in Louisiana. I had taught journalism in a college there for a short while after stints with the *Nashville Tennessean* in my native state and a travel magazine in New York. Following my Louisiana experiences with post–Huey Long politics, raw plantation racism, and the reactionary *Shreveport Times,* Little Rock seemed a good place to be.

The *Arkansas Gazette,* where I worked briefly and for which I later wrote features and book reviews, was an enlightened newspaper with Harry Ashmore and J. N. Heiskell at the helm. Sid McMath, one of the promising young progressives of the South, had just become governor. A few years before, an erudite former president of the state university, J. William Fulbright, had moved up to the U.S. Senate. Brooks Hays, a courtly, liberal Baptist with a fine sense of humor, represented Little Rockians in Congress where, with Senator Fulbright, he left the legacy of the Fulbright-Hays International Scholarship Program. In light of these considerations, the political climate in Little Rock appeared quite promising.

I had grown up in Wartrace, Bedford County, Tennessee. My father's grandfather had lived in the first brick home in the state in the early 1800s and had owned slaves he inherited from his father in North Carolina. Family accounts said that the distress my great-grandfather felt over being a slave owner contributed to his mental breakdown late in life, but this was not discussed around me as a child. Instead, I was taught to be proud of my grandfather, a Confederate captain in the Civil War. His sword was kept behind the front door in the living room of the country home where my three aunts and great-aunt, all unmarried, lived. They tended to look down somewhat on my mother, whose father had been a Union sympathizer. My father lived with us in town and supported both households from his farm.

People in Wartrace (population four hundred) got to know each other pretty well across racial lines. We occasionally shared the bounty from our summer gardens and strings of fish from a nearby creek. When illness or a death occurred, we visited each other. During the Depression, everyone, black and white, in that part of the South suffered financially. Yet even then, in that tiny place, the town had two of everything. There were the humiliatingly unequal schools (the black school stopped at the eighth grade), separate churches, separate cemeteries, and even "white" and "colored" waiting rooms in the small Wartrace train depot. Children on both sides of the color line were injured by the knowledge that this way of life went counter to all they were learning in school about democracy and in Sunday school about all men being brothers (women were not then mentioned).

I heard my father, who was a Presbyterian elder, once tell a joke with racial overtones, much to the dismay of my mother (who voiced her disapproval so clearly that he did not do it again). One night she took me outside to see the sky reddened by the flames of our county courthouse burning ten miles away. A lynch mob had set fire to the building, thinking a black man accused of rape was still inside in the basement jail. The intended victim had been whisked away to Nashville when the mob began gathering. My mother and my church instilled in me a strong belief that all people are connected as human beings, but neither she nor the church questioned the Jim Crow realities of our society.

When I was fourteen years old, I organized through my church youth group a vacation Bible school for the black children of Bugscuffle. This community, which was named by my grandfather and was located at the back of our farm, was where the descendants of slaves, some of whom still worked for my father, lived. I went door-to-door, inviting the children to attend. Some of the mothers told me their children could not come because they did not have shoes to wear. I went out and found shoes for them. It was a sobering experience for me: although I was growing up without much, I did have shoes.

I worked my way through Peabody College (it later became a part of Vanderbilt University, where I also took courses). I learned little at either place to encourage me to break with my segregated past. Donald Davidson, my brilliant creative writing teacher at Vanderbilt, was a member of the Agrarians, a group of Southern writers who believed the South could recapture some of its former grandeur by returning to things as they had been. He was the author of an article that appeared in the *Sewanee Review* that compared two men, one black and one white, sitting in separate train-station waiting rooms and explained why each deserved to be where he was.

It was not until I went to Columbia University to graduate school in journalism that I gained some perspective on what I had taken for granted about race in the South. I got acquainted there with a black classmate from the West Indies with whom several of us sometimes ate lunch. One day Dave and I discussed the fact that we could not walk down the street together in Nashville without being disapprovingly stared at as an interracial couple and possibly arrested. It was a sudden, big mindshift for me. I finally understood how badly out of kilter things were in the South. That was in 1946. I did not act on it until much later.

■   ■   ■

After two years of apartment living in a lovely old neighborhood full of large but aging homes in Little Rock's central city, Pat (my husband) and I became part of a great exodus of whites to the western suburbs. We were lured by the fact that we could get large mortgages on the small new homes readily available there. At the same time, under the guise of urban renewal, the Little Rock Housing Authority began to clear black neighborhoods in the area we were leaving. Large concentrations of black families moved into the eastern-most sections of Little Rock, and the city became increasingly split into black and white enclaves. The central city itself began growing "blacker" to the east and southeast and "whiter" to the west. An all-black housing project, called Tuxedo Courts, was already in use on the southeastern edge of the central city. New housing projects for blacks were going up in two areas much farther east near the airport and beyond—a middle-class black subdivision was to be built adjacent to the most distant one. On the other side of the central city, but safely distant from the highly desirable Pulaski Heights area, poor whites were being placed in an all-white housing project.

■   ■   ■

My initially favorable impression of the Arkansas political climate was not undeserved. But I was unprepared for the lack of intellectual stimulation for women in Little Rock's white, WASPish, and wary-of-outsiders suburbs in the 1950s. The pressure for conformity in those Eisenhower years decreed that, except for getting involved with the PTA, volunteer work, bridge clubs, garden clubs, church work, or Razorback games on Saturdays, women were expected to stay home with the children.

White women in other cities were also evolving along the same patterns of isolation. Betty Friedan hit a nerve that many of us felt as suburban women when she called it "the problem that has no name."[1] More affluent white women experienced family pressure to be a part of their cities' white elites, joining country clubs and Junior Leagues that excluded both Jews and blacks and that placed additional constraints on acceptable behavior for women.

Until 1950, small colonies of Little Rock blacks lived at West Rock, at the foot of Cantrell Road hill, and on Hays Street (later University Avenue) in the western suburbs near the site of Little Rock's first shopping mall. Many of these were black women who worked as housekeepers, cooks, or baby sitters in the white homes at the top of Cantrell Road hill in the new suburbs. For them, urban renewal meant urban removal from these areas, and many of these women wound up in eastern Little Rock, a one-and-a-half-hour bus ride to and from their domestic jobs (one of these displaced domestic workers told me wistfully that she never saw her own children in the daylight).[2] The city fathers, who endorsed the racial reordering of city housing patterns through urban renewal and suburban development, were at the same time acquiring a certain reputation for progressiveness. For many years they had sanctioned the steady integration of Little Rock's parks, hospitals, buses, and public library, all of which had occurred peacefully before the time of the 1957 Little Rock school crisis.[3] There were strange and twisted limitations as to how far black rights extended, however. For instance, blacks after World War II were able to visit the amusement park and the zoo at the white Fair Park "in small groups," but they could not use the swimming pool until 1965.[4] Hotels, theaters, restaurants, rest rooms, and drinking fountains in Little Rock remained segregated in the 1950s. But unlike officials in deep South cities who were helping the civil rights movement get off the ground by stonewalling any integration of public facilities, Little Rock leaders were moving ahead on a few fronts.

As a member of the Little Rock Public Library board in 1948, Adolphine Terry began pushing for opening the main library to blacks since all that was available to them was a small Negro branch stocked with outdated, castoff books. Terry had the support of fellow board members Rabbi Ira Sanders and J. N. "Ned" Heiskell, the *Gazette* publisher and library board president.

Some of the other members, however, were less enthusiastic about opening the doors to blacks without preparing them for it. One suggested that if this happened, the board should send notices to black churches urging them to tell their people to behave like ladies and gentlemen at the library.[5] Terry was indignant. "I asked him who on earth he thought was coming and what people were coming for. I felt they were coming to read and take out books . . . , not to disturb anything or anybody." That year the board reluctantly agreed to allow a few black adults, but no children, to sit "unobtrusively in the back" and use books at the main library on a trial basis.

A board resolution formally integrating the library finally was passed in January 1951. Present at that meeting were Terry, Heiskell, Mrs. Edward Cornish, and Shields M. Goodwin. The board resolution read: "Resolved, first that the adult department of the main library be open to Negroes beginning with students of the seventh grade and to all Negroes over the age of sixteen. Second, that Negroes be required to make application for a library card in the same manner as white patrons." At the same meeting, the board approved the installation of a lavatory in the small room adjoining the county stack room at a cost of one hundred dollars, presumably for their black patrons, although the minutes omitted saying that. Black children continued to use the branch library and were not admitted to the main library until a new building was opened in 1963.[6]

When Terry was invited to speak at a meeting of the Arkansas Medical Society in 1954, she saw a sea of white faces around her. "Why are there no black doctors here?" Terry asked one of the white doctors during her remarks. "Because no black doctors have applied to join," he replied, somewhat chagrined. A reporter at the meeting covered that exchange. The next day, after it appeared in the *Gazette,* the AMS received applications from four black physicians. They were Dr. Hugh Brown, superintendent of the McRae Tuberculosis Sanatorium; Dr. Oba White; Dr. J. M. Robinson; and Dr. G. W. S. Ish, who graduated from Harvard Medical School in 1909. Prior to this, black doctors had to turn over their patients to white doctors to get beds for them in the predominantly white hospitals. "They [the black doctors] were accepted and received hospital privileges and other amenities connected with the Society. We always said that Mrs. D. D. Terry was responsible," recalled Dr. Evangeline Upshur, who herself was Little Rock's first black female dentist.[7]

The newly named Citizens Coach Company integrated in 1956 without incident, when an Iowa owner took over the Capital Transit Company, which had been plagued with strikes. The new owner from the north announced that, in view of a Supreme Court decision in late 1956 outlawing segregation on buses, local segregation of passengers would end immediately. The mayors of Little Rock and North Little Rock said the police would "pay no attention" to racially mixed seating.[8] That decision grew out of earlier legal battles at Montgomery, Alabama, and a year-long boycott led by Dr. Martin Luther King Jr.[9]

■   ■   ■

In 1953, the Little Rock School District acquired a new superintendent, Virgil Blossom. He was an ambitious and zealous man who decided to make the most of the U.S. Supreme Court's 1954 *Brown v. Board of Education* decision ordering school desegregation. He and his board were not enthusiastic about integration, but Little Rock, an upper South city with a seemingly good record on racial matters, was expected to weather the change without incident. The Little Rock School Board announced five days after the *Brown* decision that it would comply as soon as the Supreme Court gave further directions to districts on what should be done. Blossom developed several plans, the first of which would have begun at the elementary school level, but that was soon scrapped in favor of a phased integration plan beginning at the high school level. Blossom expected the latter plan to boost his political and professional stature by becoming a model for the entire South.[10]

The school board hastily approved the building of a new, handsomely equipped black high school, which went up remarkably fast after the 1954 decision. A millage request the year before for a new white high school in the western suburbs had made no mention of the need for a new black high school. "Separate but equal" suddenly rose to the top of the school district agenda. On April 8, 1956, a local newspaper headline announced "600 Negro Students Moving Tomorrow into New Million Dollar High School." Named for Horace Mann and located in the eastern part of the city, where contrived housing segregation had already taken many blacks, it replaced the older central city Dunbar High School, which was downgraded to a junior high school. The Blossom integration plan was scheduled to go into effect after the completion of Hall High School in the western suburbs in 1957.

The caution with which Little Rock leaders approached desegregation was at least partially related to how the South's political leaders were reacting to the *Brown* decision. In 1956, 101 Southern congressmen signed the defiant Southern Manifesto, which labeled the *Brown* decision a "clear abuse of judicial power." These men pledged themselves "to use all lawful means to bring about a reversal of this decision which is contrary to the Constitution and to prevent the use of force in its implementation."[11] The signatures of Rep. Brooks Hays and Sen. J. William Fulbright appeared on the list with those of a majority of Southern congressmen from every state of the old Confederacy.

Pres. Dwight D. Eisenhower's own segregationist leanings stopped him short of offering enthusiastic support for the *Brown* decision. "The president's voice was missing from the national chorus that greeted *Brown* as an act of judicial statesmanship," Harry Ashmore wrote later. As "massive resistance" grew in the South, and the Southern leaders who were attempting to build support for obeying the law urged the president to support them, he still maintained an essentially negative position. At one point Eisenhower even remarked that the "worst damn fool mistake I ever made was appointing Earl Warren chief justice" of the Supreme Court.[12]

■   ■   ■

Shortly before the planned beginning of school integration in the fall of 1957, a discussion group to which my husband and I belonged invited Blossom to speak at a meeting held in our home. By then he exuded confidence as he laid out maps on our living-room floor. These maps showed where he planned to locate both junior and senior high schools and where small neighborhood schools would be built to keep integration at a minimum. Blossom proudly pointed to the black and white pinheads on the map that color-coded where every child in town lived. I was surprised to see how much the segregated housing patterns of the city had increased in a matter of seven years. The white and black pinheads were mixed in the middle, but the black pinheads significantly thickened to the east while the white ones mushroomed to the west.

We asked him why he had not begun integration in the elementary schools. The superintendent replied that he did not have the smaller schools in the "right" places to minimize integration yet. One member of the group asked him if he was not afraid the courts might see his plan as too minimal. Blossom peered over his horn-rimmed glasses and declared sharply: "My first responsibility is to provide quality education for all the children of this community. Uncontrolled integration would lower the quality of the schools."[13]

He made it clear that the new Horace Mann High School in the east end would register only black students. Hall High School in the western suburbs would have only whites, and the older, predominantly white Central High School would have as few blacks as Blossom and the school board could manage to get away with in court. That magic number turned out to be nine in a student body of two thousand; still, it was a beginning. Our group decided this plan deserved community support, but we were not quite certain how to go about it. Blossom, seemingly confident that his plan had no flaws, did not ask us for any help.

The central part of the city around Central High School was changing to a neighborhood of predominantly working-class whites who could not afford the move to the Heights. They had no intention of going to school with blacks that urban renewal had left in what they considered "their" part of town.

Historian Numan Bartley noted that the new suburban Hall High School, by drawing students from elite Pulaski Heights families away from Central High School, cushioned the community's white leadership from direct participation in integration. This fact was not lost on whites still in the central part of the city: they were quite aware that it left their children to do the integrating. Bartley said that the Blossom "Phase Program":

> insured that much of Little Rock's civic leadership was effectively isolated while those white citizens most likely to hold strong racial prejudice were immediately involved. This arrangement added an element of class conflict to the racial controversy and allowed segregationist spokesmen to charge that integrationists were sacrificing the common citizen while protecting the wealthy. More important it amputated the center of white moderation from direct involvement.[14]

Bartley also observed that Blossom spent a "disproportionate amount of time" selling the plan to civic clubs, churches, and other groups frequented by Pulaski Heights parents whose children would not be affected by integration. He presented it as a finished product, not asking for input either from them or from those whose children would attend Central.[15] John Pagan later called Blossom's "failure to involve the community in the formulation of the desegregation plan" a "catastrophic tactical misjudgement."[16]

Blossom later wrote that he originally thought integration should be started in the earlier grades, but found parents of young children more opposed to integration than those of older students. His fervor for keeping integration to an absolute minimum (as indicated to our group) prompted him to launch the high school building program, through which he felt he could contain desegregation for a while to one school.[17] It also led him to frame his position in negative terms by giving assurances to audiences that both he and the school board felt opposed to integration. Many black parents felt he was more concerned about the feelings of segregationist parents than he was with proceeding in good faith to follow the Supreme Court's decision on integrating the schools.[18]

Although these were serious flaws, the Blossom plan probably would have survived and succeeded had it not been for the surprise intervention of Gov. Orval Eugene Faubus. Blossom was at least partially responsible for that because he had repeatedly urged the governor to make a statement supporting the minimal integration that was to take place at Central High School. His pleas became more frequent as his own fears that there might be trouble at Central rose.[19]

Governor Faubus had shown no signs of extreme racism prior to the school crisis. While he endorsed segregation, as did all other Arkansas politicians, he was considered a moderate and had enjoyed the support of liberal Democrats and the *Arkansas Gazette* in both his 1954 and 1956 campaigns for governor. Faubus acquired his middle name because of his father's admiration for Eugene V. Debs, head of the American Socialist Party of which he was a member.[20]

Four small Arkansas school districts were successfully desegregated following the 1954 decision during Faubus's first term. One of them, Hoxie, in northeastern Arkansas where the black population was sparse, fared so well that it received favorable publicity in *Life* magazine. This press exposure unfortunately caused professional racists from inside and outside the state to swarm into the town in 1955. Among them was a former southern Arkansas state senator, Jim Johnson, who founded the White Citizens Council of Arkansas to help launch himself as a candidate for governor against Faubus in 1956. Johnson resorted to the use of crude recruiting tools, including a tape supplied by the Mississippi branch of the Association of Citizens Councils and purported to be made by a nonexistent black Howard University professor. A description of the tape in his Citizens Council newspaper said it proved "the NAACP [National Association for the Advancement of Colored People] and their insolent agitators are little concerned with an education for the 'ignorant nigger'; but, rather, are 'demanding' integration in the white bedroom." The Hoxie School Board held fast and continued the integration of its classrooms. However, in a few small towns up and down the Arkansas delta, where blacks resided in greater numbers, several segregationists turned out to hear the Mississippi Citizens Council tape confirming their worst fears.[21]

The Blossom plan came under attack from another source. NAACP president Daisy Bates was incensed by the foot-dragging she perceived the school board engaged in under the guise of the

Blossom plan. She appeared on the doorstep of the Little Rock School District administration building in early 1956 with twenty-seven Negro students, demanding that they be enrolled immediately in all-white schools. The district court upheld the Blossom plan; the NAACP appealed the decision.[22]

Meanwhile, the closer Little Rock got to the Blossom plan deadline, the more segregationist activity increased. Arkansas voters passed three anti-integration measures at the polls in late 1956. In February 1957, four segregation bills sailed through the state legislature and were quickly signed by Governor Faubus. These new laws set up a State Sovereignty Commission, removed compulsory attendance at integrated schools, required names and financial records of certain individuals and organizations to be registered with the state, and allowed school boards to use school funds to fight integration in court.[23]

By June, the local Capital Citizens Council (CCC) leader, Amis Guthridge, was recruiting segregationists at an Oklahoma rally, shouting there would be "hell on the border if they try to integrate at Little Rock in September."[24] Little Rock's CCC had only five hundred members, two hundred of whom lived outside the city, but the noise they were making was having its intended effect on leaders both at the local and state levels.[25]

Georgia's governor, Marvin Griffin, spoke to a cheering CCC crowd at Little Rock in August. He vowed that if the federal courts ordered integration in Georgia and threatened to pull out school lunch programs if the state did not obey, he would "tell them to get their blackeyed peas and soup pots out of Georgia."[26] Rural whites who came to Little Rock for the rally left asking themselves if Georgia's governor was so brave and forthright, why not their governor, too?[27]

The next morning Griffin had breakfast with Faubus, who was still vacillating about which side to support. With his lackluster second term as governor approaching the halfway point, Faubus was looking for a way to drum up support for a third term. He did not like Johnson or some of the other hard-core segregationists who had previously opposed him, but he disliked even more the elitist Little Rock leaders who had snubbed him and called him a Communist during his first race for governor. At that time, liberals and the *Arkansas Gazette* defended Faubus for what they considered an unfair McCarthy-like attack. He remained bitter, however, that most of the city fathers joined in Gov. Francis Cherry's attempt to smear him for having attended an obscure Arkansas labor school, Commonwealth College. Faubus defeated Cherry, but as a former resident of a mountain town in Madison County, he remained an outsider in Little Rock.

Some of the women who found themselves in confrontation with Faubus often speculated about why he shifted positions. Lillian Smith, the Southern author who spoke at Little Rock during that time, told Ruth Arnold Ray of the Arkansas Council on Human Relations that "her experience had been that things always turned on the personal." She wondered if that might be true for Faubus. Ray told Smith about a school nurse at Central who had said that "the Faubus boy [the governor's son, Farrell] . . . didn't fit into Central at all and that Faubus never forgave Virgil Blossom for that."[28] His son's troubles at the school did not directly affect the governor's political decisions, according to Roy Reed, who interviewed Faubus many times.[29] The way the school handled Farrell left Faubus with a disgruntled feeling about Central High that was still apparent more than thirty years later:

> I thought he [Farrell] was just discontented and I made him stay in school. I didn't know what was going on or I wouldn't have. I would have let him drop out right then and go back to Huntsville which is what he did the next year and he stayed there until he graduated. . . .
>
> I went with Farrell . . . when he enrolled in Central High School in the second semester in January 1955. I never was treated more coldly in my life by the school personnel. . . . So then I found out later on that they [students] harassed him, they bullied him, they beat him until he finally fought two or three of them back and got along pretty well. But see, I was telling Farrell, behave, don't fight, you're the Governor's son. You can't be like an ordinary student. I didn't know what they were doing. They didn't tell me, no one told me. I didn't know until

years later or I would have let him drop out right then. No young person should have to endure that, black or white or Asian or whatever. They are entitled to be treated with courtesy and respect.[30]

Faubus seemed unaware even in 1992 of how his words sounded in light of the treatment that he had accorded the nine black students at Central in 1957.

Other personal feelings also made their impact on Faubus; for instance, his envy of the Cherrys and the influence they were able to exert as Little Rock insiders lingered many years later. He recalled how strong Cherry was in Little Rock and how Mrs. Cherry, "a gracious hostess," had a wide circle of friends and belonged to bridge clubs. He added that Cherry went to basketball games and other athletic events with his friends and "naturally was acquainted with the [school] personnel."[31]

Sam Faubus, Orval's father, said he instructed Orval as a boy "not to hate anybody of any race. I told him people would think he was narrow-minded and would look down on him. That's one thing Orval always hated—to be looked down on."[32] The elder Faubus later confessed to Harry Ashmore that he had written letters to the *Gazette* editor under the name of "Jimmy Higgins" taking issue with his son's actions in the school crisis.[33]

Whatever his reasons, Faubus displayed little sympathy for the untenably vulnerable position Blossom and the school board members were in as they tried to sell a plan for integration while convincing people that they favored keeping the schools as segregated as possible. They needed his help, but he knew what rural Arkansas thought of the Blossom plan and would think of him if he supported it.

After weighing all aspects of the situation, Governor Faubus decided shortly after the Griffin visit to throw his political lot with the Citizens Council. While acknowledging the political expediency of Faubus's decision, historian Bartley did not see him in retrospect as "a conniving politician coolly manufacturing a crisis," but as "a much worried man fearful of being pushed to the unpopular side of a major racial controversy." When he decided to join the racists, however, he became "increasingly demagogic and irresponsible."[34]

With the governor now on their side and feeling the need for the more benign public image that a group of women might offer, Capital Citizens Council leaders encouraged some of the CCC female members to organize the Mothers League of Central High School. These women piously declared their opposition to violence as well as to integration and said they would work "as a group of Christian mothers in a Christian-like way" to keep the blacks out. One speaker, less inclined toward nonviolence, told the Mothers League that Communism was behind the NAACP and "a nigger in your school is a potential Communist in your school. . . . Stand up and fight for your children and never cease as long as you can breathe."[35] The Mothers League seemed made to order, as some suspected, to help launch a third term as governor for Faubus in a state with a voting majority of church-going segregationists.

# ■ 3 ■

# Crisis at Central High

I had been home from the hospital only a week with my third child when I settled in on a hot Labor Day night to watch the ten o'clock news while I fed the baby. Little Rock Central High School was scheduled to enroll a few black children the next morning, and we expected all to go well. We had read about the governor's testimony in court the week before, in which he supported the Mothers League recording secretary, Mrs. Clyde Thomason. She had sought and received an injunction to stop integration on the grounds that there would be violence.[1] We had, however, written that off as a politician's attempt to grab headlines. We expected Governor Faubus to revert to a more reasonable stance in this speech after a federal court overruled the state court injunction.[2]

*Gazette* city editor Bill Shelton recalled that one of his reporters, Ernie Valachovic, had finished up and left the office just before the Faubus speech that night. "To go home, he passed Central High," Shelton said. "And there were the troops. He stopped and called us and we sent some people out, including a photographer and that way we got a picture in the paper the next morning. We got a few minutes' head start [before the Faubus speech]. Faubus did not call us."

"I was shocked," Shelton recalled. "I was totally shocked. Even watching the news, the testimony in chancery court and all that stuff for a week or two, I just thought it was a sham. I never dreamed anyone would interfere with the public schools."[3]

Gaston Williamson, a law partner of Archie House, the school board attorney with whom he lunched each day, said neither he nor House had any inkling Faubus would take such action. When Williamson watched Faubus make his announcement on television that night, "I remember just leaping to my feet saying, 'Oh no, the s.o.b.,' and I really laid into him. I was absolutely furious and I must say I haven't cooled down much since then. That's the most horrible example of demagoguery that I have ever seen in my life or ever will."[4] Williamson was speaking thirty-five years after the fact.

Like Williamson, Shelton, and many other Little Rockians that night, I listened in stunned disbelief as Governor Faubus declared that the Arkansas National Guard was at that moment gathering at Central High, with this explanation:

> This is a decision I have reached prayerfully. . . .
>
> The mission of the State Militia is to maintain or restore order and to protect the lives and property of citizens. They will act not as segregationists or integrationists but as soldiers called to active duty to carry out their assigned tasks.
>
> But I must state here in all sincerity, that it is my opinion— yes, even a conviction, that it will not be possible to restore or maintain order and protect the lives and property of the citizens if forcible integration is carried out tomorrow in the schools of this community. The inevitable conclusion, therefore, must be that the schools in Pulaski County, for the time being, must be operated on the basis as they have been operated in the past."[5]

"This is madness," I muttered. "He can't get away with this."

My lawyer husband, Pat, whose Louisiana roots pulled him back from a wholehearted endorsement of integration just then, was nevertheless appalled that the governor would take such an action. "The *Brown* decision, whether you like it or not, is law, and we've got to live with it," he said. "You can't defy the United States Supreme Court. That was settled once and for all when the South lost the Civil War."

I had the disquieting feeling that Little Rock was about to replay another version of that war. The next morning, I telephoned a likeable, supportive neighbor whose sons played every day with mine. Assuming her concern about Faubus's actions would match my own, I minced no words in telling her how I felt until I noticed the silence at the other end of the line. "What else could he do with all those guns and knives being sold?" she finally said. "He had to preserve the peace. Those Negro children will be better off at their own school. It's newer and better than Central." I put down the phone and cried.[6]

FBI reports confirmed that Mothers League members, even before the governor spoke, had also been on their telephones to encourage their friends to gather outside Central High School the morning school opened.[7] Firebrand segregationists from across the state were also coming in to join those recruited locally. The mob that Faubus had predicted on television grew to the menacing size of four hundred people. Women from the self-proclaimed non-violent Mothers League and their children were there, screaming "nigger, go home," at a fifteen-year-old black girl named Elizabeth Eckford, who was turned away by the National Guard. A news photographer captured the moment as she made her way, somber and dignified, through a sea of hate-filled faces. The picture appeared in newspapers around the world and even yet is in many history books in this and other countries.

The new medium of television did its part in elevating the Central High School struggle to a place of international prominence. In fact, "the prolonged duration and military drama of the siege made Little Rock the first on-site news extravaganza of the modern television era," Taylor Branch wrote later in *Parting the Waters*.[8]

■　■　■

Seventy-four-year-old Adolphine Terry and her husband, Dave, were visiting their oldest son in Colorado Springs when the news about the Central High School crisis first broke in September 1957. The front pages of the newspapers there carried stories about Arkansas governor Orval Faubus calling out the National Guard to prevent nine black students from entering the previously all-white school. Adolphine Terry wrote in her diary that she was aghast at what she saw on the television screen:

> There was some rioting and the newspaper photographers caught
> a number of the most unedifying pictures: good-looking white
> children, their faces distorted with hate, shrieking insults at the
> Negroes who conducted themselves very well indeed. Before

we returned, the name of our town had become a byword for lawlessness and race hatred all over the world. . . .

For almost fifty years, the Terrys had worked for better race relations and so much had been quietly accomplished. I felt that my life had been in vain; I really wanted to die. For days I walked about unable to concentrate on anything, except for the fact that we had been disgraced by a group of poor whites and a portion of the lunatic fringe that every town possesses. I wondered where the better class had been while this was being concocted.[9]

Terry was to find out that the "better class," including the city fathers, had retreated into a sustained period of silence. Despite the repeated phone calls that she made to many of them upon her return from Colorado, they did not step forward in any significant way for nearly a year and a half. By then, the city had been reduced to a psychological and political rubble, and the three public high schools had been closed.

There were a few stirrings of decent white reaction during those first days. In addition to Harry Ashmore's *Gazette* editorials every morning, ministers issued statements and set up a day of prayer. One religiously oriented statement issued September 9 came from the local Council of Church Women, who took issue with the Mothers League on what was Christian and un-Christian. It said in part:

> It is our Christian conviction that enforced segregation of any group of persons because of race, creed or color is a violation of Christian principles. The national and state bodies of the denominations which we represent are all on record with statements saying that the Supreme Court rulings regarding segregation in the public schools are in keeping with Christian principles. . . . We are shocked and dismayed that the governor of our state has placed military troops within our community to defy the order of the federal court instead of upholding the law of the land. . . . We deplore the un-Christian acts of some of our citizens expressing hatred of others, which have made headlines around the world.[10]

Campbell and Pettigrew, in *Christians in Racial Crisis*, cited this statement as an indication that these church women were far ahead of all but a few of their local ministers and were in fact pushing the clergy to take a much stronger stand. "No public statement issued by Little Rock ministers attacked segregation on religious grounds with the strength of [the] statement adopted by a local Council of Church Women on September 9," the authors wrote.

The church women also called for a citywide prayer service addressing the crisis for noon, September 12, a full month before the mainline ministers scheduled theirs on Columbus Day, October 12.

The Mothers League and others of like mind began to circulate a petition asking that Virgil Blossom be fired as superintendent of schools. Two of us from the discussion group to which Blossom had spoken countered with a petition supporting him. We carried it without publicity door-to-door in the suburbs.[11] Approximately three hundred people signed, but at least that many more slammed doors in our faces or gave contorted excuses for why they could not sign. We took the signatures to the Blossom home where Mrs. Blossom promised to give them to her husband, but we never heard from him. Circulating the petitions accomplished little except to make us more aware of the sharpness of lines being drawn in our own neighborhoods between those whites who agreed and those who disagreed with Superintendent Blossom on Central High School.

■    ■    ■

Daisy Bates, who had earlier tried unsuccessfully to enroll twenty-seven black students in all-white schools, was now working with the nine black students attempting to enter Central High School. Adolphine Terry, who was a friend of Bates, called her when she heard that temporary tutoring was being set up at the Phyllis Wheatley YWCA when the students were denied entrance at Central. According to Bates, Terry said, "Count me in!" Bates told her the tutoring was set up to keep the nine in a holding pattern for Central rather than to allow them to retreat to segregated Horace Mann. Ernest Green, one of the nine, said that really "serious tutoring was impossible with the newspaper reporters and all that business" around. Having it available, however, nevertheless served its purpose of keeping the nine students poised for their entry into Central.[12]

The Central High School situation grew increasingly tense as the National Guard continued to surround the school for the next three weeks. After much legal wrangling and a meeting arranged by Brooks Hays between Governor Faubus and President Eisenhower, Federal Judge Ronald Davies handed down a ruling on September 20 that said Faubus had not acted to preserve law and order when he barred the black students. Davies enjoined both Faubus and the National Guard from further interference with integration. The governor abruptly pulled out the Guard and left for the weekend to attend the Southern Governors' Conference at Sea Island, Georgia.[13]

A week after the Council of Church Women offered prayers deploring the governor's action, Mothers League spokesperson Margaret Jackson declared to the press: "We hope to have a big demonstration on Monday to show that the people of Little Rock are still against integration and I hope they [the Negro students] don't get in."[14]

On Sunday, Little Rock's lame duck mayor, Woodrow Mann, met at his home with his lawyer, Henry Woods. Woods had been Gov. Sid McMath's chief of staff. Woods and McMath in fact were responsible for bringing Orval Faubus down from the hills to work in Governor McMath's office, an action they both later said they regretted. Mann, who was shortly to be deposed by the changeover to a city manager form of government and who commanded little respect in the city, nevertheless was concerned that another mob might gather at Central High School the next morning. Mann had called the fire chief to bring out fire trucks and high-pressure hoses, but the chief, a segregationist, had refused. Mann then called Marvin Potts, the chief of police, who said he was ill and would not get into it. Ultimately, Woods called in Virgil Blossom; Congressman Brooks Hays; Edwin Dunaway, who knew Daisy Bates and could find out what her plans were for the black children the following morning; Harry Ashmore; and former governor Sid McMath. After Bates confirmed that the children were indeed going to school, the group began to worry about mob control. They got in touch with Gene Smith, the assistant police chief, who said he would head the police force at Central the next morning.[15]

On what came to be known as Black Monday, Smith and his policemen battled more than one thousand angry, potentially violent people at the school as the mob attacked both black and white reporters and cameramen who had come from around the world to record the event. Moving furtively among the mob members, conferring and giving directions, was the governor's friend Jimmy Karam, a Little Rock clothier whose wife had accompanied the Faubuses to Sea Island.[16]

The black students arrived in a police car and were slipped in a side door. Mothers League members hysterically screamed and sobbed before the television cameras that they wanted to get their children out when they heard the black children were in the school. The mob was pushing the inadequate police lines back farther toward the school.[17]

Assistant Chief Smith reported to the anxious moderate leaders who had reassembled at the Woods home Monday that several of his policemen were expressing sympathy for the mob. One had even thrown down his badge and resigned. Smith was afraid a full-fledged race riot was in the making if the mob broke through to the school. He decided to withdraw the black students for their own safety, and the Woods group put through a formal request to the White House asking for federal help.[18] Ashmore, from his *Gazette* office, also told Deputy Attorney General William Rogers "the city police had done all they could and the situation was beyond their control."[19]

President Eisenhower a few hours later ordered the crack "Screaming Eagles" 101st Airborne Infantry Division into Little Rock to provide whatever protection was necessary to get the nine children safely into their classrooms at Central High School.

At dusk on a September evening, army trucks and jeeps loaded with more than eleven hundred riot-trained paratroopers rolled across the Arkansas River bridge and headed toward Central High School. The convoy entered the city against the backdrop of a large billboard that poignantly read: "Who will build Arkansas if her own people do not?"[20] The chief photographer of the *Arkansas Gazette,* Larry Obsitnik, captured the military procession on film, and the story was retold on the front page of the paper. The next morning, paratroopers escorted the nine black students safely to their classrooms.

Although I have never cared for tanks or guns, we drove our children to Central High School so that they could see the paratroopers when they first arrived and lined up in front of the sprawling high school. I hoped the fact that they were there to let the nine black children in, not to keep them out, would be a memorable lesson in what this country was about. I can still remember the immense pride and exhilaration I felt when I showed the soldiers to my children.

Governor Faubus made the unsubstantiated charge that federal troops had gone into girls' dressing rooms at Central, an allegation that the White House labelled vulgar and untrue. Margaret Jackson, the Mothers League vice-president, also called on Governor Faubus to close the schools shortly after the federal troops arrived because, she said, "they are supported with our tax money. Federal dictatorship is not conducive to educational activities and we feel that the very lives of our children are in great danger in the school. They are attending classes under the watchful eyes of hardened soldiers, who are acting under stern orders."

Jackson filed a petition with Federal Judge Ronald Davies, which he dismissed, asking that the troops be removed. Her lawyer, Kenneth Coffelt, then asked for the impeachment of Judge Davies. Faubus said the state itself might seek the removal of the troops.[21]

The 101st Airborne departed late in November but not because of pressure from the Mothers League or the governor's office. The job of maintaining order inside Central was transferred to the Arkansas National Guard, federalized by Eisenhower for that purpose. The Guard thus was removed from the command of Faubus, who had used the same troops earlier to keep the black students out.[22]

Mothers League members were back on the telephones in early October, attempting to "persuade parents to have their children join in a big 'walkout' demonstration at the school." Rumor had it that Faubus was hoping that if one-half or more of the students failed to attend school, he would be justified in shutting it down. The walkout, which involved only about eighty-five students, fizzled, but the Mothers League continued its concerted campaign to stop integration at the school.[23]

The Mothers League, acting in opposition to the Central High Parent Teacher Association, which was attempting to make the black students feel welcome, publicly criticized school officials in the *Arkansas Democrat* each time they tried to discipline white students, who harassed the black students on a regular basis.[24] Bomb threats at the school were frequent, and they were often followed by Mothers League members, who had heard them on the radio, coming to pick up their children.[25]

Margaret Jackson charged in an angry letter to Principal Jess Matthews (also published in an ad in the *Arkansas Democrat* on December 23) that he had banned the singing of "White Christmas." The letter said, in part: "Mr. Matthews, we think you owe the white people an explanation on this matter. . . . How far shall white people be expected to go in appeasing the whims of the African race?" What gym teachers at the school had actually done was discourage a parody that segregationist students were singing: "I'm dreaming of a white Central," Blossom explained.[26]

The events at Central High School troubled Adolphine Terry, but she thought that surely the city fathers would get them under control. Grainger Williams, who had worked as an administrative assistant to Congressman Terry and who now as a businessman was vice-president of the Chamber of Commerce, remembers he could predict, when the phone rang, who it would be. "Grainger, Adolphine Terry here," the voice would say after each new event at the school. "What are you men going to do about this?"[27]

Terry was immersed in letters from friends elsewhere who were expressing their dismay about the Central High crisis when she received an honor she would just as soon not have had. She wrote:

> To my horror, on glancing at the *Democrat* before leaving for church school, I discovered that I had been selected Little Rock woman of the year. Only once before was I so overcome: when I was chosen "mother of the year" for Arkansas. This election has been going on for ten years and I have been nominated several times—in fact, I ordered Sam Dickinson of the *Democrat* to keep my name off the list; that I didn't want to and wouldn't accept the honor if I ever received it. Considering some of the previous recipients, one's election cannot be considered the

perfect compliment. Some of the candidates put up active campaigns, buying up packages of the paper—which is, of course, the reason for the whole thing. At least we didn't do that, Bill [her son] being the only member of the family who admitted he voted for me.[28]

Terry said that she "finally broke out of her lethargy" in January 1958 when her husband, Dave, read in *U.S. News and World Report* that one of the black students, Minnijean Brown, had been expelled. The article said the black students had signed a pledge not to "retaliate" regardless of what the white students did. Adolphine Terry decided to investigate.

> I talked to teachers and was told that discipline had completely broken down, that the Negro students were persecuted daily and when they complained the principal remonstrated with the white boys and girls and nothing happened. The leaders of the student body were not permitted to discuss the situation publicly, and everything was getting worse.[29]

Terry called Daisy Bates and found that she also thought firmer discipline was needed for the disruptive students. "The constant agitation of the segregationists, plus the inert leadership in the Little Rock community, had their effects inside Central High School," Bates wrote later in *The Long Shadow of Little Rock*. "The Negro pupils became constant targets for torture, both the physical and the psychological variety." A five-part series on the crisis appearing in the *New York Post* listed "42 recorded incidents of taunts and roughhouse inflicted upon the nine Negro children" as documented by Bates, against two recorded incidents of retaliation by black students.[30]

By the middle of December, after repeated acts of harassment by segregationist students, Minniejean Brown, one of the nine black students, had had enough. She spilled some chili on the heads of tormentors blocking her way to a cafeteria table. For this act she was suspended for six days and was also later doused with hot soup herself. She was made the primary target of the segregationist students, who repeatedly attacked her by shoving her down or spattering her skirt with ink.

Upon her return after the holidays, Minniejean responded to

a verbal attack by calling the girl who made it "white trash" and was suspended for the rest of the term. Psychologist Dr. Kenneth Clark and his wife invited Minniejean to live with them in New York, where she was promptly enrolled in the New Lincoln High School.[31]

Two weeks after Minniejean's expulsion, a sixteen-year-old white girl named Sammie Dean Parker was suspended and then expelled. Parker had been involved in several incidents, including distributing cards that said: "One down, eight to go." She became an instant celebrity on television protesting her expulsion and was allowed to return to school. She also became Governor Faubus's own inside-the-school informant, furnishing him regularly with her version of the events taking place there, although she did not make it by name into most historical accounts.[32]

Sammie Dean Parker and Hazel Bryan both played major on-camera roles in the 1957 Little Rock crisis as white teenaged female opponents of integration. Although Hazel's role was fleeting, it was more permanently significant, because it is her picture that continues to appear in history books with accounts of the Little Rock crisis.

Hazel and Sammie Dean had attended East Side Junior High School together where they knew each other slightly. When they came to Central in the tenth grade in 1956, they became close friends. Sammie Dean, vivacious and outgoing, was elected president of her homeroom and secretary of the student council. She clearly was a leader.

Fifteen-year-old Hazel and her father, a disabled veteran, were standing next to Sammie Dean in front of Central High School the morning of September 4, 1957, when the nine black students appeared, only to be turned away by the wall of National Guard troops. A news picture captured Hazel, her mouth open wide and her face distorted with hate, clearly venting her wrath on Elizabeth Eckford, who was walking the full humiliating and dangerous length of the screaming mob alone. It was not exactly the kind of picture of oneself one would want to go out on international news wires and to be used subsequently in history books.[33]

Hazel did not attend Central that year. Her parents pulled her out to attend Fuller High School in the nearby county school district. But Sammie Dean, who turned her head and missed having her face in the famous picture, was conspicuously in attendance all year. Sammie Dean's goal was to excel in drama and land a part in the senior play when she became a senior, but since there was no senior play—or school—the following year, she remembered tearfully that she missed that goal.[34]

Sammie Dean instead played a starring role in the Central High crisis by, among other things, jumping out of a classroom window when the federal troops arrived with the black students later in September. Her husband, Jerry Hulett, in a biography of his wife prepared for a college course, wrote that someone shouted, "the niggers are coming and they are already in the building!" According to his account, she became hysterical when she was put in a paddy wagon and carried to the police station, but her parents quickly picked her up, and she embarked on a period of notoriety, giving interviews on television and for the newspapers.[35]

■   ■   ■

Sometime during the next year, Harry Ashmore of the *Gazette* suggested to Mrs. Terry that the Episcopal bishop Robert R. Brown, who had just written a book, *Bigger than Little Rock,* might be able to help her influence public opinion for better conditions within the school. Terry, a staunch Episcopalian, called Bishop Brown, who she reported "said someone should do something," but at that time he did not know what. Terry added:

> So I went to see the Governor's wife and suggested that since the problem would be settled by adults, not children, it would be a good idea if the Governor would express himself in favor of law and order in the school. She agreed with me and promised to discuss the matter with him. I knew her quite well: I had a party for her when Faubus was first elected.[36]

Nothing came of that visit either. Terry by then was determined to find a way to mobilize whites of goodwill to counter the outrages that continued to occur. She put together a panel of black women to speak to the guild at her church. After hearing them, Terry felt the need to become better informed herself. She accompanied her friend Jane Bragg to an interracial council meeting in

February 1958 at the Dunbar Community Center. She saw an "old colored acquaintance, Miss Jordan," with whom she had worked on the Phyllis Wheatley YWCA board, and it made her long for the time when "we were all working together for the community."[37]

In her effort to reach other prominent citizens, Terry took a copy of a *New York Times* article about school desegregation to Herbert and Ruby Thomas. Herbert Thomas was founder and president of the First Pyramid Life Insurance Company and president of the University of Arkansas Board of Trustees. Under his leadership both the medical and law schools of the university had enrolled their first black students ten years before. Thomas's First Pyramid Company also had sponsored the billboard proclaiming "Who will build Arkansas if her own people will not?"

Terry learned that Thomas had a plan for resolving the Little Rock public school stalemate. His plan called for the withdrawal of the black students from Central High School and for the establishment of a state interracial commission to develop a voluntary integration plan. "I can't believe the NAACP will accept it," Terry wrote in her diary March 31, although she was encouraged that Thomas wanted to establish a state interracial commission.

Thomas presented his plan to the state board of education on April 7. Terry reported that her interracial group, which met April 10 at the Dunbar Center, seemed "bent on having nothing to do with the Thomas plan" because it called for the withdrawal of the black students. A few days later, she was invited to another interracial meeting to hear Thomas himself discuss the plan.

> It was a very good meeting. He is a clever and politic creature and before the meeting was over, he had changed the atmosphere of the meeting from animosity to good will. The Negroes all agreed that they wanted an interracial commission to help solve the problems of integration, but were not ready to say that they would withdraw their children from Central High School and take a "breathing spell" and certainly no one could blame them.
>
> For the first time, Herbert Thomas met Mrs. Bates. Both were highly intelligent, and I felt that if the two of them sat down together without any other desire than to work out a

solution to the problem they would probably have come up with an acceptable answer.[38]

Terry continued to work with this interracial group to arrive at a compromise on the Thomas plan. Black members of the group were concerned that the governor would appoint segregationist commission members. Terry suggested a system whereby organizations would name the members, but the group still was not willing to endorse removing the black students or relinquishing the gains they had made in federal court.[39]

Terry brought Elizabeth Huckaby, the vice-principal at Central High School, to the Thomas home for dinner one evening to discuss the plan. The dinner was a gracious affair, but it did not accomplish much. "I felt that Herbert did not realize what the Negro children had had to take at the High School and I knew that Mrs. Huckaby did not think that they should be removed," Terry said.

None of the efforts to bring consensus on the plan worked out, and it died with its rejection by the state board of education in June.[40] The experience in working on it, however, brought Terry closer to some of the black members, especially Bates, of whom she wrote:

> Daisy Bates is the bravest woman I have ever known. When the first [nine] black children started at Central High, it was she who . . . advised them. . . . They were all smart and had stable backgrounds. She thought they could all do it and they came through all right except one who broke down under the terrible strain.
>
> Every day the students came to her house after school. They would discuss the day they had had and she would encourage them and tell them exactly what they were doing for their race. Almost every night rocks were thrown at her house and the windows were broken out many times. She was given no protection by the state or local police; she had only the protection her neighbors could give her but she never wavered and certainly never gave up.[41]

Terry thought at the time, as did many others, that Bates had played a role in selecting the nine students. However, according to Ernest Green, one of the nine, the selections had been made altogether by the school district itself. About forty-five black students applied for admission to Central High School, and from that number, the school district hierarchy screened out the nine. Blossom, as superintendent, had personally interviewed thirty-two black students and their parents, relying on his own assessment of the "mental ability, achievement record, school citizenship record and health record" of each student in making the final selection. Green was stunned when he arrived at the school board office one morning to find the number had been screened to only nine who would be allowed to attend Central.[42]

Segregationists spread the word that the black students had been imported by the NAACP to integrate Central High School.[43] The nine black students were in fact all indigenous to Little Rock. "We are third generation natives," Ernest Green said. "My grandfather was a postman there, my father at that time had died. Before that he had worked at the post office as a janitor and had been a waiter at the Little Rock Country Club." Green's mother was a Little Rock teacher, and his aunt, who was a counselor at Little Rock's Horace Mann High School, was the one who suggested that he apply. In the late 1940s, the two women had been active in a protest of the pay inequities between black and white teachers at Little Rock.[44]

Both the Disney movie *The Ernest Green Story* and Melba Patillo Beals's book *Warriors Don't Cry* document the ordeals and humiliations the Little Rock Nine experienced that first year. Their own baptism by fire at Central was made even harder when some of their friends at Horace Mann suggested to them that they were just stirring up trouble for all blacks.[45]

When *The Ernest Green Story* was being filmed at Little Rock in 1992, Sammie Dean Parker and her sister owned a restored 1957 Chevrolet convertible. Sammie Dean's sister offered to let it be used in the film. Sammie Dean, who happened to be in town, went with her sister and the sister's son to take it to the Disney representative. Sammie Dean said, "My nephew was telling him, 'Why is it they're always telling the Ernest Green story, or the Mrs. Huckaby story? My Aunt Sammie was there. She had a good handle on what was going on.'" She continued somewhat wistfully:

> But it's not something I look back on as something I'm proud
> of. Maybe if things had evolved differently, maybe so. . . . I

think some of the crowd, the adults that were at the school constantly, day after day, I don't even think they lived in Little Rock to be honest with you, . . . I really don't. I think they were there to create riots, disturbances, to keep something going on. Looking back at it, I really do.[46]

Although Sammie Dean's change of heart about what she had done at Central High School was only partial and somewhat ambiguous, her friend Hazel's was not. Five years after the incident in which she had yelled at Elizabeth Eckford, Hazel called Elizabeth. "I don't know what triggered it, but one day I just started squalling about how she must have felt," Hazel said. "I felt so bad that I had done this that I called her . . . and apologized to her. I told her I was sorry that I had done that, that I was not thinking for myself. . . . I think both of us were crying."[47]

■   ■   ■

Where were all the good-intentioned whites when the mobs gathered at Central High School? Little Rock at the time had a strong, readily identifiable white-male power structure. Made up mostly of businessmen, this group had raised money to get the Little Rock Air Force Base and a new industrial district in their county. As the Good Government Committee, these city fathers had just taken over city hall in the spring of 1957 with a city manager–board form of government to replace what was considered to be a corruption-prone mayor-alderman form of government. Irving Spitzberg maintained that, because of the city hall takeover, "at this time, Little Rock's one hundred top business and professional leaders had potentially more power—explicit political power—than they had had before."[48]

Everett Tucker, executive secretary of the Chamber of Commerce, issued an ambiguous statement in September 1957 warning that "any disorder over integration might hurt industrial development." A month later, after the mobs and turmoil had materialized, the only attempt at organized power-structure reaction came from the "Guy Committee"—named for Walter Guy, the man who pulled it together. Spitzberg described the disappointing results of this effort:

In October [1957] 25 business and "civic" leaders—the board and past presidents of the Little Rock Chamber of Commerce —met, at first secretly, to attempt to solve the crisis. The group found that they could reach little agreement on principles, much less action. . . . The Guy Committee took exactly two actions. . . . [T]hey went to see the Governor and they issued a statement in favor of law and order. Faubus explained that they must remember he was a politician while they were businessmen.[49]

Historian Elizabeth Jacoway came to the conclusion that "the best explanation of elite behavior is to be found in the admission by one member of the group that 'in their hearts' most civic leaders believed that Orval Faubus was right; they might not come right out and openly support the Citizens Council, but they tacitly agreed with the arguments these people were making. After all, racial prejudice had flourished for over a hundred years in Arkansas, and it could not be expected to subside overnight."[50]

The business community and its representatives on the school board repeatedly sought delays of integration. Ashmore felt the Thomas plan and similar efforts, however well intentioned, raised false hopes for "the timid businessmen" that they might ask for and get more time. He said:

[T]hey got Brooks Hays converted around to this, . . . how all we needed to do was reason together with Orval Faubus. Well . . . Orval was far gone by that time. . . . Brooks wrote in his own memoir saying he was convinced that Orval sincerely just wanted a little more time so he could make it work. . . . [He said] he got into trying to get him together with Eisenhower because he was afraid if he didn't, that Orval would wind up in the arms of the few militant southern governors. Well, hell, Orval was already there. I mean right up to his eyeballs. It was awfully late for that. I understood Brooks. Brooks was just simply a kind of Christian fellow who really thought that love could prevail and we were long past that.[51]

Ashmore maintained that the businessmen believed if they could just get "to the right people" and ask for more time, everything would be solved. "You couldn't have a more minimal program than the one the school board worked out and comply with the basic requirement of the court decision," Ashmore said. "There was no way to go compromising beyond that."[52]

Even when the businessmen reluctantly went along with limited integration later to restore their city's progressive image, they remained segregationists emotionally. For many years after the crisis, some of them were still throwing up repeated legal roadblocks to slow down school desegregation, building private or church academies, and growing rich on block busting and white-flight housing developments.

At the time of the crisis, Little Rock's most elite organizations, including the Little Rock Club (for men), the Little Rock Country Club, and the Junior League (for women), still excluded Jews and did not consider blacks as worthy of being anything other than bartenders, waiters, cooks, and maids, much less members. The Jewish businessmen, however, were expected to carry their part of the load in the postwar progressivism as fund-raisers and as part of the inner core of the city's power structure.

Irving Spitzberg noted that Arthur Phillips, a Jewish department store owner, handled the fund-raising for the land on which the Little Rock Air Force Base would be placed. Phillips's father-in-law before him had raised money for an army camp in Little Rock.[53] Despite their tradition of community service, however, Jews were excluded from places of social power. The Little Rock Junior League, for instance, continued for many years to foil efforts to bring Jews into the league. Finally, in 1968, eleven young women, some of them influenced by their work to get the school opened in 1958, resigned as a group from the Junior League in protest against the Little Rock league's anti-Semitic policy. A limited number of Jews were thereafter admitted, but it was 1992 before the first black was invited to join.[54]

It was also 1992 before the prestigious Little Rock Country Club allowed the first black into its membership. That action followed a *New York Times* story that criticized then presidential candidate Bill Clinton for playing golf there when the club excluded black members. Candidate Clinton simply moved his weekend golf games to the newer Chenal Valley Country Club, which from its inception included both blacks and Jews on its board and in its membership.[55]

■   ■   ■

Adolphine Terry was a strong supporter of the *Arkansas Gazette* as it continued to urge the community to abide by the U.S. Supreme Court *Brown* ruling. She called Ashmore, whom she found sympathetic to what she had to say, but she seldom talked with Ned Heiskell, the publisher, who was her contemporary and had served on the library board with her. "I think she leaned on the old man a little too hard on things and she thought he was not liberal enough, I'm sure," Ashmore recalled. "I got the sense she never came to argue the cause with Mr. Heiskell."[56]

By the spring of 1958, the *Gazette* was steadily losing both subscribers and advertisers because of its stand opposing Faubus and favoring compliance with the 1954 Supreme Court decision. At the same time, the newspaper's handling of the September confrontation at Central High School had won a number of prizes, including two Pulitzer Prizes—one for Ashmore and one for the two *Gazette* publishers, Heiskell and his son-in-law, Hugh Patterson.[57]

"In all the history of the Pulitzer Prizes—forty years, I think—this is the first time the same paper has won two of them," Terry said. "I could not be more pleased. There is enough glory in this for a little of it to rub off on all of us."[58]

Terry told a friend, Louise Vinson, wife of prominent businessman Jimmy Vinson, she felt the *Gazette* deserved recognition locally for receiving the prizes. She hoped to organize a dinner for the three Pulitzer Prize recipients. Vinson suggested that Vivion and Joe Brewer, who lived at Scott (a few miles outside Little Rock), might be willing to help.

Terry, whose idea had been a small dinner at the Sam Peck Hotel or the Little Rock Country Club (of which she was a member), was delighted to know the Brewers and others were thinking in "much more magnificent terms: the Marion ballroom with at least 500 guests!" The Brewers also suggested the Arkansas Industrial Development Commission be asked to promote it.

Terry began a round of contacts with community leaders to build support for the dinner. When she waylaid Bill Rock, the head of the AIDC, between services at church, he told her "the Commission could not touch it since they were interested only in industrial development." The following day, she talked with Episcopal bishop Brown and then with the president and vice-president of the Chamber of Commerce. "Receiving no encouragement, I decided to get up my own committee," Terry said. She had such high hopes for the dinner that she threw herself into it wholeheartedly.

> This dinner, if it is a success, can do many things: undoubtedly it will show the *Gazette* [staff] that a large group of responsible citizens approves of what they have done. In addition it will serve to clear the air of the cloud of fear and suspicion which has hung over the town since last September. People still whisper their opinions of segregation, integration and the Governor's conduct. Finally it should serve to defeat Faubus.[59]

She went back to Bishop Brown and asked him to serve on the dinner committee, but he turned it over to someone else, who asked still a third person to come. Terry was relieved when forty people showed up at the planning meeting at her home the next day. She had already reserved the ballroom at the Marion and had asked Ralph McGill of the *Atlanta Constitution* to be the chief speaker. Attorney Edwin Dunaway reported that he had asked Winthrop Rockefeller, later to become governor of Arkansas, to preside at the dinner and Rev. W. O. Vaught Jr., a local minister of the city's largest Baptist congregation, who had supported the black students, to give the invocation—"two inspirations," Terry said. She also noted a point of contention among the planners:

> Several stayed later to argue the point of having it integrated.
> I was adamant on that point—*no*. We are attempting to squirt around the Balm of Gilead not firewater.

The coolness that greeted her from so many of the community leaders about having the dinner at all could have been a factor in leading Terry to insist that the dinner be segregated. Ashmore, who did not remember the subject ever coming up with him, was not surprised. "She was always a realist with all the rest of them," he said. "What she wanted to do was [keep] the schools open, not desegregate the dining room at the Marion Hotel. I always used to tell blacks they were very fortunate that they would not allow them to eat at the Marion Hotel."[60]

Bad food and all, however, blacks felt differently about not being allowed to eat in the Marion dining room. Dr. Evangeline Upshur recalled that when she took her dental boards in the Continental Room of the Marion, she had to go to the kitchen to get a sandwich. "All of the help back there was black and they were looking with admiration at me," she said. "The dental supply salesmen had gotten sandwiches out of the kitchen for the two other blacks, both males, but not for her. Since she was both black and a woman, they did not see her as a potential customer," she said.[61]

Terry had attended an Arkansas Council on Human Relations integrated dinner a few weeks before and had participated regularly in interracial meetings throughout that year. But she knew she would make no new friends for the cause by integrating this dinner, even though it was honoring a stand for obeying the law and indirectly a stand for integration.

A few days later, Terry noted that the Chamber of Commerce turned down a request from the men on the committee to handle ticket sales. "They were in the storm cellar," Ashmore wryly observed later. But the *Gazette* at that time needed the endorsement of the respectable community as personified by the Chamber of Commerce types that the dinner could bring out, he added.[62]

"So I said our office would be the dining room here," Terry wrote. She also connected an additional extension from her daughter Mary's telephone. She came back from a meeting one Friday to find her dining room crowded with people mailing out announcements of the dinner. Several thousand were sent, with tickets that cost $3.50 each enclosed. She also found, to her dismay, after they had been taken to the post office, that Ned Heiskell's name had been misspelled "Heiskill." He would not be happy about that!

It was then that she heard from the AIDC director again, asking her to postpone the dinner until after the election. She was delighted to report to him that the invitations, misspelled name and all, were already in the mail.

The day before the dinner brought a deluge of last-minute people who wanted to pay for their tickets. Despite a sign Terry had put up that read, "Open, Come In," they invariably rang the door-bell. "It is 50 feet from our dining room to the front door and I've made the trip all too many times today," she wrote.[63]

The dinner, held on June 3, drew an overflow crowd of 925 people, the largest crowd ever assembled in the Marion Hotel, according to its manager.[64] After many months of listening to the rantings of segregationists on the local news, my husband, Pat, and I felt distinct relief that we could at last join others of like mind in honoring the *Gazette*. The paper, affectionately known as the "Old Lady" because it was the oldest paper west of the Mississippi, had offered us a different voice through that critical time. The turnout heartened Terry, another "old lady" with a spiritual kinship to the *Gazette*. She wrote:

> Later, I was to realize that it was the tremendous success of this affair which gave me the incentive and courage to go ahead with my activities in the area of integration and eventually to help form the Women's Emergency Committee.[65]

Terry was in fact so elated by calls of congratulations coming in the next day about the dinner's success that she forgot the United Daughters of the Confederacy meeting at her house that afternoon. She hurriedly shifted gears to get out chairs, punch cups, and food for forty UDC women, all of whom would have been happy to send the *Gazette* into immediate oblivion.[66]

When she put together the Arkansas Festival for the Arts that spring to "lift the spirits of the city," Mrs. Terry had no trouble in enlisting the support of the Chamber of Commerce, the Junior League, and the Federation of Women's Clubs. Such organizations had failed to support either the *Gazette* dinner or the integration at Central High School, but they enthusiastically endorsed and worked on the arts festival. Terry opened the doors of her own home to painters, craftsmen, and musicians, who showed their work and performed there for the public. She also carried artwork herself to festival events going on all over town.

It went over so well that the Chamber of Commerce asked Terry to chair the festival the following year, and by fall she was meeting again with civic leaders, who were enthusiastic sponsors this time. When forty of them met at Terry's August 6, it put the room air conditioner on overload, and they sweltered in the ninety-eight-degree heat.[67]

■ ■ ■

Adolphine Terry ventured once more into politics that summer, supporting Judge Lee Ward's unsuccessful attempt to unseat Governor Faubus. Joe, her son, had taken a leave from his job to work for Ward. Terry was financing some of the campaign activities he set up, including a "talkathon" on the radio, to the tune of one thousand dollars.

She met with attorney Henry Woods and a group of labor leaders at the Marion Hotel to discuss raising more money for Ward in early July. Woods recalled that Terry frequently bailed out not only that but subsequent campaigns against Faubus when other funds dried up, as they almost invariably did.[68]

Faubus won the Democratic primary without a runoff, although 115,000 citizens "who did not bow to the knee of Baal cast their votes for his two opponents. . . . All the disturbance of last fall at Central High School was created by Faubus solely to re-elect himself and he has succeeded probably beyond his own wildest expectations," said Terry, who was not a happy loser. "He is doing exactly what he would do if he were a Communist. He is fomenting dissension between groups of our people: he is working in the poorest and most ignorant state and from it his influence for evil is radiating in all directions."[69]

Mrs. Terry was appalled that Jim Johnson, an even more rabid segregationist who had run against Faubus two years before, won a seat on the Arkansas Supreme Court in the same election. She observed that "this year they were there together on a platform of 'hate the nigger.'" By this time, she was receiving junk mail regularly that was both anti-Negro and anti-Jewish, and Joe reported to her that he had heard more anti-Catholic talk than ever before. "Intolerance breeds intolerance," wrote Terry sadly.[70]

Terry read in the *New York Times* that East German Communists were putting on a "Little Rock Ballet." She felt the events at Little Rock were aiding the Communists. She wrote:

> All over the world the Communists, like bad boys, are draw-ing lines in the dust with their bare toes, and daring us to step over them. Of course, they want an atomic war no more than we do, but they have evidently found out how far they can go with us. At the present moment they are engaged in bombing the islands of Quemoy which Formosa claims. No one in this country will want to fight to preserve Chiang Kai Chek but yet can we let the Communists make another grab?[71]

Terry made a late summer trip to visit her ailing sister, Mary, in Maryland and went from there to Vermont to be with friends. "Everywhere I go, the front pages of the newspapers are covered with news from Little Rock," Terry wrote. "The Rutland, Vermont, paper yesterday had a large picture on the front page of our Governor signing a proclamation which would keep the legislature in session (on paper) until the Supreme Court can come to a decision."[72]

Later, back at Friendship Airport in Baltimore, Terry stood in line beside an "attractive, younger woman who was carrying a bunch of unusual dried flowers." They chatted and the young woman asked Terry where she was going. "I didn't have the courage to say Little Rock!" Terry wrote. Instead she said Washington, where she was to change planes for home.

"People who are returning from vacations both in this coun-try and abroad have the same tale to tell," she wrote. "Everywhere dirty looks when people found that they came from Little Rock. Several were refused accommodations in hotels and tourist courts when these were not filled."[73]

# ▪ 4 ▪

# Call Out the Women

When Adolphine Terry returned from her late summer trip to the East in 1958, she found the school situation at home growing steadily worse. After meeting with a couple of friends, she placed her hat squarely on her head, donned her white gloves, and went down to the *Gazette* to call on Harry Ashmore. She wasted no time in telling him what she planned to do. "The men have failed," she said. "It's time to call out the women."

Ashmore included Terry's legendary remark in his speech at a 1966 dinner honoring her. He confirmed much later that the visit did indeed take place and gave this version of what happened:

> Well, you know everything was falling apart and the phone rang at the *Gazette* one morning, and I picked it up and she said, "Mr. Ashmore, this is Adolphine Terry. . . . I'm coming to see you." . . . So she came in and I had no idea what [she] was up to, really. She . . . sat down and said, "Mr. Ashmore, the school situation is absolutely intolerable. It is perfectly evident that the men are not going to do anything about this. I've sent for the young ladies."[1]

By the end of July, Orval Faubus had won the biggest victory of his career in the Democratic primary with nearly 69 percent of the statewide vote. The same election ensured that the fanatical segregationist Jim Johnson, whose previous opposition to Faubus had caused the governor to move in more extreme directions, would win a seat on the Arkansas Supreme Court. Both had run vicious campaigns against Harry Ashmore, the *Gazette,* and Daisy Bates, paying little attention to other candidates in their races.[2]

With local businessmen running scared and community silence growing after the Faubus and Johnson victories, Terry was seeing only a hopeless uphill battle ahead until she received a note from a young friend, Velma Powell, the wife of the controversial assistant principal at Central High School, that spurred her on. "Whenever there's been a crisis in Little Rock in the past, you have always been there," it read. "Where are you now?"

As a result, Terry, Powell, and Vivion Brewer, who had helped with the *Gazette* dinner, met in Terry's parlor on September 12, 1958, a date that would be remembered for other events as well, some of which would have a profound effect on what the women decided to do.[3] Hatred had by then reached a high pitch in the city. Relman Morin, a Pulitzer Prize–winning reporter, wrote on September 12 that the situation at Little Rock "seems infinitely more dangerous . . . than it did a year ago. Sentiment has crystallized. Resistance to desegregating Central High School has become truly massive. . . . Now, 12 months later, the feeling looks solid, a monolithic slab of resistance against desegregation."[4]

None of the Little Rock senior high schools had opened when the elementary and junior high schools started classes after Labor Day. They were awaiting a Supreme Court decision on whether the school board could get a two-and-a-half-year delay on integration. The lawyers admitted that the time requested coincided with when they hoped Faubus would be out of office. The decision denying the delay came down at noon on September 12. "The Supreme Court said 'integrate!'" Terry wrote in the same diary entry in which she recorded her impressions of the meeting that had taken place in her parlor:

> This afternoon Velma Powell, Vivion Brewer and I had a session, as the result of which we are calling together a group of women who are concerned about the matter of race relations to see if we cannot organize an agency through which our kind of people can express themselves. The meeting will be next Tuesday at 2:30 P.M. It is high time for the moderates to be heard from.[5]

As seventy-six-year-old Terry swung into action in one direction, Governor Faubus moved in another. He signed a state school-closing bill and issued a proclamation, both on the afternoon of

September 12, that would keep the Little Rock high schools shut down until a special local election could be held.[6]

Terry noted the following day, "the sufferers will be the young people, whose college credits will be put in jeopardy." Then, on September 15, she wrote:

> Mothers are beginning to look around for schools to which they can send their high school children. Faubus is becoming more and more drunk with power; if you are against him you are a Communist. He attended the Communist school at Mena, Ark. and I personally think he *is* a Communist. He has done exactly what he would have done, promoting fear, hatred and discord, if he were a member of the Party.[7]

Mothers League members had been protesting a few days earlier the anticipated use of federal marshals at Central High School if the Supreme Court ruled for what they called "gun point" integration. They also called for the governor to sign a school-board recall bill that would require only 15 percent of the voters to sign a petition initiating a recall. When Mothers League leader Margaret Jackson got news of the Supreme Court decision, she sobbed into the telephone to a reporter that "we will keep fighting as long as there is breath in our bodies."

Dr. Dale Cowling, a Baptist pastor and president of the Little Rock Ministerial Alliance, had wrestled with his conscience and had come up with a different view. He declared bravely that it was the responsibility of the Supreme Court to interpret the Constitution and laws, and it was the duty of citizens to obey them. He suggested in a strongly Baptist vein that instead of violence and hot tempers Christians "need to generate the attitude of Christian love as exemplified by our Savior."[8]

Despite Cowling's support, the school board was feeling other pressures. On September 12, one of its members, Henry Rath, resigned in protest, he said, against the Supreme Court decision. Meyers Bakery was also getting calls from small grocery stores that refused to stock Meyers bread on their shelves unless Rath, the bakery's accountant, left the board.[9]

A petition-signing campaign by the Mothers League to get rid of all the rest of the board members except Dr. Dale Alford got lots of publicity but too few signatures even to meet the 15 percent requirement. A KLRA radio announcement had urged those wishing to sign to go to the Capital Citizens Council office or to Jimmy Karam's Men's Store, making it clear who the Mothers League allies were.[10]

"While we fight locally over the problem of integration, the world situation becomes constantly more frightful," Terry, staying grounded in international as well as local affairs, noted in her diary:

> Today Mr. Dulles and Soviet Foreign Minister Gromyko both addressed the (United Nations General) Assembly mainly on the subject of the China-Formosa area. Dulles spoke of the "Chinese Communists' armed aggression which threatens peace" and Gromyko called on the U.S. to withdraw from the two islands.[11]

Governor Faubus integrated other schools in Arkansas that September without intervention and some the year before at Fayetteville, Fort Smith, Ozark, Charleston, and Van Buren.[12] A small white-student boycott occurred at Van Buren in September 1958, which had first been integrated in 1957. However, it was soon over.[13] All were northwestern Arkansas towns where black populations were sparse. Faubus, through his resistance at Little Rock, was playing primarily to eastern Arkansas segregationists as well as to those in other Southern states where he kept being mentioned as presidential timber.

Virginia, Texas, and Florida had also adopted "Little Rock" laws that would enable them to close schools rather than allow the federal government to integrate them. Virginia governor J. Lindsay Almond did in fact close schools at Front Royal, Charlottesville, and Norfolk. The Norfolk closing affected some ten thousand white students.[14]

■   ■   ■

One of the two women who met with Terry, thirty-six-year-old Velma Powell, had no children, but her husband, J. O. Powell, was one of two vice-principals at Central High School. Both she and her husband had been distressed at the state-level resistance to the Central High integration and the disruption caused by it inside the school the year before. Velma Powell was secretary for the Arkansas Council on Human Relations, an interracial organization to which Terry belonged and which had sponsored an integrated dinner Terry had attended the previous spring. During the first year of school integration, Velma Powell had repeatedly made lists of things that could be done to make it work better, but they had remained just that: paper lists.

Powell's frustration level was high when she wrote to Terry, whom she knew well. She had once stayed in the Terry home when she was attending business school at Little Rock, and she had watched Terry more than once head successful community efforts.[15]

The other woman, fifty-seven-year-old Vivion Brewer, was a native of Little Rock but at the time was living at a family-owned Bearskin Lake home near Scott, twenty miles away. She was married but had no children (her only child had died young), and she lived outside the Little Rock School District—facts on which Faubus later capitalized. She was, however, like Terry, financially invulnerable, having inherited a substantial sum of money from her father.

Brewer's father, W. E. Lenon, had owned the Peoples Savings Bank, where she had worked for a while after her graduation in 1921 from Smith College. He had also been mayor of Little Rock. Brewer had later lived in Washington for a time with her husband, Joe, formerly an aide as well as a nephew of Sen. Joe T. Robinson from Arkansas. Vivion Brewer had strong feelings about what was happening in the city where she had lived for most of her life:

> Suddenly we were confronted by that disgraceful September day in 1957 at Central High School. . . . The stories friends told me of that violence which need never have been except for the egocentric ambition of one supremely shrewd man, served to heighten my anxiety over the "place" of the Negro in the American way of life. All that winter and the next summer, stories of the indignities heaped on those courageous young Negroes in Central High School who wanted nothing but a better education drove me to a state of illness. . . . I worried about the possible destruction of a once beautiful, peaceful and progressive city.[16]

Terry had obtained information from the Southern Regional Council in Atlanta about how Jessie Daniel Ames had put together the Association of Southern Women for the Prevention of Lynching. She told Powell and Brewer that something like ASWPL was what she had in mind for Little Rock.

Terry asked Brewer to serve as chairperson and Powell to be secretary. Then the three listed names of twenty or twenty-five women they thought might come if it were presented as a study group to improve the racial climate.[17]

While the meeting was taking place, a mother who had two daughters affected by the Central High School closing knocked on Terry's door. She was Frances Williams, whose father had been a congressman from North Carolina when she met and married Grainger Williams, who was then working in Congressman Dave Terry's office. She had gone to Adolphine Terry's house almost instinctively. She added:

> Nobody answered the door. The next day, I found out that she and Vivion Brewer and somebody else had been having a meeting. . . . I didn't know of anyone else in this town I would have even thought of [going to see].

"There wasn't any doubt that she [Terry] was the one, she could pull us together," Williams said, sensing the need to get women organized as did the three other women.[18]

Terry had another concern as she moved toward getting a larger group of women together just four days later. Daisy Bates recalled that Terry invited her to her house after the meeting with Powell and Brewer to find out what the NAACP was going to do about Faubus's order and to inform her about the plan to organize white women. Bates told her that the NAACP would probably appeal the state school-closing law, and Terry asked if she thought the schools could be opened that year.

"I don't know," Bates had replied. Terry explained that the purpose of the upcoming meeting of white women was to build acceptance for integration in Little Rock. Bates was by then a national symbol of courage as the leader of the Little Rock Nine but considered a much-feared radical by many whites at home.

"Now don't you come, Daisy, don't you come," Terry reportedly told her as they walked to the front door. "Because if you do, I can't get the other women to come." Although she could not have been happy about being asked not to participate, Bates said that because she trusted Terry, she supported what Terry was doing.[19]

Just as Terry had decreed that the *Gazette* dinner be segregated, she was deciding in advance that the women's effort also would be segregated. With a political eye developed from earlier times, she knew that to win over other whites, she needed a core of white women with enough influence, clout, and drive to pull others in.

Bates did not come on September 16, but fifty-eight white women did, much to the delight of the three founders.[20] Ashmore, in his 1966 speech honoring Terry, said:

> There was, I am sure, a symbolism that would have pleased Miss Adolphine's poet brother, John Gould Fletcher, in the trek of the matrons from the green suburban hills to the old city, up the long walk and through the pillared portico of the great house put up four wars ago by a ranking Confederate, Albert Pike. John Gould would have sensed, certainly, the flow of history, touched as always with irony, and the more marvelous for it.[21]

I heard about the meeting from a friend and called Terry, whom I knew by reputation only, to ask if I could come. Alice Gray, who worked at the Little Rock Public Library and knew Terry as a member of the board there, went with me. The two of us were mothers of six elementary and preschool children—three each. We talked about how good it felt to be going to a meeting that someone of Terry's stature had put together, where there would be other women who thought like we did.

It was my first visit inside Terry's home. Its Greek Revival exterior did not prepare me for the massive, well-worn Victorian furniture that gave it a musty, much-lived-in look. Two large parlors on the left side of the foyer had chairs set up for the meeting. A library was to the right of the entryway. Terry's father, dressed in his gray Confederate colonel's uniform, looked down, rather benignly I thought, on our gathering from a portrait above the fireplace in the front parlor.

Adolphine Terry, dignified and patrician, her wispy, white hair drawn back in a bun at her neck, was dressed in a printed dress that looked like it could have, and probably did, come off the rack at Blass's, one of the town's two department stores whose building she owned. Behind her glasses, her eyes were full of good humor and she had a whimsical smile as though she was about to share some intriguing secret with us. What came through as she spoke, along with her warmth, was a clarity about how she felt and about her intention to act. She was what I wanted to be—clear on the issues, tenacious and fearless, but with plenty of good common sense. It was the first time I had heard the story of the Association of Southern Women for the Prevention of Lynching. I was fascinated with the idea that it could be used as a model for action in this present crisis.

And I felt exhilaration that I was finally doing something. Little Rock had become the testing ground for implementing the *Brown* decision for the entire South, and up until now, we had been a miserable failure. I never doubted after that first meeting that, with Terry at the helm, we could make ourselves heard. My assignment was to make telephone calls to nonexistent but potential members, with the hope that a telephone chain would emerge. I learned to cook dinner, clean house, settle fights, and give bottles, all while holding a telephone to my ear with one shoulder.

Aside from a few older women who were friends of Terry and Brewer, the other women were mostly in their thirties and forties. I recognized several as mothers of teenagers displaced from their high schools. The rest of us had children of assorted younger ages and a heavy stake in keeping the public school system intact. Aside from Terry, Brewer, and a few others, it was not by any means an elitist group. It was made up of the kind of women who head committees at the PTA and at church, and we could not have afforded private schools had there been any, which at that point there were not.

As the meeting got underway, Terry nominated Brewer as chairperson and she was quickly voted in. Although Brewer appeared charming and confident, she confessed later that she had had misgivings about her own ability as a spokesperson. "Probably I was the worst choice to be the leader of the WEC," she wrote later. "Certainly from a political standpoint I was, although many a time I tried to convince myself that my adversaries would have found something to attack in any woman."[22] Her large, intent eyes gave her a solemn demeanor and she spoke deliberately, as though studying each word carefully before saying it.

The political concerns Brewer alluded to were related to her not living in or having children in the school district, but those were mild compared to some of the public onslaughts and attacks that followed. Terry, an experienced hand in politics, could slough them off or fight back, while Brewer seemed to suffer inwardly when the segregationist abuse came.

Because Brewer, Terry, and Powell had agreed the emphasis should be on easing racial tensions, Brewer, apparently unaware of the encounter between Terry and Bates, proposed that black women who shared the same views be called in. With that, Brewer said a few of the women who had come took their names off the sign-up sheet and slipped out, as Terry's instincts had told her they would. Brewer, following her own list of recommendations, then suggested that, since United Nations Week was coming up, the black operatic singer, Marian Anderson, might be invited to Little Rock for a concert. There were a few more departures from the room. Then Brewer described the moment when the meeting came to life:

> Suddenly a woman in the rear of the second parlor jumped up from her folding chair and cried out, "This is all very fine, but what are we going to do now, *now?* My two boys must have an education and they have already lost two weeks of school. I think we have to do something now to open our schools." There was a clatter of affirmation and I looked from one to another of the intense faces and knew there was nothing to do but throw away all my notes and start over.[23]

Barbara Shults, the mother of two elementary-aged children and who was to become a member of the steering committee, said that the women had first envisioned starting a committee for racial harmony, but because of the crisis they had decided that this in itself would create opposition, so the focus for the new group was to be "strictly aimed at saving the public schools." She also recalled the mood at the first meeting:

The funny thing, everybody was so furious with Faubus in 1958. I remember somebody got up and said, "We can't say such and such, after all, he is our Governor." The rest of the women just booed her down. It was very biased and I thought that was interesting somebody had made that comment and nobody else was willing to give an inch just because he was Governor.[24]

The discussion shifted to the fact that Governor Faubus had set a local election for October 7 at which Little Rock voters would have the option of voting for or against integration. The wording on the ballot, the handiwork of segregationist Attorney General Bruce Bennett, was such that when a voter cast a ballot against integration he or she also voted for closed schools. With the prevailing ugly racial mood in Little Rock, no one expected more than a few people to vote for integration. But before they left, all of the women who remained to the end had agreed to work on the election.

Dottie Morris, the shy, prematurely gray mother of two teenaged sons and the wife of a physician who looked after Terry's family, was sitting on the front row. Brewer caught her eye and asked her to head an election committee. Although "taken by surprise," Morris agreed to serve "with the grace and resolute purpose which characterized the women through the life of our organization," Brewer said. Volunteers were recruited for the committee meeting to be held the next day at Morris's home.[25]

A second committee to name the organization was set up by Brewer and chaired by Hildegard Smith, a retired music teacher who lived not far from the Terry mansion and who was roughly the same age as Terry. Her sister, Ada May Smith, who lived with her and who wore prim, closely fitting black hats whenever she went out, was elected treasurer. Velma Powell was elected secretary, but that was soon to be changed.

Brewer was pessimistic about that first meeting and afterward said that "it fell to pieces." She added that Barbara Ashmore had told her husband, Harry, the *Gazette* executive editor, "that it was confused and confusing, admitting she had little idea what would come of it."[26]

Terry, on the other hand, as an old politician observing the passion and energy rising out of the women who came, considered it an enormous success.[27] Brewer, Powell, and Terry, in their post-mortem of the meeting, recognized that the young mothers had reset their agenda, and they immediately began to draw up new plans.

The three also decided that they could not hope to win any elections, particularly the upcoming one, if there was any taint of their being integrationists. That meant that Velma Powell, secretary of the interracial Arkansas Council on Human Relations and also secretary of the new group, would have to go. Brewer called Dottie Morris, who, because she had agreed to do one job, got another as the new secretary of the still unnamed group.[28]

Hildegard Smith's committee, which met the next day, decided the new organization's name should be the "Women's Emergency Committee to Save Our Schools." A few days later, the name was changed to the "Women's Emergency Committee to Open Our Schools," because we discovered that a "Save Our Schools" committee was being formed in New Orleans. The name reflected both the urgency and the single-mindedness with which the Little Rock women viewed the task at hand.

Terry held onto her own larger goals for the organization, writing a few days later:

> Most of the women were particularly concerned with the school situation as of today, hence the word "Emergency" but we hope the organization will continue to function and help create a climate of good will for all groups. We have been a friendly, peaceful community and in the past year have become the center of the "hate-mongering" of the country. I have been receiving quantities of anti-Negro and anti-Jewish materials, which is being mailed right here in Little Rock.[29]

The official account of that first meeting in the organization's minutes said that "Mrs. David Terry opened the meeting with a brief statement that she had been thinking how much a group of women could do by working quietly and with no publicity to help educate our community."[30]

The formation of the WEC, however, received almost instant

local and national press attention. Terry noted a few days after the first meeting:

> This afternoon *Life* and *Time* magazines sent reporters to take pictures of the officers of our group. I have always been violently opposed to publicity in integration matters but I suppose times have changed. When I asked why our little local group rated national publicity, we were told that ours was the only group of responsible citizens in the community who had taken a stand for law and order.[31]

When the *Time* photographer got down on his knees to photograph Terry in front of the fireplace, she had no idea why he chose that position until she saw the picture later in the magazine. It included the portrait of her Confederate father overhead.

Terry had good cause to be leery of the publicity. Following the first news stories, hate calls directed toward her began arriving on a regular basis at her home, labelling members of her family "half niggers" and accusing them of wanting Daisy Bates to be the Central High principal. Threatening letters arrived by the dozen, most of them unsigned, and one from an anonymous man who claimed to have been a family friend. "You have asked for the mud to be thrown and I can assure you that a lot of it will be flying," he wrote. "The past history of your home will come to light. Especially where our great statesman Albert Pike was concerned. There are a lot of old timers who still remember the K.K.K. meetings that were held in the very home you now live in. We also remember that Albert Pike was the Leader of the Ark. K.K.K. His spirit has come to life."[32]

The kind of intimidation that had worked on the Little Rock business community, however, failed to silence Adolphine Terry. And it was Governor Faubus himself, when he set the school closing law in motion, who provided her with an organizing base of angry white mothers whose teenagers were underfoot at home. When Faubus was later asked if he took this into consideration, he replied:

> I knew it would last about a year and then it would be over with. You can't talk to people when they're riled. You can't reason with them. You have to let them have their way for a while.[33]

He admitted he had not expected the opposition of a few women to amount to much. "It was just the senior high schools [that were closed]," he said. He had not bargained for the fact that many more of us could also see the specter of no schools for our younger children too. Faubus maintained that sentiment at that time was overwhelmingly with him. Contributions to form a private high school were coming into his office, "as much as four thousand dollars a day from every state in the Union and from foreign countries," he said.[34]

Faubus had cited an 1875 state law that said public schools could be leased to private schools when he got the school closing law passed by the legislature in August. The day after the first open WEC meeting, six persons formed a Little Rock Private School Corporation, saying they were going to use the Little Rock high school buildings.[35] All but one were Faubus supporters and prominent segregationists. The women who had been at Terry's meeting were upset to learn that Willie Oates was one of the incorporators. Many had supported her as a fellow American Association of University Women member. They had assumed she was for keeping the public schools open when a few months before she won her race to become the second woman at the time in the Arkansas legislature.

One of the Terry women, Irene Samuel, felt compelled to call Oates because, like her, she was a doctor's wife. Samuel said she had worked to get Oates elected to the legislature. "She had always taken a positive, active role in the community, volunteering for everything as she's continued to do," Samuel recalled, but she added that she expressed her unhappiness about Oates serving on the board for the private school, which was no more than a segregationist ploy.[36] A letter from Vivion Brewer as WEC chairperson also went to Oates, calling on her to resign from the Little Rock Private School Corporation.[37]

The WEC women working with Terry were in for another major surprise. Governor Faubus shifted the date of the school election forward from October 7 to September 27 after he realized public pressure against him was growing, although he denied that was the reason for the change.[38] Brewer took the shift in election time to mean that the WEC was making him aware that some opposition was building. She was stunned, however, that it left only eleven days to get ready for the election. Besides that, the election now would be on a Saturday when many Little Rockians would be traveling to Fayetteville for a football game, she noted.[39]

Although Faubus chose to ignore the women on the day he announced the election change, he did lash out at a group of Presbyterian ministers who opposed his school closing policy. They were "brainwashed," he said, by "the left-wingers and the Communists" and declared some of them were left-wingers and Communists themselves. He also took a few jabs at his favorite targets, Virgil Blossom and the Little Rock School Board, because they had decided to suspend football and extracurricular activities at the four closed high schools, upsetting the sports fans who were Faubus supporters.[40]

Shortly afterward, Brewer issued her first statement to the press declaring:

> We are deeply concerned that the young people are the ones to bear the hardships of this tragic situation and we are going to do everything in our power to open the four high schools. . . . Since the ballot is to be worded . . . :
>
> *For* racial integration of all schools within the school district
> *Against* racial integration of all schools within the school district
>
> And [since] we are urging every voter to mark his or her ballot *For racial integration,* we feel we must clarify our position in this regard. We stand neither for integration nor against integration. We are not now concerned with this. Our sole aim—I repeat—our sole aim is to get our four high schools open and our students back in their classes.[41]

It was tricky business, as the wily attorney general, Bruce Bennett, had meant it to be, urging people to vote for racial integration while attempting to proclaim one's own neutrality. Brewer was suddenly out on a tightwire, a new target for the Citizens Council, the Mothers League, and the assorted hate groups that suddenly had appeared. She was inexperienced in fielding questions from reporters, which made such encounters painful for her. Brewer spoke of her "doleful likeness" in a picture that appeared in the *Gazette*. She felt that *Life* magazine had failed to run a picture of the new WEC officers because the "four gray heads did not have *Life*'s choice of hair coloring." She told about one foreign reporter who said he was tempted to take a picture of a "pretty, gay young girl on the Capitol grounds" and run it as the WEC leader. And it needled her that even the White Citizens Council said in an ad, "Don't be misled into voting for race-mixed schools on September 27 by the nice old ladies and the ivory tower preachers."[42]

Brewer often worked with Velma Powell's help at the Arkansas Council on Human Relations and narrowly escaped being caught there in a raid orchestrated by Attorney General Bennett, who sent police to the door during a routine meeting. "This caused two male members of the Council board to dash out the back door and hurdle the back fence. I was grateful to have escaped such a method of exit."[43] Charles Johnston, then an officer with First Federal Savings and one of the fleeing board members, also recalled the incident:

> Right in the middle of this meeting we became aware of this milling crowd out front, and Bruce Bennett had set up this raid. Rusty Ralston was this television huckster, and they were banging on the door. What did Fred Darragh and I do—duck out the back window. I had to push him over the fence in the back yard. . . .
>
> That's my comment on white man's courage—when push came to shove, we cowarded out.[44]

Brewer's visibility in the press began to bring hate calls and letters to her home as well. One correspondent wrote, "Food for thought, Sister Brewer. . . . You're too like Thurgood Marshall, Wiley Branton and Daisy Bates. . . . You're too far along in life to become pregnant by one of those Black Bucks or would that have been the height of your ambition? You surely don't have any offsprings [white] or grandchildren or you wouldn't think as you do."

Another letter said, "I'm absolutely dumbfounded at what you and Mrs. Terry are doing. I know her and I know she isn't a Jew or a Negro but I do not know you and by your picture in today's paper you could be either or both. Surely you are not white gentile." She received several death threats. One, reminiscent of Little Rock's last lynching, said, "You and all others who think as you do should be tied by the feet to a car and dragged the length of Ninth Street as did happen once before."[45]

Still, Brewer met constantly with the media, often at Terry's home because her own was so far away, and she attempted to give public shape to an organization whose own members had not fully defined it. For the most part she received good press, because even those who did not agree with her were impressed by her tall, straight bearing and her determination to speak out honestly at a time when so few others were doing so.

Brewer recognized, however, that she knew little about public schools. She found it difficult to explain a statement hastily drawn up by a WEC committee about Faubus's plan to turn the public high schools into private ones that read:

> The [WEC] Committee has been assured by attorneys that there is no possible legal way for our schools to be operated on a private basis without immediately subjecting themselves to further law suits which would force them to close again.
>
> Schools operated on a private basis would be deprived of all federal aid, school lunch programs, North Central accreditation, present inter-scholastic athletic competition and eligibility for college scholarships.[46]

"I feel so desperately inadequate," she said to Terry, who assured her that the only person who felt adequate to the crisis was the one who had created it—the governor himself.[47]

Brewer and Terry, however, found allies almost immediately among several young attorneys who were also opposing the school closing. Bob Shults, Barbara's husband, and Tom Eisele (currently a federal judge) put together a statement signed by sixty-one prominent lawyers for an ad that appeared on September 21 in both the *Gazette* and the *Democrat*. The ad declared support for free public education. It recognized that, while the court order for limited integration might be distasteful to some, having no public schools was even more distasteful:

It is our opinion that existing public school facilities of this District cannot be legally operated with any public funds as segregated private schools and, consequently, that the real issue before the voters of this District on September 27, 1958, will be whether we shall open our schools under the Court approved plan of limited integration or close them altogether.[48]

Although most of the younger lawyers in the major law firms signed the statement, some of the senior members did not. One head of a firm, who was then also head of the Chamber of Commerce, "equivocated and hemmed and hawed . . . but wouldn't sign it," Bob Shults recalled. "Later, after it was published in the *Gazette* [the next morning] he called me and said, 'Is it too late for me to get my name on there? It's going to be in the *Democrat* in the afternoon.' I tried and I said, 'I'm sorry. It's too late.'"[49] Little Rock had less than a handful of women lawyers at that time, none with major firms, and only one of them, Neva B. Talley, signed the ad. Shults and Eisele paid for the ad out of their own pockets, Shults said.

Conspicuously absent from the list of signers were members of the Mehaffey, Smith, and Williams firm. Bill Smith of that firm represented Governor Faubus in his legal activity to thwart the federal government's attempt to enforce federal law. Later, Herschel Friday of the same firm served as the lawyer for the Little Rock School Board through its many years of foot-dragging effort to keep integration at a minimum.[50]

■　■　■

The fledgling WEC, which almost immediately began to run ads supporting the opening of the high schools, found scattered support in the mainstream religious community. "Two ministers and the governing boards of two Little Rock churches went on record yesterday urging retention of the city's schools as public institutions," the *Arkansas Gazette* proclaimed in a front page story on September 22. One of the pastors, Dr. Dale Cowling of Second Baptist Church, had already been heard from. The other was Rev. Kenneth Shamblin of Pulaski Heights Methodist Church. St. Paul Methodist and Westover Hills Presbyterian Church boards issued statements calling for the retention of public schools. Husbands of WEC members were active on both boards.[51]

■   ■   ■

Approximately 170 women crowded into Terry's parlors and foyer, some of them sitting on the stairs, at the second WEC meeting September 23, four days before the election. Those who came were asked to sign one of the yellow legal-pad sheets going around. At the top of each sheet, a handwritten pledge read: "I will go to the polls Saturday and vote *FOR* integration in our public schools." This was done to weed out spies from the Mothers League, at least one of whom was present. The women were also asked for a one dollar contribution. The yellow sheets, still part of the WEC file, show that each married woman signed with a "Mrs." in front of her husband's name. Wives were normally identified that way in the 1950s on printed stationery, in checkbooks, and whenever their names appeared in the newspaper.

The group, described by Terry as "fairly young and well dressed," got even better billing from a *U.S. News and World Report* photographer who told her "it was the best-looking group of women" he had ever photographed.[52] One member, Gwen Booe, recalled that for one meeting Brewer and Terry had sent out the word that TV cameras would be present. "We all dressed up real pretty and she had a tea to show off this old Southern mansion," Booe recalled.[53]

Their brief encounters with the press had convinced Terry and Brewer that they needed more young mothers of school-aged children out front representing an organization to open the schools. Brewer announced the names of steering committee members, all attractive young mothers, at the second meeting, and the picture appeared the following morning in the *Arkansas Gazette*—three days before the fateful election.

Booe, who appeared in the picture with her sister, Billie Wilson, recalled that the steering committee's membership fluctuated up until the time the picture was made. One woman, a well-known local artist, agreed to be in the picture until the society editor of one of the local papers told her she was horrified that the artist would even consider doing it. Another enthusiastic woman reluctantly declined when her husband's employer vetoed her appearance. Two more just did not show up that day.[54]

Those who finally appeared in the picture were identified as: Mrs. S. W. Ross, Mrs. Charles Stephens, Mrs. L. Prentice Booe, Mrs. Edward Lester, and Mrs. Gordon Wilson. The caption also listed Mrs. Samuel Cottrell and Mrs. Nathan Graham as steering committee members.[55]

The picture caption cautiously said "the Committee believes that only by voting 'for' Saturday can Little Rock residents retain a public school system." The word "integration" was no where to be found this time.

Booe, Wilson, and Stephens were PTA presidents. Lester and Shults were the wives of law partners already actively opposing the school closing. Mary Evelyn Lester knew Vivion Brewer, who had sought advice from Mary Evelyn's husband, Ed, from the WEC's beginning.[56] And Charlotte Ross, whose husband was a physician at the University of Arkansas Medical School, was a neighbor of the Lesters.

Tables were placed on Terry's huge porch at the second meeting where women could sign up for immediate duty in the upcoming election campaign. Volunteers were given pages out of a poll tax book at one table to call eligible voters and find out where they stood. At another table, women willing to volunteer their cars to take voters to the polls were putting their names on a list. Another table solicited poll watchers, and still another asked for women to sign up to hold Coke parties at which lawyers would come and explain the ballot.

Alice Gray, Dr. Dola Thompson, and I signed up together to give an afternoon Coke party in our neighborhood. Others on the handwritten Coke party list were Miss Hildegard Smith, Mrs. Robert Wixom, Mrs. Hans Schlumberger, and Mrs. John Samuel. Samuel, who said she sent out several hundred invitations, had only nine people show up. We had only slightly better luck. Approximately a dozen friends came to hear Jim Storey explain the legal implications of the ballot.[57]

I also joined the publicity committee, headed by Frances Williams, as did ten other women. We prepared fliers, ads, and press releases. Brewer, working with Jim Brandon of Ted Lamb's advertising agency, stayed busy placing newspaper ads and arranging for television and radio time.[58] One of the first ads carried treasurer Ada May Smith's name, address, and telephone number, urging women to send one dollar and join the WEC. Smith learned some words she had never heard before from hate callers and from angry messages written across some of the ads returned to her. But her mail also brought many one-dollar to five-dollar donations and the names and addresses of new members. One doctor sent her fifty dollars.

In addition, a "clever finance committee" built a small election war chest overnight. Much of it was contributed anonymously by people who feared for their jobs and businesses, but it came. One woman brought Brewer an envelope with five hundred dollars in it, asking her to forget both where she had gotten it and the fact that the woman had been there.[59]

A letter with a fifty-dollar check came to Terry from the insurance executive Herbert Thomas on the eve of the election. "I now see the first signs of public courage and regardless of how this election goes, the willingness of people to speak out is going to grow, and with that will come a better answer than we now have," Thomas wrote.

Terry, the perennial optimist, held out hope that the still-disorganized women might win:

> We expect to bear down on the election. . . . The whole thing is set up in the interest of the segregationists: the voters have to cast their ballot "for integration," which few people want to do, and we have to carry a majority of the qualified voters, not a majority of those who vote. It will be a miracle if we win but miracles do happen. And it will be the only way to open our schools.[60]

Although all of the meetings were held at Terry's home, Brewer announced at the second meeting that office space had been rented at the old Capitol Hotel at 119 West Markham. She was grateful to Miss Cassanelli, who owned the property and "did not for an instant question our motives."[61] Brewer described it as an "early landmark with a beautiful iron Colonial facade," although it had by then become a rundown eyesore where prostitutes sometimes brushed shoulders with the earnest WEC women as they came and went.

Meanwhile, the governor was trying to sell the public on his private school plan, which he said was "sound and workable," to replace the closed high schools. In a television appearance, on the evening of September 18, he cited a congressional committee report on the Washington, D.C., schools after integration. He quoted the report as saying that "integration would bring a lowering of educational standards, [a] rise in immorality and juvenile delinquency and strife." The WEC quickly copied and circulated a well-researched booklet about the District of Columbia schools that refuted his statements and got the *Gazette* to print portions of it. The battle between the women and the governor was intensifying.[62]

Brewer called all three of the local television stations asking for equal time to refute Faubus's arguments that the high schools were better off closed than integrated. Only one, KATV, Channel 7, would agree to furnish thirty minutes as a public service two nights after the Faubus speech. Brewer met with Lester, Shults, and Walter Trulock, a young stockbroker and a friend of the two lawyers, to plan a television pro-public-school panel to be sponsored by the WEC.[63] It was the first of its kind to appear on television during the crisis.

"Are we really ready to abandon one of the finest public school systems in the United States just to keep a few Negro students out?" Margaret Stephens, president of the Central High School PTA the year before and a member of the WEC steering committee, asked TV watchers. Ed Lester followed up with, "Do you really believe that we can have schools just like before by simply painting 'private school' on a sign and hanging it on Central High?" And another attorney, John E. Coates, said, "a vote for integration would not be a vote for immediate integration of all city schools," but a vote for "reopening the high schools under the court plan."

Dr. Cowling called for not allowing "the heat of our passions in this hour to cause us to throw overboard such a priceless heritage" as free public schools. Marguerite Henry, a member of the governor's own committee on education established prior to crisis days, a staunch WEC member, and the wife of a local physician, thanked others who were working for the WEC and urged people to vote for "free public education." The moderator was W. H. Hadley Jr., who had been a television newsman sympathetic to the black students at Central High and was now in public relations. While he showed film of empty classrooms, he talked about those classrooms without students as being the "price of segregation."[64] Terry was elated by the panel's presentation:

> Our Women's Emergency Committee put on the best panel discussion on TV that I have ever heard; Two women and three men discussed various aspects of the desegregation situation as it concerns our schools. People were urged to go to the polls Saturday and vote *"yes"*; that it did not mean complete integration as the ballot read, but only the slow plan worked out last year by the School Board. My telephone continued to ring; one woman said she was coming over to burn this house![65]

No other Little Rock organization had been willing to urge citizens to vote for opening the schools in this election, not—despite the individual lawyers' ad—the County Bar Association, the PTA Council, the Chamber of Commerce, or the Ministerial Alliance. The burgeoning WEC was alone, serving as a rallying point for voicing opposition to the governor's actions. Information sheets, prepared with the help of the lawyers, were circulated through local PTAs with WEC-friendly presidents, urging patrons to vote for integration and opening the schools.

When the other two TV stations refused free equal time, Brewer decided to use WEC campaign funds to purchase thirty minutes of time on KARK-TV and KTHV for election eve, Friday, September 26. Working again with Lester, Shults, and Trulock, she met also with Episcopal bishop Robert R. Brown, the author of a recently published book, *Bigger Than Little Rock,* who urged using only ministers on television. Brewer said she felt his book "stressed too much, in my estimation, the efficacy of the ministers in the Little Rock situation." But it was Friday morning and there was no time for argument. The other men thought perhaps having all ministers would motivate churches to act. Brewer, in her account of the incident, said:

Deeply disappointed and apprehensive, I picked up my phone to seek three ministers to complete what had become Bishop Brown's panel. Many calls elicited assents from only Bishop Paul Martin of the Methodist Church and Dr. T. B. Hay of Pulaski Heights Presbyterian Church. Exhausting my list of potentials, with knowledge that the entire script must be rewritten within hours, I finally turned once more to Rev. Dale Cowling. "Of course, I'll do it," he said. "But it makes me very sad that you have found so few."[66]

Shults recalled that after he and Trulock got to the station that night, they found that Bishop Brown had changed his mind, deciding the panel was "too controversial." While Brown later became identified as a staunch supporter of what was going on, Shults could not forget that "we were like ten minutes from going on the air, and he was trying to talk us out of it.[67]

Shults said that Bishop Martin convinced Brown he should go ahead, but the results were something less than desired. Terry also voiced her dissatisfaction with the second panel and agreed the all-minister format was not as effective as the preceding one sponsored by the WEC. She viewed the second program with dinner guests J. O. and Velma Powell, and reported "we were very much disappointed in our Bishop who spoke in the most glittering generalities."[68]

Brewer pointed out that the panel was at somewhat of a disadvantage since that night it followed another television appearance by the governor. "He attacked the WEC as integrationists and promised that he had a fool-proof way to guarantee the continuation of the existing school system on a segregated basis."[69]

Later, Adolphine Terry and Dottie Morris, both Episcopalians, called on Bishop Brown, who had earlier urged his congregation to take a stand or at least discuss the integration problem, to get an interpretation of his attitude expressed during the broadcast. According to Terry, Brown had had numerous meetings with Governor Faubus, "who seems to trust him and he is not willing to lose any little influence he may have by taking too strong a stand on TV." Brown urged the ladies to continue their work to change public opinion, and upon reflection, Terry decided "he is doing the right thing."[70]

Brewer remained skeptical that the bishop was likely to accomplish much alone. Like many moderates, Bishop Brown was holding on to the hope that a solution mutually agreeable to both sides could be worked out. In light of the upcoming rigged election, however, the opening of the schools was no longer up for negotiation.

Although the women worked valiantly on election day distributing material through their PTAs and in their neighborhoods and had some semblance of a fledgling political organization, the miracle Terry had hoped for did not occur. The vote was 7,561 for integration, 19,470 against. Daisy Bates commented wryly after the election that it was heartening to know there were 7,500 persons in Little Rock who would vote for integration.[71]

Faubus, who had promised to open the public schools as private ones, found himself blocked by yet another federal court injunction that forbade the use of public school teachers or buildings for segregated private school use.[72]

The public high schools remained closed. An eastern Arkansas Faubus supporter, Vance Thompson, purchased the former University of Arkansas night graduate school facilities for fifty thousand dollars. Raney High School, Faubus's segregated private school, moved in and began enrolling students October 20. Its all-white student body named the school paper the *Rebel Rouser*.[73]

Two-thirds of the other displaced thirty-six hundred high-school students were sent out of town or out of state, placed in hastily put together church schools, or enrolled in correspondence courses set up by local colleges. Approximately one thousand of the would-be high school students, 40 percent of whom were black, dropped out permanently.[74]

# ▪ 5 ▪

# Breaking the Silence

On a November morning in 1958, as she arrived at the WEC office in Margaret Kolb's utility room, Vivion Brewer found an enthusiastic volunteer standing at her desk. The WEC office had just been relocated from its downtown rented site to the Kolb home in Hillcrest.

"I'm Irene Samuel," the volunteer said. Although she had attended previous WEC meetings, Brewer said she had not gotten acquainted with Samuel before. "I have training in organization work and I am willing to devote my entire time to running this office," Samuel continued. Brewer was overjoyed.[1]

Samuel, a small, vivacious woman with a quick smile and a computer-like mind, became, as the WEC's unpaid executive secretary, its field commander and chief strategist as well. One of the men friendly to the WEC referred to them, somewhat patronizingly, as the "little bird-like women" with Samuel apparently in mind because of her size and constant movement. Samuel, however, was as tough as she was small, keeping track meticulously of who was with the WEC and who was not. At the time of her interview in 1992, she still had a dogeared Pulaski County 1959 poll tax book with all registered voters marked to reflect whether they were reliable supporters of public schools. And she occasionally looked someone up to check her memory, which was still remarkably accurate without the book, thirty-five years later.

Samuel's second husband, John, was a Jewish physician, and they had one adopted son, Lou, who at the time of the crisis was in grade school. Samuel herself had been brought up in the Nazarene Church. Her mother, Grace Gaston, who was more than just a member of that church, also had had her own religious radio show called

"The Promise Hour." Her father was a union employee of the Rock Island Railroad. Samuel recalled that both her parents supported women's suffrage, the labor movement, and liberal candidates for public office. After a marriage in her late teens had dissolved, Samuel went to Washington to work for the Federal Housing Authority. When she married John upon her return to Little Rock in 1939, her old friends abandoned her because her husband was Jewish.

When John went overseas in World War II, Irene returned to Washington to do personnel work for the Federal Housing Authority. After the Fair Employment Practices Act passed, she had black colleagues at the agency where she worked. But prior to that, coming as she did fresh out of Little Rock, she did a double take one day when a well-dressed black man stopped at her desk and asked to see her boss. "I lost my equilibrium for a moment," she said. "Then I pushed my chair back, walked around my desk and shook hands with him and told him how glad I was to see him. I was 21 maybe at the time."

She later screened and hired black secretaries whose bosses would place them behind filing cabinets so no one could see them. The women would come back in tears to tell Samuel they were being segregated in their offices. This led her to join the Urban League in Washington, and when she and John moved back to Little Rock after the war, she brought home views about race that were far different from those she had taken with her. She was also a member of the Urban League board in Little Rock for many years.[2]

Irene quickly gained acceptance in the Jewish community, where she heard for the first time about the college and career quotas that Jewish women worried about for their children. Still, when she and John adopted their son later, he was reared in the Jewish faith. Although she never converted, Samuel was to serve as legislative chair of the Council of Jewish Women. What she continued to learn about discrimination against Jews had a profound effect on her desire to contain the bigotry that was growing by leaps and bounds in Little Rock in 1958.[3]

■ ■ ■

Samuel immediately settled into the tiny space in the Kolb's utility room. She pitched in with Brewer to create order out of the energy, determination, and good intentions of the women who were now joining the WEC in droves. The latter was due primarily to the efforts of a Jewish woman named Jane Mendel, who was Samuel's first recruit.

Mendel, a dynamo of energy who as the mother of four school-aged children had her own concerns about the closed schools, lived up the street from Barbara and Harry Ashmore and Knox and Mary Banner (Knox was head of the Little Rock Urban Renewal Program). Mendel had been appalled by the abusive telephone calls and mail the Ashmores were receiving because of his editorials in the *Gazette,* but she had done nothing. One night at the local Jewish country club she met Irene Samuel, who urged her to become involved with the WEC and "get in there and get this thing organized." Mendel recalled telephoning Margaret Kolb the next day and later meeting with Adolphine Terry and Vivion Brewer. Her inactivity soon changed.

> We met over at Margaret Kolb's bedroom upstairs because these were, of course, times when you didn't want it to be known what you were doing. We ended up in her maid's room but in between, we switched to my house and there were eight of us . . . at the round table. . . . We had two typewriters going, two phones going, from the minute the kids went to school until they came home. I remember Irene, Jo Menkus, Barbara [Ashmore], Mary [Banner], Dottie Morris, myself and maybe two others.[4]

According to Samuel, "when we met at Jane Mendel's that day to try to enlarge the membership, all day long the thing that we were watching was we didn't want to get it loaded with Jewish people. We established a certain percentage and the minute we hit that, we'd stop getting any more Jews."

While Jewish women were supplying a great deal of the conscience and effort that fueled the WEC, some of the Jewish men, who were watching the increase in the Citizens Council's anti-Semitic attacks, were urging caution. When Mendel went to call on them and other businessmen for funds, however, she seldom came home empty-handed. The president of one company turned her committee down flat in front of another executive who said nothing. As she left, the other executive whispered to her that she should meet him outside the men's room. She did, and a sizable cash contribution was slipped into her hand.

Mendel's enlightenment on racial issues came from having grown up outside the South in Toledo, Ohio. She did not have the same anxieties that some of the Jews indigenous to Little Rock felt. Her husband, Ed, "gave 100 percent approval, which was super-wonderful," to her extensive WEC involvement. "I want to give Ed lots of credit," she said. "[He was] Southern born and when we first got married, he still used the word 'nigger,' so he came a long way. And on the subject [of what the WEC was trying to do], we always agreed."[5]

Samuel's husband, who saw a significant portion of his medical practice disappear during that year, was, like Mendel's husband, a firm backer of what his wife, Irene, was doing. "John was behind me [all the way]," said Samuel. "Once, when they said they were going to bomb our house, [I called John and said] that I needed to go home real quick. John said, 'if they're going to bomb the house they'll bomb it. They wouldn't tell you they were going to.' I had a different spirit with his backing."[6]

Samuel said she herself did not get out front (as Terry and Brewer did) with the WEC because "you couldn't be out front and run it. I couldn't be down at the city director's office. I had to be out there and make sure somebody went to the city director's office, somebody went out to the legislature, and somebody got out all those envelopes." But she also maintained a low profile to avoid giving extremists a further excuse to attack either the Jewish community or the WEC because of her Jewish connections.[7] Parma Basham, who was then president of the League of Women Voters, became Mendel's stand-in on the WEC board to report on fund-raising for the same reason, but according to Basham, Mendel was the one who did the real work.[8] The personal bravery of Samuel and Mendel went far beyond that of many other women, Jewish or otherwise, who were afraid to join the WEC, or if they did join, did so anonymously.

Mendel created a pyramid process through which ten women were asked to recruit ten more women, who in turn were to recruit ten more. Mendel herself made a visit to Pat House who, with four very small children at that time, had a home "that looked like a tornado had been through it" but who promised to recruit her ten women.

Mendel also convinced the WEC women that more than a verbal commitment was needed and the membership fee was set at one dollar. Women came trudging in and out of her house with their lists of ten women and their ten dollars. The lists sometimes were the result of five times that many arm-twisting calls and visits.

Many of the women called by Mendel, fearful of reprisals against their families or of what their husbands or friends would say if they joined, simply said, "Janie, I'll call you back." She never heard from them again.

One woman, whose husband intended to run for public office, wanted her WEC materials delivered in a brown paper wrapper to her aunt's house. Another woman said, "I'll join when you get 1,000 women," so that became Mendel's goal. In a week's time, the membership roster grew from 200 to 600, and by November it was up to 850. Mendel said that the "most wonderful call she made" was the one when she reached her goal of 1,000. She told the new member, "I'm coming over to get the dollar myself."[9]

Mendel immediately organized all the members into a telephone chain that followed the same chain-letter-type system so that members could be reached in a short length of time. Mendel recalled that when she called me, I'd say, "Janie, I hate to hear the sound of your voice because that means I have to get those calls made this very minute." She estimated that the entire membership could be reached in two to three hours, as it often was, just before critical meetings.[10]

This base of names, addresses, and telephone numbers became the nerve center of Samuel's work with the WEC. From the membership list, in just a few weeks' time, Samuel assembled a mailing list for fliers and newsletters. It was the basis for the recruitment of volunteers for office work, getting crowds for meetings, establishing committees for special assignments and, even more important, getting workers for elections. Unlike the soft-spoken Brewer, Samuel pulled no punches when she talked to other volunteers. She let it be known when she called that she expected action.

House, who lived not far from Margaret Kolb's house, would arrive at the utility room office with several children in tow to pick up envelopes, which she delivered to other mothers to be addressed. "Irene couldn't understand if something wasn't ready immediately," House said. "She was the central focus. . . . She was always amazed that I could sit down in the floor and catnap while I waited. . . . If she had not done the focal point work and literally driven people to do things that needed to be done, even though they had good ideas and good motivation and intentions, it wouldn't have happened."[11]

Kolb remembered making an "off the cuff" offer to furnish a working space for the WEC at one of the early meetings. "Stupid me, I was young and not one of Arkansas's first families. I said, 'Well I have this little utility room if you can't find anything larger.'" Before she knew it, the WEC had moved in.[12]

Kolb cleared out the plastic baskets in the utility room, which her children and their friends had used as a swimming pool dressing room during the summer. Located at the back of the house, the room had an outside entrance and a half bath. Prior to its use as a utility and dressing space, it had been a servant's room occupied by a black student at Philander Smith College, who baby-sat and helped out with ironing. It was a snug, small space for the WEC office during the next few months, and impromptu meetings of volunteers often spilled over into Kolb's dining room.[13]

The Kolbs installed a telephone for the WEC, and Kolb suspected that it, along with the line into her house, was from time to time tapped. "You'd feel like the line was open and you'd go out and look and there a man would be up on the telephone pole," Kolb said. "It was like when you have two or three phones in the house and you're talking on one and someone picks up one of the other ones." If they were there as Kolb believed, the phone tappers often heard no more than Kolb, a committed Pulaski Heights Baptist Church member and a PTA worker, making her regular calls to her Sunday school class or to homeroom, Cub Scout, and Brownie mothers. Samuel said she was never aware that the telephones were tapped but does remember receiving many harassing and threatening phone calls both at home and at the WEC office.

Both Samuel and Kolb remember the cars that cruised Colonial Court on many days. Their male occupants often slowed down and even stopped in front of the Kolb home, where they could be seen taking down license numbers of the WEC women who came and went with their deliveries and assignments. Kolb also got her share of harassing telephone calls, and a large rock was thrown through her den window one night.[14]

Margaret Kolb got her perspective on racial issues from her mother and father in western North Carolina. Her father's father was a Baptist minister from whom her father acquired "these very liberal racial issues." Her mother's father had inherited a slave who no longer had any living relatives, and to whom they gave a two-room cottage and land on their farm. She continued:

> Uncle Artemis died [when I was small], but I was old enough to remember him as a little girl. In fact, we used to go out in the evenings and sit on the porch with him out from Hot Springs, North Carolina. My father and his family were from near Burnsville and my mother was from Hot Springs. That's where I went to Morris Hill Junior College, a Baptist college.
>
> It's a remarkable thing to me, our fundamentalist movement in the Baptist Church. The Baptists were so gung ho on liberty. Roger Williams took his group to Providence, Rhode Island, and established Brown University. Rhode Island was founded on religious liberty. . . .
>
> My background in the Baptist denomination engendered this liberty thing. The blacks would be liberated to acquire all the benefits of American society just like the women were.[15]

Kolb said she knew the fundamentalists were sincere, but it was hard for her to understand some of their positions on issues in light of the long history of the Baptists in pursuing religious liberty. She recalled that she "had the reputation of being a liberal on racial issues" when she was a student at Furman University in Greenville, South Carolina, in 1940–41. It was there that she got to know

Barbara Ashmore, Harry Ashmore's wife, who was just out of college and on the physical education faculty. In Little Rock, Barbara quickly became a utility room regular at Kolb's house along with Dottie Morris.

Kolb also had gotten to know Terry earlier, shortly after she moved to Little Rock. She said in the crisis "we just sort of like magnets were attracted to Mrs. Terry's leadership. You couldn't help but love her. And then we got acquainted with Vivion Brewer through her and came to respect Vivion. She had all the regal and intellectual backup to push us to say, 'We *can* see this accomplished. And we don't have to let politicians and rednecks keep stirring this furor up in town.'"[16]

Kolb and Terry often had long conversations about religion in which Terry would ask, "Do you really believe this, or is this Christian philosophy something you just inherited?" Kolb said she replied, "No, I really believe it because you have to have faith to function. If you don't have any faith, there comes a time in life when you cannot function, you fall apart if you don't have anything to latch onto."

Kolb thought that most of the women who came to the WEC meetings heard about it "by word of mouth through the church women: Westover Hills Presbyterian, First Methodist, Pulaski Heights Methodist, Pulaski Heights Baptist," and the Temple B'nai Israel. But members also came from the PTAs, the League of Women Voters, the AAUW, and many other nonreligious organizations.

Monthly general meetings were still held at Terry's home. Every Wednesday morning, WEC board members would slip in through the latticed back porch that faced on Eighth Street to gather around Terry's massive dining-room table with its ornate, carved griffin legs. In the adjoining atrium filled with large green plants, a parrot squawked incessantly. Kolb also recalled that a kinkajou, a small furry animal that Mary Terry had brought back from one of her trips abroad, stayed in the atrium for a while.

On the table beside her, Terry kept a copy of the *New York Times,* which she read when discussions got lengthy. She would confer with her cook in the kitchen about the upcoming noon meal or with her yardman outside while "never missing a beat" in what was happening in the board meeting.[17]

Mamie Ruth Williams, a colorful, oversized, freewheeling sort, came to Terry's first meeting as a substitute for her mother and later served on the board. Her mother, Ruth Curry Brown, who was connected to Terry through the American Legion Auxiliary, the Women's City Club, and the Daughters of the American Revolution, offered to baby-sit with Williams's two children if she would go in her place. Williams was unique among many of the younger women because she had grown up in the central part of the city and was still living there. She recalled:

> I remember going to the first [WEC] meetings and feeling so out of place because I was not wealthy and I didn't come from the upper class and I lived in the old end of town and I had kids I had to park around. . . . I wanted to be there so bad it didn't matter. . . . I can remember everybody there was so smart and so capable. I felt so dumb.[18]

Williams, who was a born political organizer, was anything but dumb. She ran the first ward for the WEC in many elections and hung out with news reporters who came to rely on her for information. "I remember walking those streets there. . . . I was the boss of the first ward. . . . I was impressed in every election with the support I received from my mother's generation." Williams brought out votes that no one thought could be had for opening the schools in the ward, which included Central High School itself.[19]

Although Mamie Ruth Williams came from a slave-owning southern Arkansas family, she remembers she was taught that all people deserved respect and that "human beings were human beings." She also recalled that her grandmother built a black church on the family place and that her mother furnished a home for an elderly ex-slave who lived to be 103.

Williams got thrown into the 1957 Central High fracas one morning when she delivered a friend's child to the kindergarten there. She was stopped by the troops around the school because they thought she had a weapon. It was an ice pick she planned to use to break up some ice she had in the back of the car for water at her son's school. She got so rattled that she wound up locking her own child in her car, boarding a bus with a black student being pursued by the mob to ride her to safety a block away, then walking back to get her son. "It was a traumatic time," she said. "People don't know how sad it was."

> You see, I thought everybody would feel like I did. Then all my different groups—luncheon, supper, bridge clubs—were divided right down the middle and I was very much in the minority. And the problem is, at one point you think, "I wish I didn't have to do this. I've lost a lot of friends. My kids are being snubbed." But . . . once you step out, you cannot go back to the time of non-knowing.
>
> And when you step out . . . you're on this lonely course.

At one of the WEC meetings, she had a long talk with Terry about how "extremely upset" she had been that "some people I counted on to be supportive . . . weren't" and Terry told her the following story.

When Congressman Terry was asked to run for the Senate, he was promised everything. But his friends deserted him when he lost. The defeat was devastating to Adolphine Terry because she realized he could have kept his House seat if he had not followed the advice to move up that had come from friends who no longer stood by him. Williams quoted Terry as saying:

> It made me sick. I had to go for treatment out in Denver. . . . I just couldn't get over it. One day I was in a bookstore. . . . I picked up a book. . . . It said, "If someone does you a wrong, forgive him once, then forget it. Don't forgive him every day." I have lived by that since.[20]

Meanwhile, Vivion Brewer spent much of her time calling on businessmen who, she said, "were far from eager to see me." One banker, whom she knew well and finally cornered, irritatedly said, "No, I'm not going to get into this. I've pulled Little Rock's chestnuts out of the fire time after time and I'm tired of it. . . . You women ought to leave this thing alone. You are the ones stirring up trouble."[21]

Irene Samuel's mimeograph machine was always running hot in the Kolb utility room, and it regularly turned out WEC fliers that went to organizations all over town. WEC women were also flooding their elected officials and ministers, as well as the editors of both the *Gazette* and *Democrat,* with letters and statements in support of getting the schools open. While others were huddled in fear, these women were demonstrating that they, at least, would not tolerate in silence the governor's actions against public schools.

Having learned their lesson in the "for" and "against" integration campaign, Brewer and other WEC leaders focused exclusively on urging the reopening of the schools and the support of public education. They clarified where they stood with a "Policy and Purpose" statement that read:

> The Women's Emergency Committee to Open Our Schools is dedicated to the principle of free public school education, and to law and order. We stand neither for integration nor for segregation, but for education.
>
> OUR AIM IS:
>
> To get the four free public high schools re-opened;
> To get students back in their classes;
> To retain our staff of good teachers;
> To regain full accreditation by the North Central Association.[22]

When the Arkansas Education Association incurred the ire of the General Assembly's Legislative Council by pledging to be a watchdog for maintaining public education in every county in the state, the WEC issued a public statement commending the AEA. When Claude Carpenter, a Faubus aide, solicited a five-dollar contribution from each of the state's fourteen thousand teachers for "Dollars for Democrats," the WEC and others protested publicly and the Governor backed away. The women also voiced loud objections to the payment of more than seventy thousand dollars to Raney High School from Little Rock funds before the state law allowing it was declared unconstitutional.[23]

Faubus hurled criticism at the Little Rock School Board for cancelling football at the closed high schools, calling it "inhuman."

He knew that the Little Rock male leaders, who had stayed silent about the locked classrooms, would not want their sons who were still around to miss out on sports. The school board said "it would carry out the football schedule and anything else that the Governor would return to it." So schools that had no classes or students that year did play football.[24]

Faubus also insisted that the board lease the public-school buildings to the Raney High School private corporation and allow teachers to transfer over to Raney, but the federal courts blocked both actions.[25]

Frank Lambright, whose wife was a WEC member and who worked for the Williams and Rosen Insurance Agency, replaced Henry Rath when he resigned from the school board in September 1958. Lambright, however, served only two months because the entire board, except for Dr. Dale Alford, resigned on November 12. Soon after he joined the board, Lambright said there was a movement to get rid of Virgil Blossom and that the consensus was such that "the board could not be effective with such an impasse in the community." He described a meeting to get six local bank presidents to run as a group for the board, because members felt "people for whatever reason would follow their leadership" and "because obviously the emphasis had become economic more than anything else." He continued:

> Business was falling off, Little Rock wasn't getting any industry.
> . . . We met in the basement of the old Union Bank Building
> and told them [the bankers] we were going to resign as a group
> and we were asking them to run as a slate. They wouldn't do it.
> As I recall, Dabbs Sullivan, president of the Bank of Arkansas, a
> brand new bank, was the only one who would agree to it. So
> we resigned and that's when they got a replacement board. . . .
> What we wanted to do was protect Virgil's contract. Everybody
> on that board coming up for reelection knew we were going to
> get opposition and knew [the new board] was going to try to
> break Virgil's contract and have him hung out to dry financially
> so our last act was to pay off his contract.[26]

Alford, an eye specialist, did not join the mass resignation because he was moving on to a higher job. As an outspoken segregationist, he had run as a Faubus-backed, independent, write-in candidate for Congress on November 4 and had won. He had defeated Rep. Brooks Hays, who as a Democrat had furnished distinguished service to the fifth district for nearly two decades. The vote was close: 30,739 to 29,483.

Governor Faubus, who had promised Hays just a few weeks before that he would not intervene in his race, did not make public statements but sent his chief aide, Claude Carpenter, over to run the Alford race. The WEC mobilized its members to work briefly in the Hays-Alford campaign—Alford had announced his write-in candidacy only eight days before the election—and were again bruised by another, and unexpected, loss.[27]

■　■　■

Jimmy Karam, the clothing store owner who was a close friend of Governor Faubus, announced his candidacy for the school board in October. Later, when the entire board resigned, he promised that his own slate of other segregationists would follow. By then, he was heartily endorsed by the Citizens Council.

Karam had a somewhat strange and murky history, which included joining the Urban League and the Arkansas Council on Human Relations at one point. *Life* magazine, however, photographed him in the mobs at Central High School in early 1957 and reported that Little Rock mayor Woodrow Mann called "Karam, once a professional strikebreaker, a 'principal agitator' of the mob."[28]

Karam, in his October announcement, said he would remove Virgil Blossom but "half-seriously" added that Blossom might be kept as "assistant principal of Dunbar (Negro) High School." Karam declared that he would require all students to have health examinations and would "suspend those with contagious or infectious diseases." He further said he would ask for "a high code of morals" to prevent children from "Christian homes" being "forced to associate with children of low moral standards." He said "indiscriminate integration" would bring about such associations.[29]

Karam's potential candidacy shook moderates sufficiently to cause one of them, Ted Lamb, whose advertising agency had represented the WEC in the September closed-schools election, to step forward as a candidate in favor of opening the schools. Lamb was banking on WEC support, which was all he had at that time, being enough to enable him to defeat Karam.

Billy Rector, a blustery businessman full of self-importance and with large real estate and insurance holdings, also became interested in the school board race. Rector, who "never let any strong ethical standards or theoretical beliefs stand in his way of making a dollar," according to Edwin Dunaway, had (for economic reasons) made sporadic behind-the-scenes efforts to get the school crisis solved. He began working on a list of possible Chamber of Commerce candidates for the school board after the bankers refused, and he placed his own name at the top of the list.

The year before, Rector had been in a "bitter personal feud" with the governor. It evolved after a real estate development company in Newark, New Jersey, with which he was working on a western Little Rock shopping center, pulled out because of the integration trouble. "What in the hell are you all doing down there?" said the head of the development company, according to Rector, in the fall of 1957 when the mobs first gathered in front of Central High School. "If you don't straighten this thing out we'll never be able to build this shopping center or finance it." The shopping center deal collapsed, and Rector blamed it on the school crisis.

"Of course, they immediately went and told Faubus this, at which point Faubus had double apoplexy and started calling me a liar, an integrationist, a Republican and a few other things," Rector said. "Periodically after that he used me as an example of an integrationist."[30]

Nothing could have been further from the truth. Rector, who was to build the city's first private academy as a haven for those avoiding integration, told researcher John Pagan in 1973: "I am a segregationist. I never did want to integrate that thing in 1957. I didn't have a violent feeling about it the way he [Blossom] was going to do it. He had seven or eight or ten . . . clean, intelligent blacks. I didn't mind that too much although I'd just as soon it didn't happen."

What Rector did mind, and the reason he was submitting his

name to run for the school board, was that "Little Rock's name was getting dragged around the world as the symbol of a bunch of bastards and they're not." He was reluctantly in favor of obeying the law, although he did not like what "the Warren court did." Rector, whose support of integration extended only so far as it meant new business for him, said sadly:

> We never got a new industry in this town for five years. We didn't get anybody to talk to us for three years. It was the end of our new industry. I could see it was just going to ruin us. Right after that crisis if that chamber board had stood up and said, "By God, we're not going to stand for this, and we're going to go to court or do whatever we have to stop you," they would have won that thing.[31]

Rector and Grainger Williams, representing the Chamber of Commerce, had both been involved in trying to get the six bank presidents to run as a slate when Frank Lambright let it be known that the entire board was about to resign. Rector said that he and Frank Lyon spent weeks trying to convince the bankers to run in anticipation of the board's resignation. "Every time we would get one, Faubus would turn the heat on him," he said. "He'd come unglued and then we'd go over and get another one and this went on." Williams, who was also part of the banker recruitment team and a partner in the Williams and Rosen Agency, for which Lambright worked, remembered:

> We didn't go blazing down there to ask Mr. Kahn if he would do it; we picked out someone who Mr. Kahn would listen to. McLean said no, of course, until Satterfield said he'd do it if McLean would do it and McLean [then] said he'd do it if Satterfield would. . . . All said yes except two, and they finally said no. I can understand why, because unless all of them decided to run they would have lost all their east Arkansas deposits.[32]

When the school board did resign on November 12, only three days were left before the filing deadline for a new board. Vivion Brewer was at Terry's house when Grainger Williams arrived that

Thursday with Rector's list of potential candidates. He asked the two women if the WEC would be willing to try to talk some of them into running before the Saturday deadline for filing. Unfortunately, a relative of Brewer's had died and she had to leave town. All that stood between Karam and his segregationist slate was a relatively unknown contender named Ted Lamb and seventy-seven-year-old Adolphine Terry (she'd had a birthday on November 3).

Terry agreed to take the list and start calling, provided she could add at least one woman's name to it. She called until midnight, finally getting four "yes's," one of whom was WEC steering committee member Margaret Stephens—her own addition. The other three were Billy Rector, Everett Tucker, and Russell Matson. The "moderate" businessmen's slate of six was rounded out with Lamb and Ed I. McKinley, who was also on the opposition slate. Rector insisted McKinley should be on both slates because Rector knew him as a fellow member of the Little Rock Country Club. As Rector explained later, "We thought he was an honorable, decent, intelligent guy which in retrospect was totally wrong." That was one Rector comment with which Terry and Brewer agreed.[33]

Terry got other WEC women to scurry around Saturday, getting names of supporters on the petitions for each of the candidates before the 6 P.M. filing deadline. She had only one problem: Matson, who had agreed to run, was in Fayetteville attending a University of Arkansas football game and would not be home until Sunday night. Terry was not about to let that knock Matson off the ballot after they had gone to the trouble of collecting endorsement names. She simply signed Matson's name at the bottom of the petition herself. When he returned to town, he went down to the courthouse to correct the forgery.[34]

Stephens was opposed by a highly vocal segregationist and municipal judge, R. W. (Bob) Laster. Lamb had two opponents, Dr. George Branscum of the Citizens Council and Pauline Woodson of the Mothers League. Matson was opposed by C. C. Railey, Rector by Ben Rowland, and Tucker by John Clayton and Margaret Morrison. The latter was a segregationist maverick who was president of the NAAWP (National Association for the Advancement of

White People). Karam backed down from running when opposition materialized.

Rector became the self-appointed spokesman for the slate Terry had put together for him. According to Vivion Brewer, when Rector came to see her at her office:

> He was decisively abrupt, almost belligerent, and I tried to smooth our paths a bit by telling him I had known some of his family in my banking days and that my father had spoken of him as a most promising young man. It was obvious that this mattered not one whit to him. He had no time for pleasantries. He wanted total efforts of our organization on behalf of "his" slate but he made it clear that no one should know of our alliance.

Brewer visited Ted Lamb after listening to Rector's orders about how the campaign should be run. She urged that, in exchange for an all-out WEC effort, Lamb's advertising agency not paint the candidates the WEC was supporting as diehard segregationists, to which Lamb readily agreed. When Faubus accused them of being integrationists, however, Rector, to prove he was a segregationist, announced that he had given one hundred dollars to the White Citizens Council in 1957. And Rector further antagonized the WEC leaders by running ads that called the WEC-backed candidates segregationists who wanted to open the schools.[35]

Irene Samuel by then had organized the WEC members with captains in each ward who had precinct workers under them to whom they delivered postcards and fliers for addressing, mailing, and placing on doorsteps. The precinct workers were also using names from the poll tax book for telephoning and for setting up carpools to get voters to the polls.

The women had their first taste of success: Tucker, Matson, and Lamb of the so-called businessmen's slate were elected, although Stephens and Rector were not. Rowland, Laster, and the unopposed McKinley also won. After a board meeting or two, McKinley made it clear that his loyalties were with the governor, and the women knew they should not have listened to Rector. There was now a three-segregationist to three-moderate split on the board.

Rector was bitter about his defeat and demanded a recount, which he paid for, of both his and Margaret Stephens's votes. When he was setting it up, he called Brewer and asked, "Do you have about a dozen women of *reasonable* intelligence you can send out to help count?" Brewer choked back what she was thinking, assuring him she did, but even after the recount, Rector's opponent still won.[36]

Terry invited a group of thirty people, among them Billy Rector, Grainger Williams, and Vivion Brewer, over to have lunch with the three new board members Everett Tucker, Russell Matson, and Ted Lamb to discuss what the next steps should be. Rector "laid everybody out that he had lost," according to Williams. He suddenly turned to Brewer and said, "And *you* are the chief reason I lost." Terry, whose tongue could be sharp at times, said, "Young man, I want to advise you that if it hadn't been for this group you wouldn't have got the votes you got." Rector abruptly got up from the table and left. Terry wrote him a note afterward, regretting that he was called away so soon and suggested that he go on record for opening the schools with the others. "He wrote [back] that he wanted it distinctly understood that neither now or at any future date would he do anything to promote integration," Terry said later.[37]

So badly did Rector want the schools reopened, however, that, even after he had given up on himself, he financed and set up the mechanism for a court challenge of Margaret Stephens's vote. The first results at the courthouse on election night had shown her to be 18 votes ahead, but after the recovery of a mysterious box containing 120 votes that suddenly showed up after the election, she became an 81-vote loser. The recount, done after the missing box appeared, produced 407 disputed ballots.[38]

Rector hired attorney Edwin Dunaway to represent Stephens in the election contest because, as he told Dunaway up front, he had tried to get several other lawyers to represent her who refused. Dunaway, while not an admirer of Rector, knew that the economic pinch was motivating Rector to back the Stephens challenge. Dunaway went one night to Rector's floor of offices in the old gas company building on Fifth Street, and he describes what took place there:

He had a printout made of all voters and we had it on the floor . . . , we had to take our shoes off not to mess up the papers. We decided certain votes we would want to challenge but not others, like voting in the wrong precinct. We got down to about 165 votes we were thinking of challenging. "We're going to do a poll," he said. We pretended to be conducting an opinion poll. We didn't quite ask how did you vote in the school board election but we could tell or decide from the way they answered. If they had voted for Mrs. Stephens, we wouldn't challenge them. We called that many people, Billy and I, we got all set and felt ready to go to trial. Then we found Margaret Stephens had moved out of the school district and was not eligible to serve.[39]

Heartened by their first success at the polls despite the loss of Stephens's race, the WEC increased their once-a-week flier blitz to educate people with simple messages. One of them, in recognition of Brotherhood Week, showed drawings of the four closed high schools—Central, Hall, Horace Mann, and Tech—and beneath them the Adlai Stevenson quote that said, "The world is now too dangerous for anything but the truth, too small for anything but brotherhood." When Brewer approved it, that was the entire message, but before it was printed, someone else added her own touches to the drawing, showing the schools holding hands. Since all-black Horace Mann was one of the buildings, this set the segregationists off.

"Those [fliers] were returned to us with these horrible things [written on them]," Irene Samuel recalled. "One dentist whose little girl was in school with my son Lou wrote a diatribe down the side about what he thought of us and I was sure he told his little girl not to speak to Lou." The WEC board agreed to stick with the "open schools" theme after that and Samuel said "we got them simpler and simpler and simpler."[40]

The original three founders were still working, however, on getting something done about human relations at another level in the city. Velma Powell, after being replaced by Dottie Morris as secretary earlier in the fall, sketched out "a proposal for a civic interracial committee." Brewer took the proposal to the WEC executive committee where a plan for a City Commission on Civic Unity was developed. It called for an interfaith, interracial commission to advise the city government on ways to build better community relations.

Brewer's job was to present it to the city directors who had just been elected under the brand new city manager form of government. She finally reached Mayor Werner Knoop by telephone, who was about to take off on a tour of the world with other mayors. He told her brusquely that there was no need for her to discuss the WEC proposal with him. She got a much warmer reception from the one woman on the board, Mrs. Edgar Dixon, a WEC supporter, who encouraged her to go ahead and present it, assuring her that she thought the men would go along with it.

Brewer mailed the plan to all the city directors; to Dean Dauley, the city manager; and to Warren Bray of Southwestern Bell Telephone Company, the president of the Chamber of Commerce. The detailed plan even listed organizations that might be asked to send representatives. It was covered by the newspapers but ignored by the city directors.

When a similar group was unofficially organized in 1966, it was headed by Bishop Brown, who said that its forerunner was an anonymous group of businessmen who had first organized in 1958. Brewer replied in a letter to the editor that it would have been most helpful if the WEC, which was not anonymous, could have located that businessmen's group eight years before.[41]

■   ■   ■

Irene Samuel left the WEC office for one mission—that of trudging around in the snow with Pat House, who by then was working with her regularly, to call on ministers to sign a statement. She was attempting to build on the earlier support a limited number of ministers and their churches had shown for opening the schools.

"It seemed like that winter lasted forever," Samuel recalled. "I think of it as being cold and sleeting, and we were walking around trying to get these ministers to sign this nebulous statement that said, 'I'm for public education.' That's all the damn thing said." She and House succeeded in getting only six of the forty they called on to sign.

Other WEC volunteers, including Vivion Brewer, also were visiting the ministers. Colbert Cartwright, pastor of the Pulaski Heights

Christian Church and president of the Arkansas Council on Human Relations, told Brewer that while, of course, he would sign, the Ministerial Alliance had been unsuccessful in getting its membership to agree on what to say earlier. The women finally wound up with only twenty-five signatures out of four hundred ministers in town— seven Baptists, eight Presbyterians, three Methodists, two Episcopalians, and three Christians. The town's two rabbis also signed after "synagogues" was inserted after "churches" in the statement.[42]

The WEC prepared a letter for its members to enclose with Christmas cards that bleak winter that said in part, "We know it will be a long time before the state of Arkansas can live down the shame and disgrace with which it is now viewed by the entire world. We thought you might like to learn that there is one group here dedicated to the principle of good public education with liberty and justice for all. . . . I am proud and happy to be a member of the Women's Emergency Committee to Open Our Schools."[43]

Finally, in January, an important breakthrough came. Grainger Williams, a precise, direct man with a deep Presbyterian conscience and a good sense of humor, supported both Terry and the WEC wholeheartedly. His wife, Frances, who went to Terry's on that first day and who by this time was serving on the WEC board, prodded him to do more. His strong ties to the Terry family stretched back to the days when he had been Congressman Terry's aide in Washington, and he and Frances had remained close to both Adolphine and Dave Terry afterward. And Williams was proud of what Terry had done in organizing the WEC and of Frances's involvement with it.

"We wouldn't have gotten a thing done if it hadn't been for the women," Williams said. "Because I think the women were a force to get the men to look at some things they didn't want to look at. I think they really played a role in it."[44]

Williams, who had served as vice-president of the Chamber of Commerce in 1958, was elevated to its presidency in December of that year. Those who preceded him as president had been heads of Southwestern Bell Telephone Company and the Arkansas Power and Light Company and because of their positions did not dare oppose the governor. In January 1959, when he made his president's address at the annual chamber banquet, Williams decided to digress from the speech written for him by a staff member and embark on some surprise remarks of his own:

> I cannot keep faith with myself . . . as your newly elected president, without a frank statement to you, and a plea in the interest of public education. . . .
>
> It is neither my purpose nor desire to discuss any of the political or sociological aspects of our school situation—nor do I have any solution to offer. But it is my feeling that the time has come to evaluate the cost of public education—and the cost of the lack of public education.
>
> I would urge that no matter what our personal feelings might be—each of us encourage the reestablishment of all areas of communication. . . . To achieve this climate of communication would be one of the greatest contributions we could make, and to that end I am dedicated.[45]

The chamber audience, at first stunned that Williams would mention the unmentionable, was silent for a moment and then broke into a thunderous applause. Williams, who had expected stony silence, was pleasantly surprised by the crowd's positive reaction. "It was something I had to do regardless," he said later.[46] The WEC now had a powerful ally.

Although Williams's leadership allowed the executive board of the Chamber of Commerce to find its voice again, the board members were willing to go only so far. They first proposed publicly that the schools be reopened segregated, with the school board submitting a new plan for integration to the courts. That was an improvement over the silence but not a realistic solution.

The chamber then polled its members in February 1959 and found that of those voting, 632 members did not want closed schools to continue, while only 230 did. And 819 favored reopening them with limited, controlled integration as compared with 245 voting no. The chamber executive board, acting on the strength of the poll, recommended that the schools be opened, using a pupil placement plan, and that there continue to be private, segregated schools.[47]

In a letter to the *Gazette* editor that followed, the unsigned author, who called himself "Little Businessman," commented:

I'm getting mixed up. Has the Little Rock Chamber of Commerce become a subsidiary of the Women's Emergency Committee to Open the Schools? I used to think that the chamber was dedicated strictly to improving business conditions in Little Rock and hewed to a policy of not taking part in social questions. If the people who run the chamber are eager to get into the integration controversy, they may as well expect to witness complete disintegration of that once-fine organization.[48]

Frances and Grainger Williams were active members of tiny St. Andrews Presbyterian Church "and there were times when people would hardly speak to us in the church," Frances said. The year before, an officer in the National Guard had come over to her while she was standing outside the church and said, "I know about you, it would suit you all right to have 'niggers' in the school." Frances replied that it certainly would. He continued, "You're in favor of your daughter marrying a Negro." Frances replied, "That doesn't have one thing to do with this. She doesn't go to school now thinking she's finding a husband." There were also others who thanked them after Grainger spoke out. One woman said her husband couldn't do it and another said, "My husband will lose his job if he does."[49]

■　■　■

The businessmen and the women of the WEC were taking quite different approaches to bring Little Rock out of its predicament. The chamber leaders, with the exception of Grainger Williams, were still clinging to segregated thinking while doing only what had to be done about the schools to crank up the economy. The women, on the other hand, were promoting a vision of a better community that was inclusive in the education of all its children.

An out-of-state reporter, while visiting Terry at her home and noting the portrait of her Confederate father, asked why she was involved in the school crisis. Terry threw her head back and peered at the young woman through her glasses, declaring, "My dear, I am an integrationist!" In another interview, which appeared in print, Terry voiced her views about human rights: "Whether we like it or not, human slavery and segregation are dead. We are living through

the most exciting time in the world, because the soul of man everywhere is demanding more rights and more recognition—and most
of all, more human dignity."[50]

It was the first of many lessons I learned from Mrs. Terry—
that it is better to be clear with oneself and others about where one
stood so that there is no misunderstanding. Being a closet integrationist might put one on the right side, but it did not lead to any
courageous action. That did not mean that all the women who
embraced the WEC had to be integrationists, but Terry's outspoken-
ness made it easier for some of the rest of us to stand for what we
believed as well.

# ▪ 6 ▪

# Barefooted and Pregnant

Adolphine Terry received an important letter in December 1958 from a good friend, Eleanor Reid; Reid was the legislative chair of the Arkansas branch of the American Association of University Women, which Terry had helped to found. In her letter, Reid made a strong case for getting the WEC to lead a lobbying effort in the upcoming session of the Arkansas legislature scheduled to meet in January. Faubus, just elected to a third term, would be proposing increasingly ominous legislation related to school desegregation. The general assembly, dominated by rural white males who shared his views, could be expected to go along unless other voices were heard.

Reid, who regularly slipped through Terry's back door to discuss politics with her, argued in her letter that "a women's group like the Women's Emergency Committee is most formidable. As I said to you on the phone, I can testify from personal experience that legislators turn pale when they see a group of polite but determined women descending on them. Perhaps it brings sudden memories of their mothers, urging them to do the right thing! Anyway, it is so, and I wish the women of Little Rock realized how much power they have, if only they appear in groups."[1]

Reid, a native of Pennsylvania and a blonde who could be characterized as both pushy and aggressive, had conducted a largely one-woman campaign in the legislative session two years before. "I enjoyed lobbying," Reid said. "I had to be the opposite of my natural self. I had to be tactful and patient, which are qualities I do not naturally have." She was defending Dr. Frances Brennecke, a graduate of the University of Pennsylvania and like herself, a native of that state. Brennecke was recruited to head the Crippled Children's

Department under Gov. Sid McMath and then was fired by the Faubus administration. Her offense was that she had wanted to hire more public health nurses instead of setting up clinics for young doctors. Brennecke also wanted the nurses to see that the braces and shoes fit the children before she paid for them.

Reid's lobbying did little good, and Brennecke's case dragged on for some time before the Merit Council. "Although she was one of the best orthopedic surgeons in the country, at the end of a year some of us had to buy her food and shoes because she didn't have any money left," Reid said.[2]

Reid learned a thing or two from that lobbying experience, however. Her letter to Terry envisioned a large women's coalition lobbying effort led by the Women's Emergency Committee and other women's groups such as the AAUW and the PTA. She wrote:

> Both the AAUW and PTA have accumulated numerous members who are either terrified at taking any action on anything (school teachers seem particularly rabbit-like at this thought) and/or they are "agin" any suggestions made (at least by me, whom they seem to regard as some kind of radical). . . . On the other hand, both organizations have many members who are willing to take action, but spend so much time arguing ways and means that they are never ready in *time* to do any good. It is *timeliness* which counts most. . . . The Emergency Committee seems, miraculously, to have avoided these pitfalls, at least so far.

Reid suggested demonstrations of at least one hundred women each time from all over the state, wearing "Save Our Schools" labels, and carrying signs with a leader who would speak to the press. She also called for "well-planned followup" in which each woman would call on her own legislators. "It gives a man an 'out' when, for instance, someone like Van Dalsem puts pressure on him," Reid said, assuming, of course, that the representative really wants to do the right thing.[3]

Rep. Paul Van Dalsem was a rotund, red-cheeked legislator from rural Perry County who, through longevity of service, had accumulated considerable power that he did not intend to have disturbed. As chair of the Legislative Council, he held hearings on civil rights activities and, with Governor Faubus, issued a mandate to use the state police to investigate "subversive" groups. One of those happened to be the Women's Emergency Committee, and members' license plates at one meeting were duly recorded by the police and passed on with the names of the car owners beside them.[4]

Both Terry and Brewer endorsed Reid's idea to turn out the women, and it fell Irene Samuel's lot to get the women to the legislature. Samuel was not unaware of the ways in which sex and politics often intertwined. She had once been compared by Sander Vanocur, the television news commentator, to Lysistrata, who got the women of Athens to lock themselves in the Acropolis until the men stopped the Peloponnesian War. Although the Little Rock women were not locked in, Samuel was said to be keeping them otherwise unavailable simply by working them into the night until the school crisis was settled. It did not take her long to figure out how legislators might best be reached after the WEC board gave the go-ahead to Reid's proposed lobbying effort.[5]

Samuel first rounded up the most-serious and best-informed women she could find—mostly those who served on legislation committees of the major women's organizations. The legislators were irritated by the fact that the women knew more than they did. "Then we tried the church ladies and they didn't get very far either," Samuel said. She abandoned her feminist instincts and decided after that to rely on looks rather than message content to get a foot in the door. She selected a group of attractive young WEC workers who spruced themselves up in heels, white gloves, and their best dresses to run interference for the others.

One of these, Pat House, who was twenty-eight years old at the time, said that "we were coached to go out there and be sweet and nice. Paul Van Dalsem once bought me an ice cream bar. . . . They all thought of themselves as Southern gentlemen. . . . Politicians were like that. . . . You had to have the men interpret [bills] for you. [But] they handled the money and they couldn't talk to me about the money."[6]

Van Dalsem did not maintain his gentlemanly stance for long. Later, State Rep. David Pryor (who was to become a U.S. senator) held a debate with Van Dalsem at an American Association of University Women meeting, calling the legislature a "mudhole."

Van Dalsem retorted that lobbying groups were what made it a "mudhole." He then eyed his AAUW hostesses sharply. "Nearly all [lobbyists] are willing to compromise to get some of the things they want, but the worst ever to come before the legislature are you women's organizations such as the American Association of University Women, the Women's Voters League, [and] the library group."[7]

Van Dalsem made a speech at a subsequent session of the House of Representatives declaring that the university women needed to be treated the way women in Perry County were. "We keep them bare-footed and pregnant," he said. "And if that doesn't work, then we give them an extra cow to milk."[8] Reid pounced on the opportunity to keep the publicity going. It required nine days to get it etched in the public's mind. She arranged for, among other things, the AAUW legislative chair, Katherine Hamilton, to pose for a picture with a cow, saying demurely to a reporter, "I spent all summer learning the legislative process and now I have to learn how to milk a cow."[9]

Van Dalsem a year or so later gerrymandered legislative districts so that Pulaski County, where Little Rock was located, became a part of his district. It was a mistake. The WEC and the "university" women rounded up a candidate to run against him and handed him a resounding defeat.

Reid claimed she was the only woman who finally forgave him when he later returned, with more humility and respect for women, to the legislature. "I wrote his wife a letter when he died," Reid said. "Paul never lied and he was very helpful once we [became] friends. She was grateful. She had a hard time living with him and they separated once."

Reid recalled that Van Dalsem once walked out of a legislative hearing because he declared, "I have better things to do than to listen to Mrs. Reid," he said. After he left, Reid said, "I call your attention to the fact that you no longer have a quorum," which was included in a news story. "His wife came the next morning and sat with me in the hearing," Reid said.[10] The Arkansas Women's Political Caucus later immortalized Van Dalsem by establishing annual "Barefoot and Pregnant Uppity Women" awards.

■ ■ ■

Pat House, whose brains and willingness to work matched her striking good looks, became the WEC's legislative leader for the 1959 session. Her first act in that capacity was to take a WEC delegation to call on the Pulaski County legislators in preparation for the session. Mary Evelyn Lester and Carroll Holcomb, both also attractive and smart, accompanied her on making the rounds, as did a number of other women for one of the sessions.

House prepared a detailed report for the WEC board of the visits. She observed that "through a misunderstanding, more [WEC] people came than were expected and this was unfortunate." She added that some of the women suggested that the legislators "acted like idiots" and made other "antagonistic remarks." House reported that newly elected Rep. Ben Allen "stuffed his cigarettes and papers in his pockets with the remark that this was no place for him." House's report continued:

> We soothed him with a direct question about what we could do to help. . . . He said to tell our members that . . . he certainly was not a rubber stamp (he asked if these notes were for publication). He said that we certainly were allies in that we wanted public education. [He added that] we were not without representation in the legislature but that this was not fought and won on page one. He said anything at this time brought out publicly would be ruinous.[11]

House and Lester thought Representative Allen was sincere, but some of the others were not sure. The "only outspoken segregationist" was Rep. Glenn Walther, House said. Rep. Tom Tyler turned out "not to be an ardent segregationist at all and most of us were pleasantly surprised," House wrote. Rep. Sterling Cockrill was "definitely for us and very honest and reliable." Joel Ledbetter was also rated as favorable to open schools. And the women felt they had found a real friend for their cause when they met Rep. Gayle Windsor.

Among the senators, Ellis Fagan, Terry's old opponent, seemed to have the best grasp of what the closed schools were doing to Pulaski County. He was asked if he knew that "many people were turning their houses in, just sacrificing their down payment, stopping their payments and leaving . . . not bothering to sell. Fagan said certainly he knew about it—right now one of his most valued employees had a son going to school in Pittsburgh with relatives and now he was getting ready to move up there with him." Fagan told them that his daughter was "going [to school] over to Sylvan Hills [in the county], getting up at 6 A.M. every morning with them worried to death over the teenagers driving that distance in heavy traffic and icy dangerous weather."[12]

Pat House grew up in the small Arkansas town of Pangburn, "an all white town [where] blacks had to be out before dark," and she remembers her own parents as not being all that liberal. "Race was a subject that never, never came up. I saw a black man following a team of oxen down the road, barefoot. I had never seen a black man before . . . [and] I was four or five then," House recalled.

Her mother was a town leader who organized the PTA and the library and taught Sunday school. House remembered singing in a Baptist Sunday school "Jesus loves the little children, red and yellow, black and white, all are precious in his sight" and believing it. There were no Jews in town, and while some of the preachers in the "hard-shelled Baptist Church I went to" carried on about how the Jews killed Christ, House said, "I didn't pay a lot of attention to that."

Her father made a good living as a trader and was active in local politics. "Daddy and Mack Butler controlled the town," House said. "Every election they got together and decided who was going to get it. . . . They bought poll taxes for people and [he would tell me] this man was sorry, he went over there and paid for his vote and then . . . [he] didn't vote right. In politics, your word is your bond. . . . You learn who you can count on, who you can make your deal with and who you can't."[13] Growing up in Pangburn was good training for working the Arkansas legislature.

When House went home at night, she fed, bathed, and put to bed her children, whose number grew from four to six. With the help of a black housekeeper and babysitter, House was able, especially during elections, to work into the night as she liked to do.

She had natural childbirth and nursed her babies at a time when "they wouldn't let you check the book [on natural childbirth] out of the library. You had to read it back in the stacks." She would come home often after midnight to bake cookies and fix lunches for the next day.

House said that her husband, Byron, "did not particularly support my philosophy, but he never did fuss about it or make a great to-do because I worked hard and kept up the house, kept up the children, kept up the meals."

House described how the issue of the Little Rock crisis first rose to be a family issue back in 1957:

> A group of people had come to my husband and asked him to be a plaintiff in a suit to keep the segregation in the elementary schools. . . . They had chosen him because he worked for a pharmaceutical company and he was very good at his job. He was at the top of the company many times and the company was out of Richmond, Virginia, so they thought that there would not be any local retaliation. . . .
>
> We had never discussed this, the issue had never come up. We didn't even know how each other felt about it and I was shocked, horrified and surprised that he was going to consider it. I thought this was dreadful, and so being pretty strong-minded, I overruled him that this just would not do.[14]

House went to her first WEC meeting when her husband was out of town. She said she first attracted Irene Samuel's attention because she was one of the youngest women there and Samuel felt younger women needed to be out front. House began working with the media, attempting to get television stations, two of which turned her down, to carry information about getting the schools open. She finally arranged with KATV's general manager, Robert Doubleday, to air a series on public education on the noontime interview show. She secured people such as her old Hendrix professor, Richard Yates, to speak on the program series.[15]

House was something of an enigma to the other women with whom she worked. She was not given to chitchat, and when she did talk, it was sometimes hard to figure out exactly what she meant. She was skilled in the nuances of political maneuvering, however, which most of the other women were not. As a graduate of Hendrix College, a small liberal arts school, House also knew how to sort out and hang tough on issues she and the WEC deemed important.

House and her husband eventually were divorced, and she went back to school to study accounting. And, although the legislators did not think her capable of understanding their budget deals, she later rose to become chief financial officer and vice-president of a major Arkansas corporation.

■   ■   ■

During the 1959 legislative session, Brewer wrote that the WEC had a "platoon of women and each day at least two of our members sat in the gallery of each chamber of the legislature . . . , with small badges identifying their allegiance to the WEC." Brewer, who was working behind the scenes at the office, added, "They were quiet, dignified, listening and watching."[16]

That was the way Brewer hoped it was going, but just as House discovered in her legislative meetings, the women could not always be counted on to stay so detached. As part of the WEC platoon, Jean Gordon and I found ourselves one day in the middle of a shouting match with Jerry Screeton, a legislator from a rural eastern Arkansas county. His voice rose when he found we were lobbying for opening the schools. So did ours as we chided him for not holding the same position. It was with reluctance that we returned to our notetaking in the gallery.

Despite the presence of WEC members, working with the PTA, League of Women Voters, and AAUW lobbyists, several antiintegration measures began slipping through. A pupil placement law passed, as did an appropriation of one hundred thousand dollars to aid school districts in fighting integration. Bills passed included one requiring signatures of 25 percent of qualified voters on school-board recall petitions and another allowing teachers in private schools to be covered by the state teacher retirement system. A bill requiring hospitals to label blood by race also became Arkansas law until, like the school-related measures, it was thrown out by federal courts. The legislature also voted to place a constitutional amendment that would abolish the state's guarantee of free public education on the ballot in 1960. Fighting that amendment would consume much of the WEC's energy during the following year.[17]

By March, the WEC coalition lobbyists had abandoned whatever reserve they had attempted to show at first. Rep. Tom Tyler, who turned out to be more of a Faubus supporter than House's committee had gauged earlier, introduced a bill to allow Governor Faubus to add three members to the Little Rock School Board to break the three-three tie in his favor.

Large numbers of coalition women, who called it the school-board packing bill, swarmed into the state capitol, surrounded Tyler, and demanded that he withdraw it. According to a *Gazette* story at the time, Tyler lost his cool:

> "Lady, will you please shut up?" he snapped at one persistent questioner to his side. "If I were Faubus," Tyler said, "I would not want the bill. But he thinks it might do some good. So do I or I wouldn't have introduced it."
>
> Mrs. Byron House Jr., one of the group, said she felt that the bill was uncalled for. She said it threatened the city's school system.
>
> "It may break the deadlock we have on the Board," retorted Tyler. "It may even get our schools opened faster." Tyler finally bowed out of the dispute to answer a telephone call.[18]

The women, from their balcony seats, applauded when J. H. Cottrell, another Pulaski County legislator, first tried for a public hearing, and then attempted to get the bill into committee. Mississippi County Speaker of the House Gene Fleeman "warned the women against a demonstration. He said he would have the balcony cleared if they continued."

Other members of the Pulaski County delegation, identified quite accurately by House's earlier meeting as favorable, spoke out strongly against the bill. Rep. Gayle Windsor called it a "monstrous piece of legislation." Rep. Sterling Cockrill said the governor was asking for "ridiculous power" in the board-packing bill. Rep. Joel Ledbetter said it was "unfair to Little Rock."

The bill overwhelmingly passed the Faubus-controlled House

71 to 23. Rep. O. P. Hammons from St. Francis County argued, "People all over the South and a large percentage of the North are looking toward Governor Faubus for leadership in the fight against integration."

Sen. Ellis Fagan spoke vehemently against the bill in the Senate, saying he would resign if it passed. "Never in my 26 years in the legislature," he said, "have I put a bill on a personal basis, but this bill is a personal affront to the three senators from this district." He succeeded in getting the bill tabled in the Senate and the women declared their first victory of the legislative session.[19]

When another board-stacking bill was introduced by Sen. Max Howell, also from Pulaski County, in the Senate later, the women enlisted the help of Sen. Sam Levine from Pine Bluff who filibustered it to death. He later was defeated for reelection because of his opposition to that bill.[20]

The WEC coalition was not the only group of women at the state capitol that session. Their adversaries, the Central High School Mothers League, also turned out in large numbers to support Governor Faubus and his legislation. This led to occasional, sometimes heated, confrontations between the two groups. The segregationist legislators relished the conflict between the two groups of women. It gave them further reason to trivialize and berate the WEC women by pointing out to them that they were out of step with other women as well as with most of the South.

It was important for those of us who worked in the Women's Emergency Committee to understand why the Mothers League members felt as they did. Most of us lived in the fifth ward, which was then called the "silk stocking" district, in the western part of the city. The high school students in this area then attended Hall High School, which had been planned as the all-white high school because no blacks lived nearby. On the other hand, the membership of the Mothers League, for the most part, came out of the central area of town where there were still many "salt and pepper" neighborhoods and where many formerly all-white areas were changing rapidly to black. They were feeling economically threatened not only by blockbusting but by the specter of blacks competing for the jobs they and their husbands then held, especially if blacks began to receive equal education. The less-affluent Mothers League women, who could not afford to flee west also resented other women who lived in Pulaski Heights and who did not face the same problems, telling them they had to integrate their high school. Had we understood how patronizing we appeared to them, we might have built lines of communication that would have helped reduce the emotional pitch of their prejudice toward blacks and our own prejudice toward them. But we were into feeling a liberal superiority to them just as they felt superior to blacks. As I look back, I realize how I stereotyped them and thus contributed to keeping the community divided.

When both the WEC and the Mothers League were lobbying the state legislature, I could easily pick out who was on which side. Our women were bareheaded and casually dressed while the Mothers League women were usually overdressed and wore fussy little hats, I observed with an arrogance that must have been easily detected by those against whom it was directed.

In between the Mothers League and the WEC was a vast stretch of apathetic women who simply did not discuss what was happening at Central. When it came up, they changed the subject. They blamed the outside agitators and the press for blowing the situation out of proportion and pretended things were the way they had always been. When major issues such as this one arise in a community, normally only 10 percent of the people care enough to get involved, with 5 percent on one side and 5 percent on the other. The Mothers League, however misguided, acted on what they believed, and we knew how many there were and where they stood. The more ominous ones were those in the middle who did nothing at all.

■   ■   ■

The two women in the legislature at the time were the Pulaski County club woman Willie Oates and Mattie Hackett from Stamps, who was something of a nonentity. Oates decidedly was not. She was a former University of Arkansas cheerleader with a personality to match. Oates dressed well and was given to wearing large, flamboy-ant hats, which were her trademark. She had been the *Arkansas*

*Democrat*'s "Woman of the Year" in 1955, an honor bestowed on an ungrateful Adolphine Terry in early 1958 before she founded the WEC. Oates's male counterpart as 1955 "Man of the Year" was, ironically, Little Rock school superintendent Virgil Blossom.[21]

Oates was not a Mothers League parent nor was she given to attending segregationist events. She was, however, a joiner of just about every other club and organization that admitted women in town. She was serving on twenty boards in 1992 and was still, at that time, a leader in many good community causes, including the fight against AIDS.

Although she did not know Faubus at the time, Oates said that a group of powerful businessmen had come to her and asked her to run for the legislature. She identified them as Bill Smith, Pat Mehaffey, Witt Stephens, and Harry Parkin. Smith and Mehaffey were Faubus's chief legal experts; Stephens, the head of the state's largest securities business, was a bankroller of Faubus's campaigns, and Parkin was owner of a printing company that held many lucrative state contracts. Oates said her husband, Gordon, warned her that there might be strings attached. She said, however, that the men told her there were "no strings."[22]

Oates amicably agreed to become the first and only woman on the Raney High School Private School Corporation Board, the Faubus alternative to the closed high schools. "Did Faubus tell you his main reason for starting Raney High School?" Oates asked me. "His main reason . . . and he should be admired for this, although people picked him apart in little pieces, he had money coming in from . . . all these Southern states who felt like we were fighting their battle too. We were sort of the first ones to get into this mess . . . in the integration thing." Oates went on to say, "When he [Faubus] said he was going to form a private school corporation I said well, I know there are a number that can't afford to send them to military school or out of state or don't have connections to send them anywhere else." She recalled that

> Mrs. Terry, who headed up this committee to desegregate and
> get the public schools back, . . . branded me a segregationist.
> . . . I couldn't understand why they would brand me a segre-

gationist because I really wasn't opposed to that. . . . I think as a result of integration that maybe it's taken away a lot of things that we had before, like when the blacks were in the black schools they had most of the spirit and they had more chance to excel in their schools and they have to really fight for it now.

A year later, in 1960, Oates called for a recount when she lost by a narrow margin to the WEC-supported candidate, Jim Brandon, who worked for the Ted Lamb Advertising Agency. But the recount did not alter the election returns that made Oates a one-term representative. "The women got out and worked against me," Oates said.[23]

Oates, to her credit, voted against the Tyler school-board packing bill. A WEC statement prepared during the Oates-Brandon campaign added, however, that "she voted in favor of every other piece of anti-public education legislation introduced in the single session in which she served." It continued:

> She voted in favor of 20 pieces of legislation opposed by the WEC as potentially or actually dangerous to our schools. . . . Among the most dangerous of the acts for which she voted was Amendment 52 which if passed could close our public schools by local elections and she has . . . made no public statement which would indicate that she has changed her views.

The WEC statement also cited the fact that while Oates was both a member of the legislature and the Raney High School Board, about seventy-two thousand dollars of public school money was given to that board before the federal court enjoined the state in March from doing so. After Raney failed, no public accounting was given for the money. "Mrs. Oates was one of the board members at the time it was incorporated and she remained a member until the school closed in spite of every effort on the part of many responsible groups, some of which had supported her in her election campaign, to persuade her not to lend her name to a group which endeavored . . . to undermine our public high school system."[24]

"Today a lot of those women are some of my best friends," Oates said later. "You know, you make amends over the years. But they never understood my position on going on the Raney High School Board. I felt so strong about giving those kids an education that I didn't even realize what it would do to me politically."[25] It was a tribute to her community effectiveness back then that the struggling WEC worked so hard to get her to come aboard.

■    ■    ■

A survey of eighty-five Little Rock businesses conducted in January 1959 by AAUW members found that no new businesses had moved to Little Rock since the school crisis began. Forty-four of the men interviewed said their businesses had been affected adversely by the school situation. Thirty-five said theirs had not, although six of the latter were either moving companies or filling stations. The moving companies reported one-way traffic out of town, and the filling stations said tourists who came looking for Central High School accounted for part of their increase. One prominent company president said, "Anyone who doesn't think the school situation will affect local business adversely has rocks in his head."[26]

The WEC helped give wide circulation to the business report both in Arkansas and across the South. The report countered a *U.S. News and World Report* article that came out about the same time saying that Little Rock continued to thrive economically despite the crisis. The AAUW study helped other Southern cities wake up to the fact that resistance to integration could hurt in the pocketbook, a fact of which Rector and other Little Rock businessmen were painfully aware.

"A Letter from Little Rock" that I worked on, also in January, gave a midyear report on the status of the Women's Emergency Committee and was also sent out of state to newspapers and friends. It reported that the list of members (later called contributors and participants because of a city director's attempts to get his hands on it) had grown to 1,061 by January. It pointed to the difficulty in organizing when many women, "however sympathetic, feared their husbands might lose their jobs or suffer other retribution because they were supporting this movement."[27]

The WEC filed an *amicus curiae*—friend of the court—brief in the Gertie Garrett case, which sought an injunction stopping Governor Faubus from closing the schools under Act 4. The suit had been filed by Kenneth Coffelt, an avowed segregationist, on behalf of Garrett back in September, and press accounts were vague as to why he did it. The WEC hired Tom Downie, Ed Dunaway's law partner, to file the brief in support of the lawsuit. Vivion Brewer's chief concern was that, while Downie estimated his work would cost $350, it wound up costing nearly $1,000. She noted, however, that Downie furnished much free legal help later.

While the Arkansas Supreme Court upheld Acts 4 and 5 (Act 5 permitted transfer of funds from a school district where schools were closed by the governor to another district or to a private school) on April 28, a three-judge federal court panel threw both laws out in June.[28]

■ ■ ■

During that spring, the WEC was getting harassed at another level of government. The women got wind of the fact that the new Little Rock City Board of Directors, elected the fall before on a nonpolitical, good government slate, was planning to ask for a list of the WEC membership. L. L. Langford, a segregationist member of the new board, had decided to invoke the "Bennett ordinance," (dreamed up by Attorney General Bruce Bennett and passed in 1957 to target the NAACP). At the request of any city official, organizations had to submit lists of membership and financial information. It had already been used to get lists of the Capital Citizens Council and the Mothers League by board members of a different political bent. While the NAACP was challenging the ordinance, it remained on the books.[29]

Brewer asked Mrs. Edgar Dixon, the one member of the City Board of Directors whose friendship the WEC could count on, to go with her to see the city attorney, Joseph Kemp, about the matter. He explained that all the board wanted was a list of WEC members. Brewer responded brusquely, "This is exactly what I refuse to give you. Don't you see that the only reason it is wanted is for harassment, for reprisals?" Dixon, who admitted she had not thought about that, sided with Brewer.

Kemp agreed to submit a letter from Brewer swearing that the WEC had no membership list, only a mailing list. The shoe box containing the WEC cards was moved from house to house at night for safekeeping in case someone attempted to confiscate it. It became a floating record of WEC volunteers and contributors, including those who wished to remain anonymous, and the amounts they had given.[30]

Irene Samuel was upset when she found out the shoe-box file had been turned over to the Arkansas History Commission thirty-five years later. "I promised those women I would never give out their names," she said.

While Brewer was working on the letter that she never sent, Langford was moving on his own. Dottie Morris, the WEC's secretary, was alarmed on March 29, 1959, to find two plainclothesmen at her door displaying their badges. Her first thought was that something might have happened to her husband or one of her boys. Instead, the policemen were delivering an official letter from Langford demanding extensive information about the WEC, including its membership and contributions.[31]

The women drafted a reply that included biographies of its officers, its statement of policy and purpose, and its income for the period of time since it was organized the previous September: income, $8,777.76, and a list of expenditures, $4,910.85. It did not mention or enclose a membership list.

The reply said that the WEC was "a group of women with no charter, no by-laws" and that it met "the first Tuesday of each month at 411 East Seventh, Little Rock." This was Terry's home address. It added that an executive committee of twelve women "meets each Wednesday at 10 A.M. at the same address" and gave their names: Mrs. Joe Brewer, Mrs. Woodbridge Morris, Miss Ada May Smith, Mrs. D. D. Terry, Mrs. Harry S. Ashmore, Mrs. W. H. Thompson, Mrs. J. O. Powell, Mrs. Earl Cotton, Mrs. Ed Lester, Miss Parma Basham, Mrs. Grainger Williams, and Mrs. John Samuel.

To further clarify the WEC's position, a quote was included from an article in the *Nation,* a New York weekly magazine. The article was entitled "The Brave Ones" and was written by Dan Wakefield:

> The president of the committee, Mrs. Joe Brewer, is a Little
> Rock born and raised citizen and Smith College graduate who
> seems to embody the kind of dignity and grace that is the South

at its best and is now its greatest hope. Faubus is Snopes and his kin are the majority; Mrs. Joe Brewer and the others like her, who are people of intelligence and principle, will always be, by nature, his greatest menace. . . . They—the Mrs. Joe Brewers and the Harry Ashmores—are the conscience of Little Rock in a way that no outsiders could ever be, and at a price that no outsiders would ever have to pay. The federal forces may eventually win the battle of Little Rock, but it is these local citizens who will have to win the war. It will be a very long and a very cold one.[32]

By April 13, the plainclothesmen were back at Morris's door with a second letter from Langford saying that he needed further information, giving as his reason that he wanted to see if the organization should pay an occupation tax.

Edwin Dunaway, one of the attorneys advising the WEC, suggested that it might be time for Brewer, Morris, and perhaps some other WEC members as august and proper as Miss Hildegard Smith to go to jail. Brewer and Morris, however, did not find that so funny. Samuel claims the whole WEC board voted to go to jail at one point as a way of calling Langford's bluff, but there is no mention of it in her minutes. Instead, the women, by now thoroughly annoyed, wrote another letter:

In your most recent letter you state that we did not give a statement of our net income. In our original report we showed a total income of $8,777.56 and total expenditures of $4,910.85. We had assumed that the difference in these two figures would show our net income. For your convenience we now make this subtraction:

$8,777.76
−4,910.85
$3,866.71

This balance, and any other money received by us, will be used in nonprofit activities to achieve the objectives of our organization. . . .

We wish to say that we are impressed with your zeal in seeing that proper financial support for needed municipal services is obtained from all who should be paying an additional tax. In this connection, we might point out that the United States mails are available for the delivery of communications to us. We suggest that future communications be sent by this means, rather than by taking the time of our undermanned police force to deliver your letters, as has been done on the past two occasions.[33]

Langford, however, was a persistent man and also irate by this time. He sent a third letter on April 26, grimly warning the women that not complying with his request could bring a fine of $50 to $250 for each day of noncompliance, and he asked if the women were afraid to comply. He also pointed out that all other organizations had complied except the NAACP and that their president, Daisy Bates, had been arrested and fined in municipal court for noncompliance. He smugly added that the circuit court and the Arkansas Supreme Court had upheld the arrest and fine (it did not stand up in federal court). "The Women's Emergency Committee to Open Our Schools publicly claims a membership of 1,200. Is the Women's Emergency Committee to Open Our Schools also afraid to comply with our law of the land?" his letter asked.

The WEC board recaptured its sense of humor in time to reply:

In view of the extreme personal concern which you expressed in your last letter as to the names of our contributors, the Committee feels that it should make every effort to help you obtain these names of which we have no record. We are, therefore, calling publicly upon all persons who have contributed in any way to this Committee to convey their names and the amount of their contributions DIRECTLY to you, either by telephone or by mail, if they desire to do so. In this way you will not have to depend on our busy volunteer staff to relay this information to you.

We are somewhat bewildered at the letter's belligerent and threatening tone. It has been our earnest belief that we were complying with both the spirit and letter of the ordinance. . . . The last thing that our women wish to do is to be at cross purposes with civic-minded officials like yourself, since we share with you the common objectives of the betterment of our community.[34]

This was the last the WEC heard from the zealous city director. The policy statement that they supplied him, however, got coverage in the newspapers and was mailed out to thousands of people both in and outside the state who wanted more information about the WEC.

■   ■   ■

The WEC was by now forming branches in towns across the state—Fayetteville, Pine Bluff, Conway, Jonesboro—and as Brewer and Samuel went to speak to the new groups, they carried copies of the policy statement with them. According to the statement, "The Women's Emergency Committee to Open Our Schools is dedicated to the principle of free public school education, and to law and order. We stand neither for integration nor for segregation, but for education. Our aim is: to get the four free public high schools re-opened; to get students back in their classes; to retain our staff of good teachers; [and] to regain full accreditation by the North Central Association." The statement continued:

> We know that the "school situation" at Little Rock is not simply a local problem . . . and that Arkansas has been disgraced in the eyes of the entire world. We realize that what has happened here is elsewhere considered symbolic of "American Democracy" and so has made every American citizen the object of distrust and even hate. We believe that our free public school system is essential to the future of our city and state. It is our hope to say to the world that there are many of us here who care enough to do something about this problem.[35]

The WEC continued to reach out to anyone who might help to bring a breakthrough in the continuing deadlock. Brewer was skeptical, however, when the ubiquitous Jimmy Karam called and wanted to appear before the WEC board with a plan for opening the schools. She and other WEC board members knew about his unsavory connections with the Central High mob, but Terry said, "Tell him to come. Let's use anybody we can—anybody." His plan included, according to Brewer, "segregation of students by sex; health tests for all and suspension of those with communicable diseases; achievement tests for all, with [tests for] whites and Negroes identical and placement in school on the basis of the tests; and with highest moral codes for all students with unwed mothers banished from classroom and no immoral conduct permitted." It was the same platform he had planned to run on for the school board. The women, of course, turned him down, but they remained curious as to why he had come to the WEC in the first place.

Another person of a very different sort, the Very Reverend Charles A. Higgins, dean of Trinity Episcopal Cathedral, also came forward with a plan that looked remarkably like Karam's. It was based on the British colonial system of separating students by sex. A group of WEC women—Brewer, Dottie Morris, Mary Banner, and Velma Powell—called on him to discuss the plan. Powell, who made notes on the meeting, came away feeling that "Dean Higgins thinks our American system of public education is all wrong and . . . he feels teaching 'relations' is *all* wrong." He cited the fact that public schools were teaching "relations" and connected this with the fact that he was counseling two girls who wanted to marry Jews and who could see nothing wrong with this.

"I personally believe so strongly in the rightness of the American system of education and also in the teaching of relations and understanding of all groups that I may not be completely objective," Velma Powell wrote as an apology for her strongly worded account of the meeting.[36]

Mrs. David D. Terry (Adolphine Fletcher Terry), 1962.
*From* Arkansas Democrat-Gazette.

Men of the 101st Airborne Division near Central High School, September 26, 1957. *From* Arkansas Democrat-Gazette.

Soldiers of the 101st Airborne relaxing on the grounds of Central High. *Larry Obsitnik Photographic Archive. Special Collections Division, University of Arkansas Libraries, Fayetteville.*

Orval Faubus celebrating his election to a third term as governer, July 1958.
*Larry Obsitnik Photographic Archive. Special Collections Division, University of Arkansas Libraries, Fayetteville.*

Mrs. Joe R. Brewer
(Vivion Brewer), 1958.
*From* Arkansas Democrat-Gazette.

# Get On With It . . .

# We MUST Open Our Schools!

### Join The Women's Emergency Committee To Open Our Schools

**NOT for Integration — NOT for Segregation
BUT For Education**

Mail Contributions To:   Women's Emergency Committee,
P. O. Box 122 PH Station, Little Rock

—Ad Paid For By Mrs. Joe Brewer

The WEC used
frequent newspaper
advertisements, such
as these four, to keep
the issue before
Little Rock citizens.
*WEC Files, Arkansas
History Commission,
Little Rock.*

### Join With the Women's Emergency Committee to Open Our Schools

**NOT for Integration—NOT for Segregation—NOT affiliated with any other group**
**—For Public Education**

| Sign and mail with contribution to: | Name .................................................. |
|---|---|
| Women's Emergency Committee P. O. Box 122, Pul. Hgts. Sta. Little Rock | Address .................................................. |
| Ad paid for by Mrs. Joe Brewer | City .................................................. |

WEC Leaders (Vivion Brewer, Ada May Smith, Adolphine Terry, Dottie Morris),
September 1958. *From* Arkansas Democrat-Gazette.

Steering Committee of the WEC (Barbara Shults, Charlotte Ross, Margaret
Stephens, Gwen Booe, Mary Evelyn Lester, Billie Wilson), September 1958.
*From* Arkansas Democrat-Gazette.

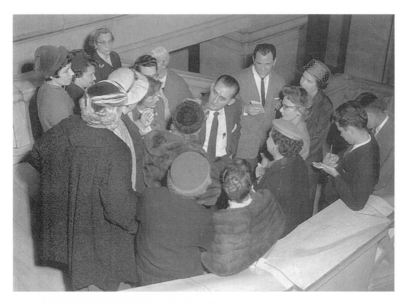

Rep. Tom E. Tyler defends the board-packing bill, March 1959.
*From* Arkansas Democrat-Gazette.

STOP campaign chairman and anti-purge school-board members (Will Mitchell, Everett Tucker, Ted Lamb, Russell Matson) on election day, May 25, 1959.
*From* Arkansas Democrat-Gazette.

The WEC continued to use newpaper advertisements to oppose the 1959 purge by the Little Rock School Board. They were joined by a group of Little Rock men, who formed STOP, and opposed by other Little Rock women, who organized the Mothers League. *WEC Files, Arkansas History Commission, Little Rock.*

WEC officers (Pat House, Irene Samuel, Kathleen Woods, Ada May Smith), October 1961. *WEC Files, from* Southern School News, *Arkansas History Commission, Little Rock.*

Leaders of the disbanded WEC (Pat House, Adolphine Terry, Sara Murphy), December 1963. *WEC Files, from* Southern School News, *Arkansas History Commission, Little Rock.*

Sara Murphy during her campaign for a position on the Little Rock School
Board, November 1962; her husband, Pat, is seated in the background.
*From* Arkansas Democrat-Gazette.

Panel of American Women (Katy Lambright, Gwen Riley, Sara Murphy, Barbara Phillips, Beth Gilmore), July 1964.
*Sara Alderman Murphy Papers, from* Presbyterian Survey. *Special Collections Division, University of Arkansas Libraries, Fayetteville.*

# ▪ 7 ▪

# A Question of Conscience

In Atlanta, as in Little Rock, the movement to preserve public education through the turbulent period of integration began with women, two of them named Maxine Friedman and Muriel Lokey. They led a parents' study group in the fall of 1958 that quickly expanded to several hundred people and eventually into an organization called HOPE, Inc. (Help Our Public Education).

Georgia had passed school-closing laws in 1956 as the focus of its efforts at massive resistance to integration. Because of this, Friedman and Lokey's group followed with high interest the actual school closings that took place elsewhere in the South and the community response to those closings.

Besides following the high school closings at Little Rock, the Atlanta women were also aware that nine schools in three Virginia cities had also been closed. This was Gov. J. Lindsay Almond's attempt at massive resistance to federal court-ordered integration. In Norfolk, where ten thousand white students were affected, the Norfolk Committee for Public Schools took Governor Almond to court for his actions.[1]

A statewide Virginia Committee for Public Schools had been set up after schools were closed in Front Royal and Charlottesville as well as in Norfolk. The field secretary, William M. Lightsey of Arlington, Virginia, spoke to the WEC executive board meeting at Little Rock in late February 1959. He was also president of the forty-five-hundred-member Arlington Committee to Preserve Public Schools set up to avert school shutdowns there.

Lightsey said the Front Royal high school had already been reopened by a federal court order but that white students were boycotting it and only twenty-one black students were enrolled. He advised the WEC "to tell about the economic importance of education. Industry and big business are going to think twice before moving into an area—such as our cities in Virginia or Little Rock—where the people they would employ have no place to send their children to school."[2]

HOPE, Inc., the organization that grew out of Friedman and Lokey's efforts, was incorporated in December 1958 and was largely responsible for steering Atlanta safely through school integration. It included both men and women from the beginning (although all the officers were women) and drew heavily from the Atlanta power structure. Like the WEC, it was an all-white organization and presented itself as being for public schools but neutral on the segregation-integration issue. Paul Mertz explained why HOPE's leaders were not altogether neutral:

> By campaigning for public schools, they were implicitly working for acceptance of desegregation. But they also recognized that saving the schools meant rallying a public that had a strong segregationist temperament, which meant they could not afford to appear to promote integration.[3]

The HOPE women were eager to learn more about Little Rock's WEC, which was already getting national recognition for its work. Fran Breeden, HOPE's president, invited Adolphine Terry to come to Atlanta in March 1959 to speak at a rally that was part of the HOPE strategy to educate the community. Terry had accepted and planned to go until an illness in the family prevented her from attending.

The WEC executive committee chose Billie Wilson, a steering committee member whose daughter, Sharon, was a displaced Hall High School student that spring, to replace Terry. Wilson, the wife of Gordon Wilson who worked for the telephone company, had never made a major speech or flown before and was a little nervous about both the size of the audience and the plane ride.

> Not until after two good Presbyterian ministers, a lawyer friend, a prominent insurance executive and my family had advised me to go did it even occur to me to wonder to whom I would be speaking and where, and how large a crowd. . . .

I was a little worried a few days before I left when my husband asked if it would bother me if a thousand people showed up—I thought that over—couldn't believe it would happen and assured him if that many came, I would simply leave off my glasses then I could only see the first couple of hundred.[4]

Wilson, however, felt deeply about having no high schools at Little Rock. She tried to explain how strong those feelings were when she wrote to Fran Breeden in Atlanta telling her she would come:

It is like sitting our three children down to a table loaded with food and telling two of them to eat and grow healthy and then telling the other one, there is plenty here for you but don't touch it, just sit there and starve to death. I know that sounds drastic but we can't help feeling that way when our lovely, new, modern, high school stands only a few blocks from our home and, although the teachers are required to sit in those empty rooms every day in order to draw their salaries, our children are not allowed to go in and feed their minds. . . .

I really feel I should have resigned as President of the P.T.A. as I am too emotionally involved to serve the best interests of that group. It tears me to shreds when the Superintendent announces that money had been saved on operating expenses by using the teachers from the closed high schools as substitute Teachers in the elementary schools and junior highs. When the Projects Chairman of my own P.T.A. announced proudly that we had been able to save a great deal of our money for redecorating our auditorium, by using the beautiful new metal chairs which had been provided, I had to fight back the tears. I knew those chairs had been taken out of Hall High School since they were not in use.[5]

Wilson began to see the Atlanta speech as a chance to say things she had kept bottled up. "I feel as if I had been released from prison," she wrote. "I have wanted for so long to do something besides beat my head against a stone wall. I have felt so frustrated that now I cannot sleep at night—my mind overflows with things I have been wanting to say to someone—anyone—for a year and a half now."[6]

She also worried what she should wear. "I suppose my 'PTA' clothes will be O.K. but do I need a dressy dress for any reason (I mean the kind I would wear to a church reception)?" she asked Breeden in a letter. "Incidentally are they in white shoes and accessories there yet? They are in the shop windows but not on the streets (here) yet, although the weather has been like spring. Are spring hats worn now?"[7]

In the first draft of her speech, Wilson repeatedly stressed the fear the crisis had created in Little Rock. "Unpleasant phone calls, boycotts of business, vicious rumors, broken friendships, strife in families, divisions in churches and social groups are some of the costs to be counted if a definite stand is taken," she wrote.

She accurately saw the power struggle in Little Rock as a battle between two groups of whites, one wanting open schools even though they would be integrated and the other wanting to maintain segregation even if it meant no schools. This observation was coupled with the less-accurate comment that there was "no apparent animosity between the two races in Little Rock." Wilson's explanation of why she came to this conclusion was true from a white person's point of view: "They shop together, ride desegregated buses, are courteous to each other and there have been a minimum of incidents. The Negroes do housework and care for the children of the whites as they have always done."[8]

This part of the speech was discreetly edited out in Atlanta by the HOPE publicity committee, which had asked for an advance copy and the right to make changes if needed. The edited version included information from the Little Rock AAUW study Wilson had taken with her that described how closed schools had hurt the economy. It also cited the fact that the Little Rock Chamber of Commerce had just completed a poll showing that 77 percent of its members favored controlled minimum integration. The edited speech gave the WEC more credit in bringing that change than had the more-modest Wilson in her original version:

> There is one bright note . . . the Women's Emergency Committee to Open Our Schools. I am a member of that committee and I am proud to state that, in spite of all opposition, I

believe we have accomplished much. I think we are primarily responsible for the recent business survey and the Chamber of Commerce action which may have far-reaching results.[9]

The edited speech retained much of Wilson's original material in slightly reworded form that cited the educational as well as the economic costs to Little Rock families of closed schools:

> Those of us who can afford it send their children away from home, out into the state or even beyond, to get their education. . . . And, of course, many students stay home and take correspondence courses, but these are restless and discouraged, deprived completely of the extra-curricular activities so important to teenagers. . . . There are no school dances—no class activities—no athletic competition.
>
> The ones who have suffered most, however, are our brightest students . . . those who qualified for scholarships and those in places of leadership. While they have been accepted in out-of-town schools, they are looked on as temporary students. . . .
>
> And there is always the worry about college acceptance. What accreditation will they receive? How will they fare in college entrance exams? . . .
>
> We have watched splendid teaching staffs sitting in empty classrooms for the past six months . . . or serving as substitute teachers in elementary schools . . . while their pupils sought an education away from home or through the mails. . . .
>
> We planned to add a room to our home . . . but if we are forced to use our funds to send our daughter away for her education next year, we certainly will not be able to build that room. Our friends are in similar positions. They are not spending freely . . . on clothes, luxuries, appliances . . . or even entertainment. . . . This curtailment of spending is just now beginning to be felt.[10]

More than fifteen hundred persons resoundingly applauded Wilson's remarks delivered at the HOPE rally held in an Atlanta movie theater that March evening. Wilson noted it was an integrated audience. Atlanta mayor William B. Hartsfield, who was also on the program, made it clear that Atlanta would be prepared to deal with those who came to town to rabble-rouse or start trouble when integration took place.

Also on the program was Ralph McGill, editor of the *Atlanta Constitution,* winner of a Pulitzer Prize, and one of the South's most outspoken advocates of moderation. So was a young newspaper editor named Sylvan Meyer from Gainesville, Georgia, who said that closing schools would kill a living institution in a futile attempt to sustain a dead one. Billie Wilson described Meyer as "a fine, handsome young man with a wonderful speaking voice, a dynamic personality and the courage of his convictions. . . . I found myself thinking 'Arkansas' each time he said 'Georgia.'"

Wilson was honored at a cocktail party and dinner and met with the HOPE board before coming home. She said the "attractive young adults . . . and the outstanding civic leaders . . . were as gracious to me as if I had truly been Mrs. D. D. Terry."[11]

HOPE's early start allowed Atlanta to educate its people and mobilize all its resources before those preaching hatred could take over the city. HOPE turned out one thousand women from fifteen organizations to discourage attempts in the legislature to pass new segregationist legislation. They got ten thousand signatures on an open school petition the following January. When trouble erupted over integration at the University of Georgia, one thousand businessmen showed up at the legislature demanding that the school closing law be changed, which it was. HOPE eventually became OASIS (Organizations Assisting Schools in September), in which fifty-three organizations worked together biracially to get the schools open and integrated without a hitch in 1961, four years after the Central High experience.[12] Billie Wilson's graphic warning about the damage Little Rock had suffered both psychically and economically when segregationists got the upper hand helped Atlanta take the kind of preventive action that ensured a peaceful school opening.

Ralph McGill wrote airmail special-delivery letters "which beat me home," Wilson said, to Wilson's three children. The letter to the oldest, Sharon, said:

> Mrs. McGill and I want you to know that you would have been
> very proud of your mother if you could have been in Atlanta

Wednesday night when she spoke to about 2,000 people in the Tower Theater in behalf of our public schools and had tremendous applause. On Tuesday evening we were with her at a dinner attended by about 15 persons, and she told us about her three children and their father and how much they had meant to her in all she had been trying to do for schools in Little Rock. She is very proud of you all, and we want you to know how proud you would have been of her.[13]

"My trip was so timely," Wilson said in her report to the WEC board. "The morning I left the *Gazette* carried the picture of the ladies, most of whom I recognized as members of my church and of this organization, protesting the Mr. Tyler School Board Packing Bill. Also that same paper carried the report of the Chamber of Commerce poll. I was delighted and arrived in Atlanta clutching the *Gazette* in my hand."

Wilson's visit received wide coverage in the Atlanta press, including one story whose headline read, "'Don't Make Mistakes We Did,' Mother from Little Rock Urges Atlantans."[14] She was attacked in only one Atlanta letter to the editor that asked, "I wonder who has the facts, Mrs. Wilson of Little Rock or the U.S. Department of Labor?" The writer, T. J. Wesley Jr., quoted Labor Department statistics from the *U.S. News and World Report* that Little Rock nonfarm jobs were up 2 percent, factory pay (weekly) up 6.4 percent, department store sales up 3 percent, building permits up 16.5 percent, and banking activity up 6.8 percent. Wesley added that "there seems to be no correlation whatsoever between the growth of any Southern state and the present school crisis."[15] Another letter writer, who identified himself only as "Jaw Bone" in the *Arkansas Democrat,* approvingly quoted Wesley and said: "The Little Rock women may as well learn that whenever they go on a mission to some other state to spread their propaganda, there will be energetic Southerners in the audience to listen to every word politely and then go out and prepare a rebuttal."[16]

Wilson also got a letter with a newspaper account of a white girl's rape by a black student in New York and a note that said: "Many of your Christian friends are shocked and saddened by your actions. We are praying for you."[17] And her aunt in Aubrey, Arkansas, wrote her saying:

I'm begging you to *study* these clippings from an unbiased paper. Please do this with an open mind and then see if you want to help open the public schools regardless of the cost to your children and grandchildren (I don't mean integration or segregation) but *domination* by people hundreds of miles away. A thing that takes place no where else except Russia and other communist countries.

I hope all of you are as well as we are. I wrote all the family news to Florence, so if you are still interested in us read her letter. I'm very fond of all of you and quite proud of you. Love, Winnie.[18]

Enclosed were several clippings from the *Memphis Commercial Appeal,* including an ad signed by R. B. Snowden, attempting to tie Little Rock's school integration and the NAACP to the Communist Party. The same Snowden had appeared with Governor Faubus and Roy V. Harris to speak at a segregationist rally at England, Arkansas, where he discussed a free presidential elector plan.[19]

During my interview with Wilson, her sister, Gwen Booe, did most of the talking because Wilson was recovering from a stroke. Wilson, however, interrupted whenever she wanted to add something. Booe said she and Wilson grew up on a plantation at Palmer, Arkansas, which is between Holly Grove and Marvell in the Delta country of eastern Arkansas. According to Booe, the sisters did not get their ideas on race from their father, who had "grown up with Negroes more than we did" and because "he didn't think like this." Fewer than six white families lived in the community, where the owner of the plantation also owned the general merchandise store and a sawmill at Pine City that their father ran, and a cotton gin. Booe recalled riding the train to and from school in Marvell each day (Wilson interjected that her teacher was Miss Lily Peters), until the community organized a school district in Palmer.

I don't know how high the grades went. I was in the seventh grade and I was teaching the ones younger than I was and the teacher lived with us. We had a Negro that came to work for us when I was born and she was twelve. She said she borned us. We moved to Little Rock when I was twelve [in 1923].

Mother was real liberal. [She had lived in Chicago as a

girl.] Now Daddy was raised to think Negroes were inferior. He got along with them fine. Pine City was all Negro. . . . The only white man that lived there was an old man in charge of the sawmill. So Daddy got along with them fine but he wanted them in their place. Mother was still living when the schools were closed. . . . She was in it right with us.[20]

Wilson remembered an incident in which her father struck a Negro for calling him by his first name, because he laughed when her father told him to address him by "Mr." and his last name.

Both Wilson and Booe were PTA presidents in Little Rock the year of the closed schools—Wilson at Forest Park Elementary School and Booe at Forest Heights Junior High School. Booe remembered that they were invited to Mrs. Terry's. "I don't know why we were invited but we were," she said. "We volunteered to be members of the steering committee."

My husband, Prentice, was very much in sympathy with what we were doing and he was very proud of us and his boss backed us up too. He worked for Maryland Casualty Company. . . . It was right in the middle of this while the troops were here, one of their associates from Baltimore had to come to Little Rock on business. He was terrified. He thought there was blood running down the streets. He wanted Prentice to meet him at the airport because he was afraid to get out of the plane. Prentice didn't have anyone who was against what we were doing in his office, but Billie's husband worked for the telephone company and he had a lot of criticism from them. [There was one fellow who gave him a hard time, Wilson explained.]

So we weren't brave to be on the committee like some of the women. We were just lending our names and our presence. We were that important, but we could stand the publicity. There was no reason why we couldn't. We could understand why some people were afraid of their positions or their husband's positions, like that woman whose husband worked for Archer Drug Company. He asked her not to do it because I think his boss, the people who owned the drug store, objected to it.[21]

Both Wilson and Booe remembered that they got strong backing from Westover Hills Presbyterian Church, which their families attended, and from its pastor, Rev. Richard B. Hardie Jr. Members of the Westover Church session, which included both their husbands, signed an ad in the *Gazette* during the Central High School turmoil the fall before "deploring the unbridled passions aroused by such mob action as now prevails in our city."[22] "It split the church and a lot of people left," Booe recalled.

Booe said that both she and her husband were greeters at Sunday morning services at Westover Hills Church. They were instructed that "if any Negroes came to church they were to be seated any place they wanted to be and not on the back row," Booe said. "And I was disappointed that none ever came but tension was high because we expected them to come and some of the members to get up and leave if they were seated by them. The situation never did happen."

Sharon Wilson Adair, Billie Wilson's daughter, was fifteen years old and supposed to be a tenth grader at the brand new Hall High School, open only a year before it was closed. Instead, she was one of three hundred students who took courses by correspondence from the University of Arkansas.

"It's a lot harder than regular school studies and it takes more time," she told a *Commercial Appeal* reporter at the time. Both she and Tommy Hill, another would-be Hall student, said they would greatly prefer to be back in a regular high school. Sharon attended a makeshift class at Westover Hills Church taught by university people so they could get academic credit. It cost her parents $180 that year. "My parents refused to allow me to go to the school that supported Faubus so they pulled together this school," Sharon recalled.[23]

"It was not an all-bad life," Sharon later remembered in an interview. She only went to school in the morning and then would go swimming at the YMCA or play tennis the rest of the day. She found it sad, however, that her friends "went every which way." Her best friend, Betty Rozzell, who lived across the street and felt as she did about integration, went to stay with her grandmother in Conway. Another went to Benton where she met boys and brought them back to Little Rock and "we'd date each other's friends. That was fun but . . . hard. After years and years of being together, we were split. And we were split on the issue."[24]

Sharon remembered her parents as being open toward blacks for "as long as I can remember." She remembered her mother's mother, who was a member of the Women's Christian Temperance Union, as also being open. "My father came from a very conservative family in Russellville, Arkansas. It was 'nigger' this and 'nigger' that. I can remember my grandfather talking like that and I can remember correcting him. It amazed me that my father came out of that environment."

Sharon thought her father's mother influenced him, just as her mother's mother influenced Billie and Gwen. When she was interviewed, Sharon was teaching human sexuality courses through her regional staff position with the Methodist Church at Dallas. She said that her mother had told her that her grandmother taught her everything about sex "because she knew so little [when she was younger]. Back then that was real unusual. . . . She was just ahead of her time in lots of ways."

Sharon remembers being active in everything at Westover Hills. Her minister, Dick Hardie, was "very outspoken" and had encouraged his church to get involved in working on the school crisis. Later, he and Frank Gordon, who served on his church board, marched with Rev. Martin Luther King Jr. at Selma, Alabama. But she also remembers, as did her aunt, Gwen Booe, the "conflict Dick and I had when I was president of the youth group on brotherhood day. I wanted to invite a group of blacks to our MYF [Methodist Youth Fellowship] and Dick said the climate is not to that point yet. And I said, 'You've been teaching me all these things all these years and now you're not willing to put them into action.' And we really clashed over that."[25]

Booe said a member of the church staff first told Sharon she could not have the blacks and she had to call them and tell them not to come. "I felt like [letting the black youngsters come] was the right thing after the stand our church had taken. I felt like that was right in line with what we were trying to do."

Adair declared, however, that Hardie had had a real impact on her. The Dallas Methodist Church that she attended in 1992 was "the exact duplicate" of Westover Hills, she added.

Hardie, whose church the Wilsons and the Booes attended, recalled, "I didn't speak on race relations Sunday, I spoke every Sunday."[26] Like Sharon, his congregants often charged out ahead of him, and Hardie was the first to recognize and appreciate this.

"The people who were courageous were the women," Hardie said in a video-taped interview in the summer of 1993. "They took the leadership. The women came forward because they were not as involved in business then. They worked inside the home rather than outside. They organized themselves and were the source of organizing some of the community groups we got going. Many were Jewish women. They were also from the Methodist, Disciples of Christ, and Presbyterian churches."[27] And many of them, like Wilson and Booe, came right out of Hardie's own Westover Hills Presbyterian Church where they had heard him expound his own views Sunday after Sunday.

Westover Hills was a *Southern* Presbyterian church as were all the white Presbyterian churches in Little Rock at the time. Only the all-black Allison Presbyterian Church was affiliated with the (Northern) Presbyterian Church U.S.A. The Southern branch of the church had split off from the Northern branch during the time of the Civil War over the issue of slavery. The Methodists did the same.

"On the defensive, morally, against the conscience generally of civilized man, theologians who were to mold the mind of Southern Presbyterianism developed a new doctrine of the 'spirituality of the church,'" according to a history of the church. Their position was that since the Bible did not specifically condemn slavery, it could not therefore be condemned by the church.[28]

The General Assembly of the Presbyterian Church in the Confederate States of America was organized on December 4, 1861, at Augusta, Georgia, and later became the Presbyterian Church U.S.[29] While Methodist churches North and South were reunited in the late 1930s, the Northern and Southern branches of the Presbyterian Church did not come back together until 1983. The Arkansas Presbytery had, however, brought the two kinds of Presbyterianism together in the state in 1974.[30]

My great-grandfather attempted to rework his conscience

along the lines of the Southern church, which told him he could be a spiritual Presbyterian and own slaves at the same time. He did not succeed. A written family account of the mental illness he suffered at one period in his life attributed it to the fact that "he was in principle an abolitionist and during the period of his mental depression he was extremely annoyed by the fact of his owning slaves." He was treated at a hospital for nervous disorders in Utica, New York, where apparently it was decided that he was not so crazy for thinking as he did, because he recovered there.[31]

By the late 1950s, there were several white Southern Presbyterian ministers at Little Rock willing to tell their segregated congregations that they should not join with the governor in stonewalling school integration. In addition to Hardie, Rev. Marion Boggs at Second Presbyterian Church (which I attended), Rev. T. B. Hay at Pulaski Heights Presbyterian Church, and Rev. Dunbar Ogden (who marched with the Little Rock Nine) were among those active in opposing Governor Faubus's actions. Ogden, whose views and actions had gotten him into trouble with his congregation at Central Presbyterian, received and accepted a call to Huntington, West Virginia, in the fall of 1958. According to Daisy Bates's account, Ogden's son, David, who had walked with his father and the black students at Central in 1957, was subjected to repeated verbal attacks by co-workers after the incident. He committed suicide in 1960.[32]

Presbyterian ministers and laymen in the Washburn Presbytery, which encompassed a third of the Presbyterian churches in Arkansas, including those in Little Rock, called on Governor Faubus the following year to change his mind about not allowing the high schools to open in September 1958. When harassment of the black students was occurring at Central High School, this was the group that Governor Faubus attacked when he said that "he knew a large number of the ministers in the Presbyterian Church have been very effectively brainwashed" by left-wingers and Communists. The ministers asked for an apology but never received it.[33]

Campbell and Pettigrew, writing in *Christians in Racial Crisis*, generally found that, with a few cutting-edge exceptions, most Little Rock ministers did not take what could be considered a courageous stand. Local ministers vigorously disputed the findings of the Campbell-Pettigrew study.[34]

A statement, however, that formed the basis for a citywide prayer service when the federal troops were at Central High School in 1957 was watered down to where it said nothing in an attempt to draw in segregationists. The segregationist churches still held their own services the evening before. Homer Bigart of the *New York Times* declared that "citizens could take their choice whether to attend a Friday night prayer service sponsored by 24 Baptist pastors who are avowed segregationists, or wait for Saturday's meeting when the praying will be neutral."[35]

■   ■   ■

A few Methodist women were on the firing line earlier as were Wilson, Booe, and other Presbyterian women at Little Rock after the schools were closed. An integrated two-day meeting was held by thirty of them in April 1958 at Camp Aldersgate, the year before Wilson went to Atlanta. A full report on this meeting was furnished to the governor by one of his anonymous informants, who relied on another informant who had actually been there.

An unsigned note attached to the front of a program and the report of the Aldersgate meeting that wound up in Faubus's files said, "It is my personal opinion that this was a 'brainwashing' session—and those select few who are capable of being brainwashed were invited. Certainly my source of information seemed to be convinced of everything that was said at the meeting." The governor had scratched across the note, "Patsy, save for me, OEF." The report did not give the names of the women, who were from both Arkansas and Tennessee, who attended, although the name of Mrs. Russell Henderson, a well-known Arkansas Methodist leader, appeared on the program. The report saved in the governor's file does, however, comment on the speakers and the fact that the meeting was integrated:

> One of the principal speakers was from Baton Rouge, Louisiana, where her husband is Dean of a colored college. . . . [M]y source of information said of her, "A brilliant person, who made me feel inferior and whom I enjoyed, however, one of the

white ladies, from Brownsville, Tennessee, remarked that the women 'rubbed her the wrong way'—and that she could do more 'good' in the North and East than in the South."

A panel of lawyers, one colored, named Mercer, who is a Field Representative of the NAACP and maintains an office on Ninth Street here in Little Rock, and two white lawyers, one named Edward Lester, who is a member of the law firm of Wright, Harrison, Lindsey and UPTON (school board) and one other white lawyer, discussed the "legal" aspects of integration. [An anthropology] professor from the University of Arkansas, Stephan . . . told them there is no difference in blood, that we are all the same, the only difference being in the hair and some other features, that it is an old wive's [sic] tale that should a colored man marry a white girl they would have a black child, etc. . . . Did not learn the subject of Dean Leflar's talk, neither was I told what Mr. Ashmore spoke about—when I asked, the subject was changed whether or not intentionally I do not know. There were approximately seven or eight negro women in attendance, and all women (white and colored) slept in the same cabin, used same facilities, and, of course, all ate together in the dining room.

A Dr. Will Campbell, from Nashville Tennessee, spoke. . . . [H]e said, "The most prominent people of Nashville took a hand in our integration from the beginning and we had no trouble, and of course, our Governor was behind us." Where upon I asked if our Governor's name was mentioned, or rather if anything was said about him—and my source . . . stated, "Not by name but by implication, AND THEY ARE OUT TO GET HIM."

My source . . . stated that she came back convinced that the NAACP is *not* subversive, and when I questioned why she was convinced, she stated that they were told that it is not . . . and that J. Edgar Hoover says it is not. . . .

When I asked if the church is going to integrate, I was told, "Oh, no, the colored people want their own churches." Then I said, "Well, I wonder why they want to live next door to us." And then this—"one of the colored people present said that just as the white people don't want to live next door to a lower class, neither do the colored people want to live next door to their lower class and they want to improve them-selves." It was admitted at this meeting by the colored people that it may take another generation or two to accomplish com-plete integration, socially and otherwise, but that it will come.

The white lady from Brownsville, Tennessee, remarked that her husband did not know she came to Little Rock to attend an integrated meeting, but she thinks the colored people are "mistreated." She stated that they have no integration problem in Brownsville . . . where the negroes are 4 to 1, because the negroes don't want to integrate. This meeting, as you know, was to have been secret . . . but it did leak out—and it is my understanding that this is not the first . . . integrated meeting.

One negro woman in attendance lives in Danville, Arkansas, has white hair, so must be elderly—and she told the meeting that they don't have an integration problem in Danville, that her people are happy the way things are—but there aren't a hundred negroes in Danville.[36]

The informant also noted that Herbert Thomas Sr. spoke to the group but that Dr. Ethel Alphenfel, author of *Sense and Nonsense,* and who was listed on the program, did not come.

More than three hundred Arkansas Methodist segregationists "including a sprinkling of women" pulled in former governor Homer M. Adkins to tout a move to reestablish the Methodist Church South in October of the same year. They cited the earlier meeting of the Methodist women as one reason they thought such action was needed. Adkins and other speakers, who included Ed I. McKinley, also attacked "members of the Methodist clergy, the United States Supreme Court, the NAACP and a former Philander Smith College professor" named Lee Lorch. McKinley said the Supreme Court deci-sion was based on Swedish sociologist Gunnar Myrdal's *An American Dilemma,* not on law.[37] How McKinley slipped by the moderates and the WEC to be accepted as their candidate at the insistence of Billy Rector a little more than two months later is a mystery.

Other religious leaders who were segregationists were heard from frequently in their support of Faubus's actions. Rev. Wesley Pruden of the Broadmoor Baptist Church was president of the Capital Citizens Council. Rev. M. L. Moser Jr., pastor of the Central

Missionary Baptist Church, rose to prominence as a segregationist leader during the school board recall election in May 1959.

■　■　■

Rev. Colbert Cartwright of the Pulaski Heights Christian Church had helped form the Arkansas Council on Human Relations earlier in the 1950s, along with Fred Darragh and Harry Ashmore. Prior to the crisis, he wrote articles for both secular and religious national publications and spoke to local groups about the need for Southern ministers to be involved in preparing their communities for desegregation.

Cartwright was at Central High School as a journalist on the eventful morning that the black students were turned away from Central High School in 1957. In his own account of what happened, he said:

> I was present standing by the black students when they were turned away. I heard what the guard told them. I found out Elizabeth Eckford was turned away. She walked the full block from one end to the other [with] young white mothers hurling language at her that I had never heard even in a locker room. She was quite poised, clutching a notebook in her ging-ham shirt, with great dignity and bearing, walking . . . to a bus stop, waiting for the bus.
>
> A white woman helped her on the bus. She was Grace Lorch, known as an academic, theoretical Marxist. A Marxist woman comforted her, then disappeared into the crowd.
>
> I went back to the black newspaper. I met with Mrs. Bates. I asked what they would do with the students turned away. She said Wiley Branton of the NAACP was taking care of the legal aspects of it. She had two requests of me. She said, "one, we want to protect the black students. Here are the names and addresses of all black students. I'm not giving it to the press or the public. I'm giving it to you because you will know what to do with it. Two, go to the FBI and give a deposition so there is a witness that you heard the students were turned away.[38]

He gave the deposition and then teamed up with a reporter from the *New York Herald Tribune* who had heard he had the names and addresses of the students. Cartwright had met with the students at Dunbar Junior High School, and that evening he took the reporter with him to several of the students' homes. In most, they were not admitted, but the Eckfords let the two of them in.

Cartwright asked Elizabeth how she had stood up under such tension, and she said her mother had read her the Twenty-seventh Psalm the evening before and she had read it again that morning. She read a part of it again to the visitors, "If a host encamp against me, I shall not fear. My God shall vindicate me." Her story was printed in the Sunday *New York Herald Tribune* and became the human interest story that moved many people to identify with her stand.

Cartwright lost thirty-one church members, 10 percent of his three-hundred-member congregation. However, he was kept on in Little Rock until 1964 and, through his writings and sermons, provided insights into the events that occurred during that time.

"In the end, the law could not do it," he said. "A group of very dedicated people—women, . . . Methodist women [among them] marshalled . . . grassroots support to take back the schools and work on the desegregation problem. The lesson is that people themselves had to take responsibility for what they wanted their community to be. . . . They had to rally the good forces in the community to take back the schools, do more than a lackluster desegregation effort to abide by some edict. This was work that should have been done prior to desegregation."[39]

Rev. Dale Cowling, pastor of Second Baptist Church, went down to his farm to struggle over what he would say about integration the Sunday before the black children were to enter Central High School. In order to preach the sermon he had struggled with he said, "I had to make up my mind I'd rather dig ditches. I thought I'd be fired." His congregation said nothing. "I'd been there long enough, people knew what I said came out of my heart."

Because of his stand and because he was president of the Little Rock Ministerial Alliance, Cowling was frequently asked to make public statements, including one on CBS the day the Central High crisis began. He was also a close friend of Governor Faubus, who he pointed out had "previously integrated colleges and the Democratic

Central Committee." Cowling recalled, "I knew the mob was going to be called in. I asked him [Faubus] why. He had tears in his eyes. He said you could never know the pressure. Then when he got into it, it became a political bomb." Cowling remained friends with Faubus despite their differences on this issue and performed the ceremony at Faubus's second marriage years later.[40]

A group of black persons led by Albert Hudson attempted twice to attend services at Cowling's church in the fall of 1958 after he protested the school closing. They were turned away the first time and were offered a seat in the basement the second time. Some of the group admitted they were paid to come, and Daisy Bates said Hudson was being used by someone, although he denied it.[41] Similar attempts were made at other white churches where the ministers had been outspoken in supporting the black students.

One of these was at Pulaski Heights Methodist Church where the minister was Rev. Kenneth Shamblin, who had protested the "rigged election" held in September 1958 as a ploy to keep the schools closed. Cowling also had made a similar plea to his congregation to get the schools reopened "even though this means integration." The boards of Westover Hills Presbyterian Church and St. Paul Methodist Church had passed resolutions asking members to vote for "continuing our system of free public education" and "for the preservation of public schools in Little Rock" prior to the September election.[42] None of the statements asked outright that the "for integration" box on the ballot be marked as the WEC had done, although it was implied.

Margaret Morrison, a member of Kenneth Shamblin's church, was also the president of the local unit of the National Association for the Advancement of White People. She said she was asked in 1958 to start it by the attorney general's office and there were only three members, who were women friends of hers, besides herself. The press, however, used her releases without knowing that.

"I took my maid to church one Sunday because the minister, Kenneth Shamblin, up and said we had to integrate the schools," Morrison said. "I said, 'Let's integrate the church.' When I took my maid, he [Shamblin] said, 'Margaret, you're just trying to embarrass me.'" Morrison said a friend whose husband was on the church board told her Shamblin tried to get her put out of the church, but another fellow spoke up and said, "She's just trying to get you to practice what you preach." Morrison continued:

> The Sunday I took Pearl, the T. J. Raneys were having their grandchild christened. People thought Pearl worked for the Raneys and that's why she came. The Raneys [he was a founder of Raney High School and the family was a large financial contributor to the church] thought I did it to embarrass them. I didn't. I just wanted to make Shamblin face up to what he was saying.
>
> Pearl went with me the following Sunday as well. They seated her with me each time. The *Gazette* was covering it and by then I was getting calls from all over the world . . . and we were on a TV program shown in Denmark. Nobody knew it was just the four of us doing all this.
>
> The last time I took Pearl, Shamblin just put his head down on the pulpit. He kept his eyes on her the whole time. I was just doing it to upset him. How did I get her to go? I paid her, just like I paid her to iron.[43]

Morrison had a distinct distaste for the WEC women, who she said acted "very superior. . . . They were rude to us. They tried to imply that we were ignorant, uneducated white trash." Morrison later worked for Pat House in a business office and "we got along fine. I'm a good secretary. And we just never discussed this." She added that "I still think the way I did and Pat still thinks the way she did."

Although Morrison liked Margaret Jackson, whom she called "a very nice person . . . level headed and well organized," she and her three supporters never joined the Mothers League. They preferred their own guerrilla warfare.

Bomb threats were made in anonymous letters to both the *Gazette* and *Democrat* against Rabbi Sanders's Temple B'nai Israel and the Synagogue Agudath Achim on October 18, 1958. The bombs were supposed to be exploded during Friday night services, but the two rabbis held services according to schedule and nothing happened. Few members of either congregation knew about the threats until later.

In November 1958, a few months before Wilson's visit, 312 ministers and rabbis from sixteen denominations in Atlanta had signed a strong statement calling for the preservation of public schools and maintaining communication between "responsible leaders of the races."[44] Only two church boards and a handful of ministers had gone on public record in favor of getting the schools open before the September 1958 election at Little Rock. "The WEC was the only organization in the city publicly to urge an affirmative vote in the referendum on September 27, 1958, for the racial integration of all schools within the school district," said Henry Alexander, a government professor who, for the Eagleton Institute, analyzed events leading up to the recall election in 1958–59.[45] By assembling a critical mass of women willing to address the problem head on, the WEC could act forcefully, whereas churches and other organizations, with their broader constituencies holding mixed views, were less likely to do so. When individual ministers took strong stands, they invariably lost church members and often had to move elsewhere.

# ▪ 8 ▪

# Stop This Outrageous Purge

While teachers sat in empty classrooms in Little Rock's four closed high schools, rumors began to spread in early 1959 of an impending teacher purge. When the report first surfaced in a *Gazette* story on February 8, it had an ominous and ugly ring to it. According to the rumor, if the Little Rock School Board would dismiss certain teachers, it could get back the state aid being withheld while the schools were closed. The Women's Emergency Committee fired off a letter to Ed I. McKinley, school board president, urging him to "renew the contracts of the teachers in the four closed high schools without delay."[1]

According to Ted Lamb, the proposed deal was offered to the three moderate board members, Lamb, Everett Tucker, and Russell Matson. If they would agree to fire Jess Matthews, J. O. Powell, and Elizabeth Huckaby, the three principals at Central, as well as LeRoy Christopher, the black principal at Horace Mann, then the legislature would return the state aid that had been withheld when the four high schools were closed. When the offer came up for discussion at a board meeting, McKinley called it a "ridiculous falsehood."

McKinley and Bob Laster, however, indicated they would especially like to get rid of J. O. Powell, one of the vice-principals at Central.[2] The reason they gave was that he had spoken on a panel at a meeting of the Women's Emergency Committee to Open Our Schools. Laster said that "was very improper because people place great significance on what a school principal does or says." Two days later, Governor Faubus denied that he knew anything about a deal to give the school aid back in return for a purge. He declared at a press conference, however, that if he were a school director, he would not renew contracts for Matthews, Powell, or Huckaby.

"They did everything they could to discriminate against the white students, at the behest of Virgil Blossom I suppose," he said.[3] Rowland said the three segregationist school board members also wanted to see all three principals go.[4]

The year before, when harassment of the nine black students was at its peak inside Central High School, Rep. Paul Van Dalsem, chairman of the Legislative Council, asked Governor Faubus to send the state police to investigate. They had interviewed at least fifty students, teachers, and principals.[5] Some of the white students, because they had been disciplined for their continuing torment of black students, concocted stories about the partiality of the principals to blacks.[6] Van Dalsem predicted that a Legislative Council hearing would "link the Little Rock Central High School integration crisis to a Communist plot."[7]

There was no question but that the Little Rock School District in early 1959 was hurting financially. Superintendent Terrell Powell reported a $139,000 shortfall in February caused by the withholding of state aid and said he expected the district to be $200,000 in the hole by the end of the school year.[8] But the idea of bartering state aid for teacher dismissals was so preposterous that most people could not believe that those suggesting it could be serious. Further rumors were going around that there were at least one hundred high school teachers the segregationists wanted to see dismissed.

It was during that spring that the erosion of other Arkansas teacher rights began to occur. Act 10, passed in a special session of the legislature the summer before, went into effect in early 1959 and required all teachers who wanted contracts renewed to sign affidavits listing the organizations to which they either belonged or had given contributions. One of the original purposes of Act 10 was to ferret out NAACP members who were barred by another state law from being allowed to teach. Act 10 applied not just to public school teachers but also to college faculty at state-run institutions.

Although Act 10 and the law prohibiting NAACP membership for teachers were eventually thrown out by the federal courts, Act 10, when it went into effect, created consternation among educators at different levels all over the state. The dean of the University of Arkansas Law School, Ralph Barnhart, said Act 10 was "obnoxious as invading the right to privacy and doubly obnoxious as picking out teachers as the special subject for it."[9] Psychology professor Hardy Wilcoxon said that "Act 10 is a bad law . . . that if it remains in force over the years . . . will do great damage to the University and all other educational institutions in Arkansas." Central vice-principal J. O. Powell, who was already under attack, furnished a list of his organizational affiliations but refused to sign the affidavit, calling it "totalitarian."[10] For him it was the last straw among many indignities he had endured during his last two years at the school. By summer, he and his wife, Velma, a WEC founder, were headed west to Corona, California, where he had accepted another school administrative job.

The WEC's February meeting, at which Central vice-principal J. O. Powell appeared on a panel, was the biggest of the year, with three hundred people in attendance. A film about successful school integration in Saint Louis, *A City Decides,* was shown, emphasizing the need for preparing black and white teachers to work together, for neighborhood black-white parent meetings, and for community leadership support.

Serving with Powell on the panel that reacted to the film were attorney Ed Lester; Rev. W. A. Wilcox, an Episcopal minister; Dr. Lewis Long, a psychologist at the state mental hospital; and Chris Barrier, a displaced high school student. Powell had been quoted as saying that "the smoothness of integration would be in direct ratio to the amount of public relations or community orientation." It was not exactly a radical observation. Dr. Long, when asked if "Negroes are really equal to whites biologically and emotionally," replied succinctly, "Yes."[11] Rev. Wesley Pruden of the Capital Citizens Council and certain members of the Mothers League, who came to the WEC meeting to monitor what was said, heard the response in person although it was in the *Arkansas Democrat* the next day as well.

Before the week was out, Dr. Long (whose wife, Barbara, was a WEC board member) had been dismissed from the state hospital, and Powell was targeted to be at the top of the teacher purge list. Vivion Brewer offered to prepare a public statement protesting the action against Dr. Long, but he and his wife declined. They moved shortly thereafter to Washington, D.C.[12]

A survey conducted by the Chamber of Commerce in February

showed that, by a vote of 632 to 230, its members were against continuing with closed schools. Overwhelmingly in the same survey, by 819 to 245, chamber members favored opening the schools on a controlled minimum plan of integration acceptable to the federal courts.

Acting on the results of this survey, plus some prodding by the WEC of individual chamber members, the chamber board of directors passed a resolution that asked for immediate action by the state supreme court on the legality of Acts 4 and 5 of 1959 that made possible the school closings and the withholding of funds from Little Rock. The resolution pointed out that "time is running out for executing teachers' contracts in the Little Rock School District for the coming year."[13]

A later resolution, passed unanimously by the chamber board at its March 23 meeting, called for using a controlled, minimum pupil placement plan of integration to reopen the schools and urged the school board to assure "all teachers that their contracts will be promptly renewed; in order that we do not lose our valuable and loyal staff." The resolution also took aim, however, at the supreme court decision which it said was binding but "erroneous and . . . a reversal of established law [based] upon an unprecedented basis of psychology and sociology."[14]

■   ■   ■

On May 5, the Women's Emergency Committee was having its last meeting of the school year and was looking forward to taking a break for the summer. The approximately fifty women present had just heard a report from Barbara Shults that the WEC list of members had grown officially to 1,340.[15] Her committee had sent out 365 letters and had made more than one hundred telephone calls during April.

Irene Samuel had reported that the office was moving to its new location in the Pulaski Heights shopping center. Brewer had asked the women not to be discouraged over the failure of the state supreme court to declare the school closing act illegal. She had said that with the help of the AAUW and other organizations, a growing movement of women was shaping up over the state to counter the multifaceted attack on teachers and public schools.

Suddenly, the telephone rang in Adolphine Terry's hallway, interrupting a program on the history of public education in the state.[16] Someone whispered to Vivion Brewer that it was urgent that she take the call. When she came back, ashen and shaken, she announced that Billie Wilson had called to say "the school board is firing our teachers right and left down there."[17]

Wilson, a WEC board member, was attending the fateful school board meeting at which the teacher purge actually got underway. The WEC immediately sent other representatives to the meeting. Representatives of the League of Women Voters, the Mothers League, and the Capital Citizens Council, along with those from various teachers' groups, were also present.

The school board meeting had begun at 9 A.M. with all six board members present. Tension was high because it was the last meeting for considering teacher contracts for the coming year. The board accepted thirty-four resignations submitted by teachers and listened to Superintendent Terrell Powell's report that a survey indicated 175 teachers would not be returning. It then split three-three to move Terrell Powell out of the superintendency and back to his old job as Hall High principal, with Ed McKinley, Ben Rowland, and Bob Laster for and Ted Lamb, Everett Tucker, and Russell Matson against.

The Lamb-Tucker-Matson contingent walked out at noon after it became apparent that, instead of rehiring all the teachers recommended for the coming year, board president McKinley intended to go through the list one by one and attempt to fire those he wanted terminated.[18] Lamb told the WEC board the following day that he, Matson, and Tucker had left on the advice of their attorney who felt that, in the absence of a quorum, the meeting would be declared illegal in court.[19]

Barring legitimate termination by the board ten days before the end of the school year, teacher contracts would then automatically be reactivated for the coming year under a state teacher tenure act and a 1955 Little Rock administrative ruling. None of the teachers recommended for termination had received the required prior due-process notification that they would not be rehired.[20]

The purge began at 1 P.M. McKinley, Rowland, and Laster declared themselves a quorum and threw out the administrative ruling. They then voted not to renew the contracts of forty-four of Little Rock's most highly respected teachers and administrators at the afternoon rump board session. The casualty list included thirty-nine whites and five blacks: thirty-four were teachers, seven were principals, and three were in other positions; twenty-seven were from Central High School, and seventeen from ten other schools.[21] The possibility was raised that some of the names might have come from the Van Dalsem state police investigation earlier.[22]

The three board members appointed the elderly T. H. Alford, father of the segregationist former school board member, Dr. Dale Alford, who defeated Brooks Hays for Congress, as the new superintendent. After the three board members fired the principals of the two schools that Wilson's children attended, she rose to ask: "On what basis were they dismissed, may I ask?"

McKinley looked at her sternly and replied, "At this time we are not open to discussion from the floor."

"As soon as they fired Frances Sue [Wood], I got up and went out . . . and I called Frances Sue at school," Billie Wilson recalled. "I said, 'Did you know you were just fired?' And of course she was just dumbfounded. I told her who they were firing and she was just amazed."[23]

Before it adjourned that day, the WEC became "the first organization in the city formally to condemn the dismissals."[24] Women attending the meeting voted to empower Vivion Brewer and the board to do whatever was possible to save the teachers who had been fired and gave its full "confidence and support" to all of Little Rock's public school teachers. The WEC statement appeared the following morning in the *Gazette* alongside the story of the purge.[25]

Immediately, other voices joined in. The attorney for the Little Rock Classroom Teachers Association said the board's action was "patently illegal and wholly indefensible," and added that legal action would be taken. Forrest Rozzell, the executive director of the Arkansas Education Association, declared that the firings "violated both state and school board administrative policies of long standing." Rozzell was a neighbor of Wilson's and his daughter, Betty, like Sharon Wilson, was a displaced student that year. [26] The first public demand that a recall of the purgers be considered came from the

Little Rock PTA Council's executive committee, which included several WEC members. The executive committee got together at Pres. Jean Hoffman's house on May 6 to pass without dissent a resolution that criticized the three segregationist board members "for attempting summary dismissal of school personnel without cause." The resolution declared that "we feel that board members who attempt such high-handed tactics are not qualified to hold offices of such responsibility." It further urged voters "to carefully consider all legal measures allowed by Arkansas law to achieve recall of officials who use their positions to jeopardize our public school system."[27] Since the council represented a membership of roughly thirteen thousand members in twenty-six schools, this was no idle request.[28]

■   ■   ■

The recall law had been passed by the state legislature in 1958 to make it possible to get rid of school board members unfavorable to segregation, but there was nothing that said it could not work the other way. A recall election could be held if petitions, signed by at least 15 percent of the qualified voters of a school district, were submitted. In Little Rock it was estimated that approximately sixty-three hundred signatures would be necessary for a recall election.[29]

The pent-up feelings in the city about the year of closed high schools began to explode. A storm of protests against the purge came from the League of Women Voters, the Greater Little Rock Ministerial Alliance, Chamber of Commerce president Grainger Williams, and several individual PTAs.[30] The following day the AAUW and the Junior Chamber of Commerce also followed suit.

Teachers at two elementary schools, Forest Park and Franklin, had met on May 5 as soon as they heard about the purge. They were considering not showing up at school the day afterward because their principals, Frances Sue Wood and Opal Middleton, had been among the forty-four fired. Wood and Middleton talked them out of it, but the teachers at Forest Park set a meeting for the evening of May 6 to consider what action to take.[31]

Forest Park School was located in the most elite part of the Heights, and both Wood and Billie Wilson, who was president of the Forest Park PTA, got many calls from distressed parents. "We're all so very upset about it," Wilson was quoted as saying. "We cannot believe this action was legal. Several parents wanted me to call a special PTA meeting to give Mrs. Wood a vote of confidence. We might do this."[32] Frances Sue Wood also happened to be the sister of Irene Samuel, the mastermind of the WEC infrastructure, who was now ready to deploy the troops that she had been training in minor skirmishes for a major showdown with the segregationist forces.

After the PTA executive meeting, Billie Wilson made good on her word to call a full PTA meeting in addition to the teachers meeting at Forest Park on May 6. Bobbie Bauman, a WEC and PTA member, rallied help to call all PTA members that afternoon, and the WEC telephone chain swung into action.[33]

Meanwhile, Ed Lester and Bob Shults had rounded up Tom Eisele, another lawyer; Charlie Johnston, an officer of First Federal Savings and Loan; and another businessman friend. Together the five drafted a resolution calling for petitions to be circulated, which Eisele, a school patron, would present at Forest Park Elementary School that night.[34] They also called Dr. Drew Agar, a physician with three children in the school who also was PTA vice-president and president of the Dad's Club, to decide how their resolution could be worked into the PTA meeting.

Four hundred people showed up at the Forest Park PTA meeting at 7:30 that evening. "I was amazed when I walked in and saw all those people there," said Billie Wilson. "I didn't know they had been called. I was interviewed that night about 6 P.M. by the *Gazette* [and one of] the TV stations. The next night my picture was in the paper. I remember the dress I had on.

"While I was being interviewed all these people kept passing me and when I came in, it just amazed me. The place was full and people were standing at the back."[35]

Wilson presided over the PTA meeting while two resolutions were unanimously adopted by the PTA, one condemning McKinley, Rowland, and Laster and the other commending Wood and her staff for "their high standard of instruction." Agar then came up and told her that when the PTA meeting was over they were going to have another meeting.

"There wasn't anybody to ask anything about so I just stood back and said, 'This concludes the meeting of the PTA,' and he [Agar] jumped up and said, 'We're going to organize a committee,'" Wilson recalled.

Agar, a dapper man with black curly hair, had at the time a minor ailment that caused him to wear a white patch over his left eye, making him look somewhat like the Hathaway shirt man. He called on Eisele, a brisk speaker, who quickly offered his resolution asking that petitions be prepared and circulated to recall McKinley, Rowland, and Laster so that teachers could "be forever protected in their just rights and expectations." Calling the action of the three board members in firing teachers, "many with long tenure and distinguished careers . . . high-handed and un-American," the resolution said it "demonstrates their lack of qualification to serve this district" as board members.

Cheers and shouts greeted the resolution, which was, like the two from the PTA, unanimously adopted. Agar, who was elected chair of the ad hoc group, said he would appoint a committee immediately to begin work on the petition drive. By the next day five hundred of the three thousand recall petition forms ordered had been delivered. Agar's committee was made up of Frank Gordon (chair), Olga Frick, and Jennie Harrel. All were Forest Park patrons and the latter two were WEC members. They immediately enlisted others to help them begin collecting names.[36]

The morning after the Forest Park meeting, the young lawyers and businessmen, and a few other friends met at Breier's, a favorite downtown gathering and eating place mostly frequented by men. With the recall now underway, they were regrouping to assess where they stood. One of the men, Gene Fretz, a *Gazette* feature editor, came up with an acronym for the recall campaign: STOP, for "Stop this Outrageous Purge," and the name stuck.[37] The men knew that the organizational strength of the WEC was behind them; the women were already revving up to get voter signatures on the petitions and to do the immense amount of other work that would be necessary to win the election.

What they did not have, as young men just starting out in their careers, was the clout that the older men of the power structure, who had been silent for so long, could bring to the upcoming fight. While they met, however, Grainger Williams had also gotten the Chamber of Commerce board together to act on a resolution that stated "this abortive abuse of power is . . . without honor and human decency, and is a disgrace to this community. We urge the people of Little Rock . . . to join with us in demanding that this attempted purge be erased." This time there were no negative qualifiers on the chamber statement.[38]

When word came over to Breier's that the Chamber of Commerce board had approved the resolution, the young men were euphoric. The pieces were falling together: having the organizational strength of the WEC in place meant the immense work of the campaign would be done; and having the chamber's support meant other campaign resources, financial and political, would be there as well.

That afternoon a larger group of twenty-five men, including Chamber of Commerce members, labor representatives, and the original group, got together a few doors down from Breier's at the old Grady Manning Hotel—without publicity and again with no women—to agree on how to put together the STOP campaign. Will Mitchell, the distinguished older lawyer who had at first not signed the young lawyers' statement back in September and had then later tried to get his name on it, was present at the meeting, along with the originators of the idea and their friends. The men set the date for a meeting the following afternoon, May 8, at the Union National Bank, with the agreement that Agar would become the permanent STOP chair. The men also decided on who they would invite to a larger open meeting to be held at the Union National Bank Building the following afternoon.[39]

Without waiting for action by the men, Jean Hoffman had gotten most of the sixty-member PTA council together on the morning of May 7 to approve the STOP executive committee's censure and recall resolution. The council approved it 41 to 9 and voted unanimously to send the resolution to the local PTA units for their action.[40] Eighteen units, including all those in the affluent fifth ward, voted for both the recall and the censure. Three approved the censure only, two units disapproved both, and three took no action.[41] Nearly all the positive votes could be traced back to WEC influence in educating and organizing its constituency of women. Meanwhile, individual PTAs were holding overflow meetings of alarmed patrons, with the help of the WEC telephone chain, at each of the schools to decide whether to join in the recall.

The site of one of two meetings held May 7 was Forest Heights Junior High School, where the principal, Harvey Walthall, and a teacher, Don Bratton, were among the forty-four fired. Gwen Booe was the immediate past–Forest Heights PTA president and was among the organizers of the meeting. Two segregationist patrons, W. H. Goodman, a member of the private Raney High School board, and Margaret Morrison, president of the National Association for the Preservation of White People, spoke against the resolution to recall McKinley, Laster, and Rowland. When a heckler criticized Morrison, she turned to him and said with sarcasm, "Thank you, sugar."

Ed Lester, whose son attended Forest Heights and who was presiding at the meeting, had tried to limit speaking time for each person to two minutes, but there was some confusion about the rules. He had to take the microphone away from Goodman after four minutes to end his speechmaking. Other segregationists charged later that the meeting was rigged. Lester, who announced that 802 people had signed in at the meeting, said he was simply trying to keep it orderly and under control. When the vote on the recall was taken, the crowd roared out its approval. Since only Goodman and Morrison could be heard voting against, Lester asked that the vote be recorded as 800 to 2.[42]

It was a different matter at the Hardin Bale Elementary School not far away, where the new facility was being dedicated with school board president Ed McKinley as the speaker. He chose the occasion to defend the purge and to attack Ted Lamb, Russell Matson, and Everett Tucker. Billie Wilson, who was attending as a visiting PTA president, got physically sick listening to McKinley and left. Following behind her were seventy-five others, who along with her were accused of staging a planned walkout.[43] Wilson apologized to the principal in a letter afterward:

I want to apologize to you and your teaching staff for my rudeness in walking out of your lovely school during your dedication ceremony. . . .

I was emotionally disturbed and unable to think or act wisely under strain. I had sat through the School Board meeting on Tuesday, outraged at the action taken against the teachers; presided at the very emotional meeting at Forest Park School on Wednesday nite; then participated in the controversial discussion at the PTA Council meeting Thursday morning.

I had thought the program, up until the Dedicatory address, was lovely . . . , I was particularly moved by your tribute to Mr. Romine. . . . What you were saying . . . made me very ashamed of the pent-up emotions I had been clutching to me. . . . Suddenly I felt weak with humility and shame. . . .

What was said [by McKinley] in the next few minutes so shocked . . . and angered me that I was actually physically sick and knew I had to get out in the fresh air. I did leave by the back door and did not realize anyone had left until I came around the side of the building and saw people pouring out the front doors. I have questioned everyone I know who was there and can find no one who knows anything about a "planned walkout." . . . My sudden departure may have triggered the others into action but I sincerely believe it was spontaneous.[44]

The first half of McKinley's talk also included "sharp jabs at the United States Supreme Court" and at welfare staters, economic planners, social schemers, judicial supremacists, and one worlders. After a large part of the audience left, he claimed that Principal Frances Sue Wood of Forest Park School had accused three boys of stealing a purse at school and then searched the home of one of the boys looking for it. Wood said later the accusation was a fabrication.[45]

More meetings followed at other schools, with the WEC telephone chain turning out crowds each time. The board of the Williams Elementary School PTA met at my home to plan a meeting for May 8. My son's third grade teacher, Jo Ann Henry, a Central High math teacher who was filling in when his teacher had to resign, was on the purge list. She was a quiet, efficient teacher who favored reopening the high schools so she could return to Central. We prepared a strongly worded statement from the PTA board but were warned that the segregationists might try to take over as they had at Forest Heights.

That night my husband, Pat, and I met with a group of men to select a chair for the meeting. Pat and Bob Lindsey, a senior partner in the law firm to which Lester and Shults then belonged and a Williams School patron, worked out a system of limited speaking on only the motion at hand, which they hoped would forestall a reoccurrence of the Forest Heights incident in which the chair had had to cut off a speaker. The chair would explain the ground rules in advance, limiting the debate to three minutes per speaker on the motion before the group, and then firmly enforce the rules.[46]

One man, a doctor who later became active in right-wing politics, insisted that we did not have to let the segregationists speak if they came. "Just cut them off if they try to speak," he said. Pat was not comfortable with that nor was Bob Lindsey, who was chosen to preside at the meeting. They wanted to keep the meeting under control but felt that everyone had a right to be heard.

Rumors were rampant and a threat was even made over the telephone that Ted Lamb would be assassinated at the Williams School meeting. When the WEC telephone chain went into action, callers added the message that extra men and women were needed in case someone attempted to start trouble. WEC members and their husbands created an overflow crowd.[47]

When I got to Williams, two friends, Chad Gray, whose wife, Alice, had gone with me to the first WEC meeting, and Rep. Sterling Cockrill, who was a member of the state legislature, were already scanning the Williams School halls. I noticed a suspicious-looking man in khaki work clothes, whose age and dress indicated he was probably not a school patron, hovering near the door closest to the stage. I went over to talk to him and learned that he was one of many plainclothesmen who were also patrolling the halls, the auditorium, and the grounds outside. The good school board members, Tucker, Matson, and Lamb, addressed the crowd of 355, but except for cheers and applause, it was an uneventful meeting. Lamb remarked that the crowd looked friendly but added, "I was wondering where you people were three months ago." The PTA resolution passed, and nearly everyone who attended signed the recall petition. None of the well-known segregationists showed up at the meeting. The plan Pat and Bob devised, however, was adopted for use at several subsequent school meetings.

The following Monday night at a Pulaski Heights Junior High and Elementary School rally of 800 people, an oily haired boy beside me in the balcony kept punching the button on a switchblade knife and flashing its blade in my face, causing me rather quickly to find another seat. Amis Guthridge, a leader in the Citizens Council, had announced before the meeting that he would "name names among the school teachers whose contracts were not renewed and reveal the subversive organizations to which some belong." He said he would also identify "communist-fronters . . . now in Little Rock helping Daisy Bates and the Women's Emergency Committee and the Chamber of Commerce . . . to race-mix our schools." Instead, he merely railed at the chair when offered the three-minute speak-out time on the motion at hand and sat down.[48]

■   ■   ■

According to the *Arkansas Gazette* of May 9, "one hundred and seventy-nine Little Rock residents, including many of the city's best known and most influential persons, formed a committee yesterday to organize a budding recall movement against the three Little Rock School Board members who voted Tuesday to fire 44 employees." The invited list of "influential persons" who signed the STOP statement of principles included 178 men and one woman, Jean Hoffman, president of the Little Rock PTA Council.[49]

Ed Lester unofficially invited two other women to the Union National Bank meeting—Vivion Brewer and Irene Samuel. Brewer found it a bittersweet climax to all the WEC's prior efforts, for the WEC was conspicuously absent from the organizations the men announced would be involved in the STOP campaign. Dr. John Samuel, Irene's husband, attempted to add the name of the WEC to the list, but his suggestion was ignored. Irene assumed that the new STOP committee did not want to be too closely identified with the WEC because of the licks the women had already taken from the segregationists; but she intended to barrel in and work on the recall anyway, knowing that what the WEC did would determine the election's outcome.[50] Brewer, however, said Lester told her after the meeting, "You go home and stay there, Vivion. Your being known in this will only hurt us." She said she found his request painful, but she understood that her name had become identified with integration and would be extra baggage for the new committee to carry.[51]

Eight women other than Brewer and Samuel (but most of them with WEC connections) were appointed to the thirty-four-member STOP advisory board, including Adolphine Terry. This board chose Will Mitchell, who later was to become president of the Arkansas Bar Association, as its prestigious campaign chair; along with Agar, Mitchell became a solid community voice speaking for STOP. "Will Mitchell was very much involved [with STOP]," Bob Shults recalled. "I think early on, when he had some reluctance, it may have been because he was president of the Chamber of Commerce. Later he became very active."[52]

Agar, who as the overall chair of the ad hoc STOP group that appointed the advisory board, said many professional and business men had previously declared they could not join such a movement because it would be bad for business. "I was one of those myself," he declared. "But now it is obvious that the fear no longer exists." This was what the WEC had worked for and waited to hear. More than six thousand dollars was raised at the meeting to begin the financing of the campaign.[53]

Petitions to recall Lamb, Matson, and Tucker began to surface around town by Saturday, May 9. Margaret Jackson, president of the Mothers League, said her group was responsible for them, but news accounts credited Rep. Dale Alford, the former segregationist school board member, with getting the countermove started.[54] The new group formally emerged as CROSS (Committee to Retain Our Segregated Schools) on May 16, although the Mothers League had been collecting names on the recall petition for more than a week before.[55]

Margaret Jackson had called for "patriotic citizens who believe in states' rights, constitutional government and racial integrity" to circulate petitions asking for the recall of Lamb, Matson, and Tucker. This was not the first time the Mothers League had attempted to secure names on recall petitions: the group had tried to get enough petitions to recall all members of the school board in 1958 but then abandoned the effort.

The formation of CROSS merely spurred on the STOP petition circulators. STOP leaders felt it was important to be first, because the law was unclear concerning whether more than one recall election could be held in the same year. STOP workers set up an outdoor drive-in office at War Memorial Stadium from 1 to 5 P.M. Sunday, where circulators could bring the signed petitions to get them notarized. Margaret Jackson's segregationist group was across town at the Arkansas Livestock Show Grounds doing the same. By Sunday evening, when STOP still had only 6,000 signatures, Samuel and other WEC members laid out a plan to circulate the petitions in restaurants, shopping centers, banks, office buildings, post offices, and grocery stores the next day. They decided they would need 388 women to help and the WEC telephone chain again went into action.[56]

Most of the 400 STOP workers who showed up for assignments the next morning were women the WEC chain had called the night before. Agar, who chaired the meeting, recognized their efforts this time:

> This meeting today is the combination of long and hard and weary and discouraging efforts during the past several months for such organizations as the Women's Emergency Committee to Open Our Schools, the League of Women Voters and PTA organizations which have worked with little reward up to now. But now there has been touched off a fire that is unquenchable.[57]

This group of petition collectors brought the number of signatures up to 9,603 by the time they were officially filed the next morning. Working through the evening until midnight, twenty-five WEC workers had checked 7,000 of the names against the poll tax books. The number of qualified voters signing the petitions ran well over the 6,100 names required by the law.[58]

Going door-to-door with the STOP recall petition had introduced me in a new way to my neighbors. There were some who eagerly signed, some who slammed their front doors in my face, and one vociferous woman who followed me down the street shouting at me about the evils of race-mixing and the immorality of the board members I supported. "You don't know what you're doing, honey," she said. "They haven't told you the truth. A nice girl like you wouldn't be mixed up with those Communists if you had the truth like I do." An equally nice girl, whose children sometimes played with mine, was walking the same street with a petition for CROSS to recall the three board members who had walked out of the purge meeting.

The women who had worked so hard brought their children along when they showed up at the filing of the petitions at the county clerk's office Tuesday, May 12. They were identified in a news picture as members of the League of Women Voters, the AAUW, and the PTA, but they were also WEC members.[59]

Margaret Jackson hedged on Sunday when the press asked her how many signatures the Mothers League had collected for CROSS. By Tuesday afternoon, however, seven hours after the STOP petitions were filed, she and her cohorts filed petitions with 7,754 names. The county clerk completed his signature count on both sets of petitions on May 15 and certified them for the board of election commissioners. This board set the recall election for both the three STOP-opposed and the three CROSS-opposed school board members on May 25.[60]

Now that CROSS was in the battle, its leaders felt obliged to give reasons for the teacher purge. Rev. M. L. Moser Jr., the chair of CROSS, ran an ad in the *Democrat* which said the forty-four teachers had not had their contracts renewed for one of the following reasons: "Teaching alien doctrine, incompetency, breaking and entering, trespassing on private property, invasion of privacy, improper punishment, intimidation of students, immorality." McKinley continued to maintain that for most of them the firings had to do with their stand on integration and they would be hired back if they recanted. However, Gene Warren, the attorney for the Classroom Teachers

Association, claimed that several dismissals were related to the low grades some of the teachers had given to children of some of the extremist leaders. Warren also represented thirty-nine of the purged teachers in a $3.9 million libel suit against Moser and McKinley that was eventually dismissed three years later.[61]

Charges and countercharges between STOP and CROSS became heated. Agar said those who signed the CROSS petitions favored the "shabby treatment" of the purged teachers, and Jackson said that the uproar over the teachers was an attempt by STOP and the *Arkansas Gazette* to "hoodwink the people into accepting integration."[62] Will Mitchell, in a TV speech, made a plea to the governor: "Leave us alone. Let us return our community to a rule of reason." The CROSS supporters circulated a list of the STOP signers that identified each one by the business or firm with which he was connected as a sort of suggested boycott list.[63]

■    ■    ■

One of the first things attorney Henry Woods, the former administrative assistant to Gov. Sid McMath, did when he accepted the request to become the STOP campaign's chief strategist was to ask Irene Samuel to meet him at a drugstore in the Heights. The STOP office had been set up in the Pyramid Life Building downtown where Samuel had worked for a day or so checking in petitions.

"I sat there and those men were running around like chickens with their heads cut off," said Samuel. "They didn't know what they were doing . . . and [this minister] was standing there smoking his pipe, thanking everybody and encouraging everybody." What really set Samuel off, however, was the fact that an executive secretary hired by the men called a prominent black dentist by his first name when he brought his petitions in.

"[When] she called him Garman, it embarrassed me and I . . . went over to . . . him . . . and said, 'Dr. Freeman, I'm glad to meet you.' . . . He had been in jail overnight when they bombed Mrs. Bates' house. He lived next door to Daisy Bates. . . . I couldn't stand the way she [the secretary] was treating black people. . . . I guess that was on Saturday and I stayed down there until about midnight.

Sunday I picked up my chips and went . . . back to the WEC office [in the Heights].

"At that time they did not want Vivion's name mentioned and they did not want Henry's name mentioned," Samuel continued. "Henry called me and said, 'Mrs. Samuel, I'm Henry Woods. You're controversial and I'm controversial but I think you and I ought to meet because I understand from Mr. Ashmore that you are a good organizer.' So we met at Smith's Drug Store. That's when he told me about 'saints' and 'sinners' and the shoe box thing."

In precomputer days, all information on cards had to be individually typed and sorted by hand. Entering Little Rock voter names into a computer and sorting them by wards, precincts, and political persuasion would still be a formidable but manageable job. But with only typewriters in 1959, it was a herculean undertaking, especially with the election less than two weeks away.

Woods explained that the names, addresses, precinct numbers, and telephone numbers of the thirty thousand voters should be put on cards. They would then be coded as "saints," those who could be expected to vote for STOP; "sinners," those who were known CROSS supporters; or "savables," those whose leanings in this election were unknown. The cards would then be distributed in shoe boxes to the appropriate ward captains, precinct leaders, and ultimately, block workers. It would be the job of the block workers to see that they got the "saints" out on election day, did nothing to arouse the "sinners" to go to the polls, and worked in the meantime on the "savables," hoping to win them over.

It was an old but effective technique for winning elections by getting one's own vote out while attempting not to stir up a large vote on the other side. The problem was that it required a precision-tuned organization and, in this case, an almost endless stream of womanpower. If the ward teams were not in place, the cards could not be circulated, or if the clerical help was not there, the cards could not be prepared in the first place. As an old political campaigner, Woods knew it would work if the WEC could pull it off.

Before her meeting with Woods was over, Samuel had bought in. A good many of the ward captains, precinct secretaries, and block workers were already in place from previous elections. And the WEC telephone chain already had functioned almost flawlessly in getting large crowds to WEC meetings and STOP rallies at the schools. She knew the WEC could round up the necessary workers for this phase of the campaign as well.[64]

Fifty-four women volunteers immediately set to work on the first group of cards listing the fourteen hundred WEC supporters, two hundred STOP members, and others known to be friendly. While this was going on, the League of Women Voters and the WEC worked together, making use of their overlapping memberships to identify the rest of the ward captains and precinct secretaries. They filled four of the five ward chairs and forty-one of the forty-three precinct secretaries with their own members. They also furnished lists from the two organizations of suggested judges, clerks, and poll watchers for each precinct to be used on election day.

By now, there were two STOP offices, the one in the Pyramid Building and the WEC office to which Samuel had retreated when she departed from downtown. The WEC space, for which the women paid twenty dollars a month, was up some steep stairs over a store in the Heights where it was moved from the Kolb utility room shortly before the recall election. The WEC address was 5709 Kavanaugh and its telephone number, which most WEC volunteers knew by heart, was MOhawk 4–1607. Once they had agreed on the game plan, Irene Samuel and Henry Woods were pretty well running the show at both locations and the action was intense.

Using telephone directories, crisscross directories, and city maps, hundreds of women volunteers undertook the job in the limited time before the election of getting all thirty thousand names in the Little Rock poll tax book onto cards. WEC workers secured from the county clerk's office names of those who signed the CROSS petitions. They coded the "sinner" cards with this information, and they coded the "saint" cards with STOP petition signers and WEC members. The "savables" were coded onto the rest of the cards. This, plus adding telephone numbers and precincts, required hand-merging the information from several sources and then dividing the cards by wards and precincts. After all this preparation, however, when the ward, precinct, and block workers received the shoe boxes filled with their sorted cards, they could get right to work. The ward leaders set up training meetings with their workers over the weekend before the election, and the workers then took their cards with them to get out the favorable vote.[65]

Jane Mendel's telephone chain hit its peak when it turned out two thousand people for the STOP rally at Robinson Auditorium on the evening of May 19, six days before the election. All of the audience members were white. Across town at the Dunbar Community Center, blacks held a rally of five hundred people to support their five purged teachers. Black political leaders, including I. S. McClinton, spoke, as did Sylvia Carruth, president of the segregated City Teachers Association, which included black administrators, teachers, and other school personnel.

The day before the STOP rally, Dr. Malcolm Taylor, a Citizens Council leader, announced that "Many Negroes, including Negro teachers, are planning to attend the integrationist rally . . . these Negroes will be seated alongside the whites in all parts of the auditorium." Letters with Dr. Drew Agar's name on them circulated widely the next day in the black community, inviting "our colored friends" to come to the Robinson Auditorium rally. Agar went immediately to the prosecutor's office to investigate and discovered that the letters were the work of the CROSS forces. He called the letters "a new low" and a "scurrilous deed" and said if any Negroes showed up at the rally, they would be "gently turned away." After much last-minute television and radio notification, the black community got the word they would not be welcome. Only two showed up, and they were indeed asked to leave.[66]

It was a troubling experience, full of irony, to be working for integrated schools at a rally that was as rigidly segregated as were the churches and all other phases of public life at that time. It was the same dilemma the WEC had experienced earlier as it tried to educate whites about integration while not being integrated itself. We focused on the evil evidenced in the language and actions of the segregationists; but we were blurring the fact that our own mores made us a part of that evil, with our black maids, our socially segregated lives, and our reluctance even to include blacks in our efforts to integrate the schools. Still, our growing realization that the evil was there produced the desire and conscience to do something about it. And in changing the system, some of us changed ourselves.

One of the ads of the STOP campaign read: "Hatred? You can have it," and went on to say, "People are sick of this campaign of hatred, of trying to set one section of our community against another, one religion against another. They have had enough of these purge tactics."[67] The ad, by attacking the excesses of the other side, was also a way to confront and begin to eradicate our own bigotry.

One of the speakers at the STOP rally in Robinson Auditorium was a young fourth ward mother, Jo Jackson, who was the upcoming president of the Franklin Elementary School PTA where Opal Middleton, another of those purged, was principal. Samuel called Jackson and asked her to speak at the big STOP rally after hearing about Jackson's talk at the Franklin PTA meeting the night before.

Jo said her bridge club was meeting at her house right then but she would think about it, and a little later she got another call saying someone from her part of town was badly needed. The fourth ward had many working whites who showed every sign of voting for the other side. "Which is how I got involved in the whole thing," she recalled. "I lived in the right place. They desperately needed people in ward four which was a kind of swing vote." Jackson had no idea the rally would be so large—"it was formidable—that microphone and all those people."[68] Approximately three hundred white teachers, including those who had been in the purge, were sitting on the stage behind the row of speakers. Jo Jackson went on from there to become fourth ward captain and worked with a man who was an engineer and her co-captain. "We put in a terrible amount of work into that election," Jackson said. She also became vice-president of the WEC board.

Jackson had married before finishing Oklahoma University in her home state and dropped out to accompany her serviceman husband to his new post. When the war was over, they came back to his native state. She had two sons and became active in the PTA and other community work such as the Red Cross, but she had not joined the WEC. When Samuel asked her after the rally, "Jo, how come you aren't a member of the WEC?" Jackson said, "No one has ever really asked me." Samuel said, "Well, I'm asking you. Send your dollar." And she did.[69]

WEC women did many other things in STOP. Billie Wilson prepared biographical information on and secured pictures of each of the forty-four dismissed teachers for newspaper ads that were run one or two a day throughout the campaign. The WEC volunteers also worked, often till midnight and afterward, to mail out a daily newsletter called the *STOPLIGHT* that a young labor lawyer, Jim Youngdahl, wrote. And they participated in the mammoth "saints" sweep to get out the vote on election day.

Three days before the election, Governor Faubus appeared on television to support the segregationist slate of McKinley, Laster, and Rowland and to charge that Negroes could see how they were being used by wealthy whites to integrate them with "honest white people of the middle and lower classes." He continued, "It begins to look like the charge of the Cadillac brigade, with many good, honest, hardworking Negroes in the front as shock troops."[70]

Governor Faubus also attacked several of the leaders in the STOP campaign, including WEC president Vivion Brewer, whom he said had no children and did not live in the Little Rock School District. Although she was under attack for participating in a campaign she had been asked not to join, other voices praised Brewer and the WEC. In a letter to the *Gazette* editor, three male officials of the Arkansas Industrial Research Center said, "Too little homage has been paid to the Women's Emergency Committee to Open Our Schools for its role in the STOP campaign." They gave the WEC credit for "initially defining the only problem with which Little Rock can . . . effectively cope—opening the schools, [for] demonstrating that an organization could be formed and held together to wage this fight and [for] performing much of the 'hard labor' connected with the [STOP] campaign."[71] Even the Little Rock business leaders, who wanted Brewer and the WEC to stay in the background, were ready to acknowledge that they could never have put together such a massive effort in so short a time without having the WEC already in place.

Rev. Will Campbell of Nashville, Tennessee, a white minister and writer who had walked with the Little Rock Nine nearly two years before, came by to visit the WEC office whenever he was in town. Campbell, in a letter to Brewer, called her "St. Vivion of Little Rock," a title he bestowed, he said, "despite being a renegade Southern Baptist." In an earlier letter, Campbell, who was a national figure in the struggle for human rights, said that the work of the WEC was encouraging others to act throughout the South and the country. Of the STOP campaign, he said, "Let all the people say AMEN, or perhaps, ah men, it's about time."[72]

# ■ 9 ■

# A Community Divided

T he headline in the *Gazette* on the morning after the election in May 1959 proclaimed the good news: "STOP Wins Recall Victory; Purgers Thrown Off Board." The headline appeared above a picture of Ted Lamb, Russell Matson, and Everett Tucker being hoisted to the shoulders of other men in the midst of an exuberant crowd cheering their victory.[1]

The victory mattered in other places as well. I had made my election day telephone calls to favorable voters, had voted myself, and had then left that evening with my husband, Pat, for a meeting in New York without knowing the outcome of the election. Shortly after midnight we found a newsstand near Times Square with an early morning edition of a tabloid whose entire front cover proclaimed in giant letters, "Faubus Loses."

I pointed at it in disbelief and grabbed the sleeve of the news vendor. "I worked in that election, but I never thought this would happen," I said. "You don't know how happy this makes me." The fellow behind the stand looked at me strangely, and I realized there were tears streaming down my face. "Congratulations," he said softly.

The announcement of the victory, which spread across the country, was somewhat premature because precinct 4-A, a blue collar box expected to be heavily segregationist, was still out. It was not until 4 A.M. when it finally was counted that Irene Samuel, although she had left her office to go to the party at the Marion Hotel much earlier, breathed easily again.[2]

The three STOP candidates had won by a hair. Out of roughly 25,000 votes cast for and against his recall, Ted Lamb had squeaked through with only 431 votes more against (50.8 percent) rather than for his recall. Russell Matson had 651 more (51.3 percent) and Everett Tucker received 1,224 more (52.4 percent) against rather than for their recall. Ed McKinley (52.9 percent), Ben Rowland (54.3 percent), and Bob Laster (55.5 percent), the three purgers supported by CROSS, were ousted by only slightly larger percentages.[3] It was far from a landslide, but it was Little Rock's first gleam of light in two years.

The precinct-by-precinct voting results showed that the fifth ward upper-income voters had teamed up with the black voters to cast a significant enough percent of their ballots in support of the moderates for them to win. The voting in the rest of the precincts leaned toward support of the segregationists, some heavily, some with surprisingly close splits.[4]

Attorney Henry Woods, who directed the strategy he laid out in the STOP campaign, said much later, "We got our vote out. And the other side was not that successful. If everybody had voted, we would have lost. It was a matter of identifying the people who were with us and getting them to the polls. And we did the best job on that that's ever been done in any election."

Woods also said, looking back later, that "the WEC won that STOP election and never received the credit they should have."[5] Ed Lester, according to Irving Spitzberg, echoed Woods's sentiments: "STOP could never have been successful if the Women's Emergency Committee had not been organized and ready to work."[6]

The WEC, however, did not do it alone. STOP forged together a community coalition of businessmen, labor, education groups, blacks, and women (including those in the PTA, the AAUW, and the League of Women Voters) that picked up on and used the organizational prowess and expertise the WEC had spent a painful year acquiring. But Woods and Lester were also right. The coalition could not have won the recall election without the efficient structure the WEC already had in place.

The Women's Emergency Committee learned much from the STOP campaign that helped it increase its own effectiveness. WEC workers found it was crucial not just to get voters to the polls but also to educate them to the intricacies of the ballot so that their votes would not be lost. STOP voters, for instance, were cautioned repeatedly to vote "FOR" the recall of the school board members they were against and "AGAINST" the recall of the ones they were supporting.

The WEC also learned that massive efforts to reach favorable voters with a personal contact was a critical factor in close contests, as this one turned out to be. By election day, WEC volunteers, aided by other STOP workers, had made some twenty-three thousand calls and visits to identify "saints" out of "savables" and then, just before or on election day, to offer rides and polling place information.[7]

Many fifth ward women knocked on doors in parts of town where their social forays had never taken them before, often being met with "uncouth and obscene insults." One woman said she was "literally swept from the porch with a broom." They drove in carpools that carried people to the polls, and they did trouble-shooting by phone and in person on election day as calls of election irregularities were received at the WEC office.

Henry Alexander, in *Little Rock Recall Election,* gave this description of what the WEC did on election day:

> Election day activities at WEC headquarters began at 8:05 A.M. when a stand-by election official by telephone reported her inability to "get sworn in"; ended at 7:10 P.M. with a telephone call reporting that election officials at one polling place, out of and awaiting delivery of ballots, were allowing voters to wait in line after 6:30 P.M., legal time for polling places to close. An officer of WEC estimated that "about 1,000" volunteer workers took part in efforts "to get out the vote" for STOP.[8]

The STOP campaign was the WEC's first experience in working to get out the crucial black vote for STOP. Pat House recalled that she worked for the first time in the black community in the STOP election as chair of the third ward. Henry Woods had arranged through black leaders for one hundred drivers and cars for the black carpool effort. House, who had jurisdiction over the heavily black precinct 3-C, was introduced not only to the intensive cars-to-the-polls effort but also to the use of black Philander Smith College students who as runners went door-to-door to get people out for rides to the polls.[9]

■ ■ ■

Although Little Rock was still a divided community, the STOP victory had finally shifted control and influence away from the extremist diehards and into the hands of those who supported open schools. The STOP leaders, a new and for the most part younger group of men who gained stature and prestige from the victory, recognized that integration was part of the bargain, even though their personal views ranged from begrudging acceptance to enthusiastic support. These men, under Will Mitchell's seasoned guidance, provided what Irving Spitzberg called the "titular leadership in STOP," which combined with WEC's "well developed and skillful organizational nucleus" and the black community's "strong bloc vote" to bring victory.[10]

STOP was a major turning point because the citywide grass roots effort caused citizens to reject not only the teacher purge but also the increasing repression that it signified. "If [the STOP election] had been lost, I think you would have had a Jim Johnson [an extreme segregationist] as governor and we would have sunk to a lower level than Mississippi," Woods declared.[11]

The work of the WEC earlier during the year of closed schools had helped educate some of the citizens that the racist leadership of a governor and his fellow segregationists was leading the city down a dark alley of hate and fear. By refusing to follow, Little Rock had killed its dragon and reclaimed its conscience and dignity.

People spoke to each other of how good it felt to be rid of the fear, to be doing the right thing, to be on the right side. Even today, many of those who worked for STOP still identify others by where they stood at that time. And if they forget, they can call Irene Samuel who will look up a name in her ancient, coded 1959 poll tax book to see whether there was an "X" for STOP or "T" for CROSS by the name. The "X" has now come to be regarded as a mark of honor, signifying someone who performed a valuable service at a critical time.

A decade or so after STOP and after Marilyn Criner moved to Little Rock, she remembered finding an unusual camaraderie among certain women in the two opposing camps. Some of these women were working for John McClellan and some for David Pryor in a political race for the U.S. Senate that engendered much divisiveness.

"I couldn't figure it out," Criner said. "There was real trust between these women even though they were on opposite sides. A woman on our [Pryor's] side would say to me, 'You can call so-and-so over at the McClellan campaign office and she'll tell you the truth. You can depend on her.' That happened over and over. I asked around and found out it went back to this women's organization, the WEC, that they had all worked in together. The bond among those women was like something I had never seen before."[12]

Governor Faubus, who had made a strong pitch for the CROSS slate just before the election, backpedaled afterward, saying the results settled nothing. He said, although it had been "heralded as a victory of those who favor integration . . . there was no such clear-cut issue." He was vague about reopening the schools, suggesting that if it were done, it should include a plan for those who want integration and a plan for those who do not. School was out for the summer, he pointed out, so we did not have to worry about it right away.[13]

By the middle of June, a three-judge federal court had thrown out both the state school-closing law and the student aid transfer act (Acts 4 and 5). Faubus, although he said "federal force" and "live ammunition" would be required to open the schools integrated and that he might appeal the federal court decisions, knew he had lost the shaky legal crutches he had used to justify keeping the schools closed and transferring the money elsewhere.[14] There was still apprehension, however, that he might try some other ploy, such as calling a special session of the legislature to pass more laws.

The WEC's first concern was getting school board members favorable to open schools to replace McKinley, Laster, and Rowland. The appointments were to be made by the Pulaski County Board of Education, which the WEC learned had at least two Faubus supporters on it. Spitzberg reported later that all the board members were segregationists.[15]

The WEC made phone calls and sent the county board suggested names that were ignored. The board said it would appoint only selections on which it could be unanimous, implying WEC nominees would not meet that criterion.[16]

One of those appointments, announced on June 11, was

B. Frank Mackey, who had formerly worked for Herbert Thomas's First Pyramid Insurance Company and who later became sheriff and then county judge. The second was J. H. Cottrell, a state representative who later served as Faubus's county campaign chair. The third appointee, H. L. Hubbard, a building contractor, proved to be an embarrassment when he brought a letter to the first meeting telling that he had served sentences two times in the 1930s for grand larceny and was therefore ineligible to serve.[17] Governor Faubus later arranged a pardon for him on July 6, restoring his civil and political rights, indicating whose side he was on.[18] It showed also whose side the Pulaski County board, which had given him a unanimous vote, was on. He was replaced four days later by W. C. McDonald, the manager of a paper company who pleased the WEC by committing himself to opening the schools in his first statement.[19]

The new board rehired thirty-nine of the forty-four purged teachers and reinstated Superintendent Terrell Powell. The five teachers not rehired had refused to comply with Act 10 in submitting lists of organizations to which they belonged but were given a grace period to do so. The board also announced that it intended to reopen the high schools in the fall, using the state's new pupil placement laws.[20]

Not long afterward, Everett Tucker, who had been elected president of the new school board, Superintendent Powell, and Herschel Friday, the board's attorney, left for Charlotte, North Carolina, and Norfolk, Virginia. It was a much-publicized visit to see how pupil placement succeeded in keeping integration at a minimum in those schools.[21]

The *Gazette*, in examining Arkansas's two pupil assignment laws, listed "16 administrative hurdles that must be passed before integration suits ever reach the courts, each of them intended to further reduce the number of plaintiffs who ultimately run the administrative gamut without falling." These hurdles ranged from the psychological qualifications of black students to the morals, conduct, health, and personal standards of the pupil. But the *Gazette* also ran an editorial endorsing pupil assignment, hoping to ward off a special session of the legislature and a flurry of additional segregation laws.[22]

A debriefing for the STOP campaign, to which a number of WEC leaders were invited, was held on July 2. According to WEC notes made at the meeting, Will Mitchell, the campaign chair, attributed the victory "to timing [the firing of the teachers] and organization [the use of cards]." He added that "a lot of missionary work is yet to be done in Little Rock to convince the people we must have public schools."

This prompted the group to brainstorm ways the community could be prepared for the upcoming school opening. Dr. Jerome Levy suggested that the WEC might conduct an economic study of the cost of the closed schools. Acknowledgment of the role the WEC had played and could yet play had given the women a seat at the table for future planning and action. Adolphine Terry was not hesitant to use the advantage and suggested some actions for the men to pursue as well. "When is someone going to sue for the money turned over to Raney—$71,905.50?" she asked. As for ensuring a nonviolent school opening, she also suggested that "100 young men go down to be sworn in as deputies" and asked about the procedure for getting sworn in. Will Mitchell demurred on challenging the transferred funds. "What we need is harmony and we should postpone all suits," he was quoted as saying. Neither was he ready to endorse lining up deputies.[23]

Other women followed Terry's cues in cutting through to the heart of what was going on. Grace Malakoff asked, "Are there any political analysts who could tell us what the current financial support for Raney and any other private school is?" There were none. Janet Johnston, a WEC board member, said it was time for responsible people to refute Faubus's lies. A man replied that was what ex–Governor Cherry, who was defeated by him, did. Pat House suggested a large meeting of some sort and another woman suggested neighborhood discussions, using the precinct contacts from STOP. The women said they wanted "peace and harmony" for the opening, but they also wanted to "dispel rabble rousing propaganda" and make adequate preparation to protect the students this time from possible violence. Dr. Sam Thompson said that perhaps a men's auxiliary to the WEC might be the way to go.

Maurice Mitchell, an attorney who was one of the young STOP leaders, gave a report at the meeting that said the election would have gone the other way had it not been for the black vote. In the fifth ward, the vote was 2.2 to 1 for the recall of the segregationists, but that would not have offset heavy voting to the contrary in other white parts of town alone. Out of almost six thousand black poll tax holders, four thousand voted. Nearly three thousand of them were for the removal of Bob Laster and against the removal of Ted Lamb, and that made the difference in how the election went. Mitchell attributed it to the black college students who drove cars and to the fact that many employees gave their black workers time off to vote.[24] That information was not lost on the women, who had also begun peripherally to help get black voters to the polls and who already recognized the difference a solid black vote could make.

The women's seat at that table proved to be a not altogether comfortable one. Vivion Brewer spoke with Will Mitchell at the end and was "stunned to hear him say, 'I think it is time for the leadership of all the interested groups to change. We ought to have new names before the public.'" She interpreted that as directed at her.[25] She had already received a letter from the influential businessman Herbert Thomas criticizing an ad that the WEC had run. Thomas's letter said in part:

> I think the ad in today's paper, or any further ads under present conditions, are and would be damaging to our cause. . . .
>
> It is my belief that this morning's ad made no new friends and would irritate the extreme segregationists and possibly the Governor. . . .
>
> I favor that all organizations think hard and be prepared for any move the extreme segregationists make—but don't do anything unless we have to.[26]

Thomas had been a financial contributor and supporter of the WEC and his two daughters were active WEC participants, so his criticism had to be taken seriously. He added that he had heard others express the same opinion. Brewer was painfully sensitive to criticism of both her own role and of that of the WEC, but she was far from ready to capitulate. She replied in a letter to Thomas that she did not know if "silence and inactivity will be more effective than raising a voice in our efforts to preserve our public school system. I do fear that silence and inactivity may not serve to hold together the splendid organization that the Women's Emergency Committee has built." A few days later, the WEC board thought it over and voted to continue to run its ads in both newspapers.[27]

Some of the concerns raised at the STOP debriefing came from a morale survey of teachers that the WEC had conducted but did not officially release until July 8. Survey results showed the teachers were anxious and confused about whether the schools were going to open. The teachers said they wanted to hear more statements from community groups in favor of public schools, that they wanted to be assured that there would be no violence around the schools, and that they wanted something definite done to refute Governor Faubus. Telephone calls to the WEC about what integration would entail, together with some answers given in a publication called *Action Patterns in School Desegregation,* were circulated to WEC members.[28]

Velma Powell, shortly before her departure for California, came up with practical suggestions to prepare for a peaceful school opening. These included: preparing students, teachers, and parents in advance for desegregation; having school board members tour the high school buildings to consider what discipline measures were needed; and developing a disciplinary plan for dealing with students who harass other students. It was taken to Superintendent Terrell Powell, then explained to school board members Tucker, Matson, and Lamb at a meeting at Terry's home. Apparently, however, the plan was never used.[29]

Meanwhile, Odell Smith, a tough, plain-spoken labor leader, invited the austere, proper Mrs. Brewer to speak before a new organization of about fifty labor-union representatives he and Victor Ray, editor of the *Arkansas Union Labor Bulletin,* had organized. The purpose of the meeting was to organize a Labor Committee to Preserve Free Public Schools. It was a follow-up to the hard work Smith and Ray had done in pulling a sizable amount of the labor vote out of the segregationist column. Brewer was in awe of Smith's handling of the meeting. "Mr. Smith was a chairman non-pareil," she wrote, using a word most likely not in Smith's vocabulary. "Despite noticeable opposition, he maneuvered the discussion and the voting as a magician pulls a rabbit out of a hat, and before I could follow or apprehend his methods, he had triumphantly secured the passage of a resolution to maintain the public schools." The Citizens Council newsletter coverage of the event declared that "Odell Smith, Victor Ray and (of all people) Mrs. Joe Brewer . . . went into the now familiar song and dance routine to the tune of 'We favor public education (mixed, of course).' . . . We do know many, many card carrying members of organized labor and to a man they are dead set against Negroized white schools."[30]

Brewer presided at a meeting on July 15 around Terry's massive dining-room table that included not only other WEC leaders—Terry, Powell, Samuel, Dottie Morris, Anne Helveston, and Barbara Ashmore—but men as well: STOP's Ed Lester and Henry Woods; Brewer's labor friends, Odell Smith and Victor Ray; Joe Hardin, who was still at Arkansas Louisiana Gas Company but who later ran against Faubus for governor; Boyd Ridgeway from the Chamber of Commerce; Lefty Hawkins, who handled the STOP public relations campaign; and Forrest Rozzell, Arkansas Education Association secretary.[31] It was the beginning of the coalition that later included blacks and was to become a force in future elections. The important thing at this meeting, however, was that it was the WEC's table, complete with the parrot screeching in the sun room, around which the negotiating took place.

Brewer, unaccustomed to such a diverse group, let the meeting wander at first until the aggressively blunt Odell Smith, used to bringing noisy teamsters under control, announced, "What the lady wants to know is how we can help them. Let's get down to business." Brewer then raised some major questions. Did the men want to work with the WEC or separately? What should be done to prevent violence? What happens if a special session of the legislature is called? Was a statewide organization needed? The group came up with several ways to prevent violence at the school opening by preparing the police to deal with it, by having the city manager and the police chief make statements in advance, by having the Chamber of Commerce help build police morale, and by having sermons preached against violence the Sunday before.[32]

Also on July 15, the WEC sent a statement to the newspapers that read, "The Women's Emergency Committee—now 1,572 strong . . . [has] the utmost confidence that Little Rock is a law abiding city and that adequate protection for the peaceful opening of our schools will be provided."[33] Two days later, on July 17, the formation of the Committee for the Peaceful Operation of Our Free Public Schools, with Gaston Williamson, a prominent attorney with the Rose Law Firm as its chair, was announced. That same day the Little Rock City Board of Directors revised its policy toward possible violence at the schools, making it slightly more direct and affirmative; they directed the city police to deal "firmly and quickly" if trouble occurred when the schools reopened. And the *Arkansas Union Labor Bulletin,* of which Victor Ray was editor, reported its poll of readers voted 93 to 90 against continued closing of the schools. A report on the Little Rock school situation in August described these events as the beginning of "a campaign to support the idea that the public school system must be maintained and peacefully operated," adding that these groups had "joined the ranks of the Women's Emergency Committee to Open Our Schools, formed in September 1958; the Little Rock Chamber of Commerce, which adopted a reopen-the-schools policy in March this year; and the *Arkansas Gazette,* in support of the school board."[34]

Williamson could not recall exactly who called on him to ask him to be chair of the committee. "It may have been a committee from the Women's Emergency Committee, but it also had a man or two. . . . [I]n any event, a committee approached me in my office and asked me if I would take it on," he said. "I can't remember exactly who it was. I wouldn't be surprised if one of them wasn't Mrs. Terry. . . . She would have either come by personally or called."[35]

Although Gaston Williamson's family was not directly related to Terry, he and his wife, Wrenetta, always called her Aunt Adolphine because she was the best friend of Sue Ogden, with whom Wrenetta lived after her mother died when she was nine. Williamson, like

Grainger Williams, was a Presbyterian elder with firm convictions about right and wrong. He did not hesitate when the committee asked him to serve. He continued:

> I'd been absolutely furious at Faubus throughout this whole thing and on all occasions expressing my opposition very publicly to Faubus and I had no fear of him at all. . . . I don't remember expressly thinking about what effect it might have on our practice but had I given it any thought, it wouldn't have amounted to anything because our firm through Archie [House] was already heavily involved in support of the school board position. I was just flattered and pleased to be asked.[36]

Archie House was the Rose Law Firm lawyer whom Herschel Friday had replaced when the split school board took over in December 1958. Williamson ate lunch with House each day. Five days after the Supreme Court *Brown* decision in 1954, the Little Rock School Board, on the advice of House, had presented the community with a plan for compliance, even before *Brown* had been handed down. Williamson heard daily reports on the Little Rock plan as Archie House, Superintendent Virgil Blossom, and the board moved it forward up to the time of the grim Central High School events in 1957. "Archie's advice was that Faubus's posturing would never prevail, couldn't, as long as we have constitutional law in this country," Williamson said. Williamson had another reason to be furious with Faubus the following year when the schools were closed. His son, Jim, was to have attended Hall High School that year but instead, had to be packed off to McCauley School in Chattanooga, Tennessee.[37]

A *Gazette* editorial said that the first order of business for the Committee for the Peaceful Operation of Our Free Public Schools was to see that the schools did indeed open. The second was to "cut through the fog of emotion and bring the plain facts of the school crisis to the people."[38] When an advisory board was named to the new group, 21 of its 132 members this time were women, an improvement from the STOP board. Brewer's name was absent from the Peaceful Schools board, although the names of Adolphine Terry, Irene Samuel, and Pat House, along with many others from the WEC, were there. The new group met July 29 at the Lafayette Hotel.[39]

Williamson, in his speech before the Peaceful Schools advisory group, declared that the "public schools must open in September," and they must be "in compliance with Constitutional law." He described a city divided "class against class," where the closing of the high schools denied many children any education at all, and families were split by students forced to leave home. He said these developments were not the will of most citizens in Little Rock, but had come about because "people . . . have not stepped forward to do anything about it."

Williamson took issue with the governor's latest proposal to integrate Hall and Horace Mann but to keep Central segregated. "The Supreme Court has made it crystal clear that no citizen shall be denied entrance to any public school because of color," Williamson told the advisory group. "It is my personal opinion as an attorney, and I believe the opinion of a large majority of the lawyers in our City, that this plan would not meet the constitutional test, and would not be considered by the Courts a good faith attempt by the School Board to comply with the Court orders under which they must act."[40]

When the STOP office had shut down, the WEC had inherited the responsibility for mimeographing, doing mailouts, and telephoning for the new committee. The women once again were doing the detail work, and Brewer's invaluable past involvement in the controversy caused her to be left off the advisory board. Nevertheless, the WEC was moving into a partnership that gave it a voice in setting the fragile policy that would steer the community onto a better course. The magic of the men's names and their experience and prestige were necessary to make it work, but so were the good, sound thinking and effort of the women. In a report for the U.S. Commission on Civil Rights concerning the reopening of the schools, attorney Gaston Williamson said: "These two Committees [the WEC and the Peaceful Schools group] were particularly useful as a voice for the silent majority of the people of Little Rock, who abhorred violence and preferred integrated public high schools to no public high schools at all."[41]

Amis Guthridge, attorney for the White Citizens Council, called on "white Christian Americans" in Arkansas to oppose the

"Communist-inspired determination to destroy our white civilization in Little Rock just before the schools were to reopen." He lumped together three "fronts": the WEC, STOP, and the Committee for the Peaceful Operation of Our Free Public Schools. On July 14, Guthridge declared that the council "would take action, and not in the courts, to prevent any more school integration at Little Rock."[42]

An anonymous *Gazette* letter writer, who identified herself as a Hall High School patron, suggested that it would be more equitable to integrate Hall as well as Central when the schools reopened. "Such a move would give evidence of our good faith, would relieve some of the bitterness of the CROSS people and might serve to prevent that violence that Mr. Faubus keeps suggesting."[43] Billie Wilson picked up on this theme in a letter to the editor and strongly endorsed, as a Hall High parent, integrating Hall as well as Central and told the *Gazette* to be sure and sign her name to it.[44] Others followed suit.

The board members took this under consideration, and when registration time rolled around in mid-July, they had decided to integrate both schools. The *Gazette* reported that registration proceeded without any "untoward incident," and that "there is every reason to believe that this routine function can be completed without disturbance."[45] The board received sixty requests from black students for admission to white schools—thirty black students sought to enroll at Central and five at Hall. By the time all of the sixteen harsh pupil-assignment restrictions had been applied, however, only three black students remained at Central and three at Hall. The WEC found it unbelievable that the board they had worked so hard to elect would go backward instead of forward. This was three less than the nine black students that had been assigned at Central the year before the schools were closed. Wiley Branton of Pine Bluff, challenging the placement restrictions for the NAACP, asked that the rights of black students to attend Central, Hall, and Tech be limited only by the areas in which they lived, a new legal contention.[46]

■   ■   ■

The WEC continued to work throughout the summer to prepare for a successful school opening. Meanwhile, a summertime newsletter I worked on was distributed on July 30 as an affirming statement, with the headline "Little Rock's High Schools to Be Open in September." We proudly noted recent favorable notices for the WEC in Eleanor Roosevelt's syndicated column, in the YWCA magazine, and in a *New South* article by Nat Griswold of the Arkansas Council on Human Relations. Our supporters were encouraged to contact their legislators and request that they oppose any interference in the Little Rock school situation. Our newsletter continued:

> Since the aim of our committee is to reopen our four closed high schools in accordance with law and order, we approve of every definite move toward this goal. All the world is watching us. . . . We are convinced that nothing could be more important to the future of Little Rock than the peaceful opening and operation of our public schools. [47]

The school board pulled its biggest surprise on August 4 by abruptly deciding to open the high schools August 12, nearly a month earlier than scheduled. Brewer called this change of plans "an ingenious idea of Ted Lamb's" to avoid possible further legislation that might keep the schools closed. A subsequent account agreed that the early date was "clearly a maneuver to foil any plans Gov. Faubus might have had for a special legislative session such as he called the last week of August 1958." Lamb confirmed his motives on a national news broadcast show, where he seized the opportunity to label the governor a "demagogue."[48]

The new school board members who took office after the defeat of the segregationists proved not to be much better than the deposed members. The board narrowly escaped disaster on August 4, when the new members wrote a letter to the governor as a demonstration of their desire to cooperate and "to explore the possibility of our leasing and operating Raney High School as a part of our Little Rock public school system, with no tuition to parents." After J. H. Cottrell left the meeting to deliver the letter personally to the state capitol, the other members soon learned that Dr. Raney had just announced Raney High School would not open because of a lack of funds. Although out of town at the time, Brewer later learned what transpired:

The four members dashed to their cars to pursue Cottrell in order to reclaim the letter. With good luck they overtook him in the press room of the Governor's office just on the brink of disaster. As Lefty Hawkins remarked, "It was a Marx Brothers comedy," and it was funny, but it could have been betrayal leading to ruin. We took another look at the school board.[49]

On August 5, Faubus commented on the board's decision to open the high schools a month early: "They put off the opening of schools before to try to get the Negroes in. Now they are moving up the opening date to get the Negroes in."[50] The same day, Dr. Malcolm Taylor, president of the Capital Citizens Council, accused the board of being "reckless daredevils" in opening the schools during a polio epidemic. Dr. Mason G. Lawson, city health officer, rejected the idea that there was increased danger of an epidemic, saying that most of the polio was in children under ten years old. To help dispel the rumors, Ted Lamb resourcefully solicited advice from Dr. Jonas Salk, discoverer of the polio vaccine, who said the early opening was not likely to increase the risk, adding that "advanced students of epidemic diseases have long abandoned the recommendation or use of isolation quarantine or closing of swimming pools, theaters, schools and so forth for control of polio epidemics."[51]

With rumors of a special session rampant, eight of eleven Pulaski County legislators met with the Committee for the Peaceful Operation of Our Free Public Schools on August 6 and voted to ask Faubus to give at least ten days advance notice on any proposed legislation for a special session. Many members of the delegation were still angry at having only thirty-two-hours' notice of the governor's plans before the 1958 special session was convened.[52]

Faubus remained coy about his plans until August 11, the eve of the schools' reopening, when he went on television to discourage violence the next day; he told segregationists they had "largely lost in last September's election and in the recall election of this spring" and urged those opposed to integration to carry on their fight at the polls. The *Gazette* reported that much of the governor's fifteen-minute speech was in an "I told you so" vein, as he criticized board members Tucker, Lamb, and Matson as "integrationists" and lashed out at "puppets of the federal government" including Harry Ashmore, the NAACP, and the Little Rock Police Department. Faubus emphasized that he was not "throwing in the sponge," and added, "if token integration is effected there are many ways in which you who are opposed can still resist. The struggle is not by any means ended. Regardless of the outcome tomorrow you must resolve to continue the struggle for freedom."[53]

Segregationists scheduled a rally for 10 A.M. the next morning at the capitol, while Amis Guthridge of the Citizens Council called for a "buyers strike" (later deemed a failure) against downtown businesses that supposedly were promoting integration. Although Little Rock police chief Eugene G. Smith promised he would put up with "no foolishness" around the schools, Brewer described the mood in the city as "jittery," and said many parents and WEC sympathizers feared renewed violence. When WEC staff checked the Little Rock police force, the statistics were not reassuring: twenty-three had signed CROSS petitions during the recent election, while only six had signed the STOP petitions; twenty-six lived outside the school district, and two were members of the White Citizens Council.[54] A *Gazette* editorial on the morning of August 12 offered a hopeful tone that "those who assemble to protest the lawful re-opening of Little Rock's public high schools will do so peacefully, as they have a right to do. Here again, Little Rock has an opportunity to restore its good name and to demonstrate for a watching world that we are a people who respect the law and bear no hatred for our fellow men."[55]

Hall High School opened the next morning without incident with three black girls attending. Meanwhile, a noisy crowd estimated at one thousand persons had gathered at the capitol to listen to speeches from various segregationist leaders for fifty minutes before Governor Faubus appeared, to an ovation, and delivered a brief talk. Amidst Confederate flags and sound trucks blaring the "King Cotton March" and "Dixie," adults and children were seen carrying signs that read "Arkansas Is for Faubus," "Race Mixing Is Communism," "Stop the Race Mixing," and "We Want Americanization Not Red-ucation." City police arrested three white youths during the morning rally at a car containing nine tear-gas bombs, but since the incident occurred on the capitol grounds, the city police turned the youths over to the state police, who released them. Nothing more was heard of this incident.[56] Janet Johnston provided a written account of what then happened:

> The crowd of about 200 left the capitol grounds and marched to Central High School, carrying American flags in the front row and bouncing placards reading: "Governor Faubus, Save Our Christian America." They were asked by police to stop a block away from Central, but proceeded to try to go through police lines. The police then turned fire hoses on them, which broke up the march. Central High opened peacefully, without further incident, with two Negroes in attendance."[57]

The attempt by the segregationist and Faubus forces to jettison the peaceful reopening with a rally and a march toward Central High School was unsuccessful because this time the city police and fire-fighting forces, with the full backing of the city government, were ready. Police arrested twenty-one members of the crowd on charges that included loitering, disturbing the peace, resisting arrest, and assaulting an officer. Police dispersed the marchers, and after a year of being empty, the high schools reopened, integrated.[58]

Amis Guthridge and Rev. Wesley Pruden of the Capital Citizens Council soon accused the police and city board of "callousness and brutality," "Hungarian Gestapo tactics," and picking on women and children. Mrs. Dale Alford wrote to Mayor Knoop, and Margaret Jackson of the Mothers League sent a telegram demanding that the board take action on charges of brutality against Chief Smith. Gaston Williamson, chairman of the Committee for the Peaceful Operation of Our Free Public Schools, condemned the charges as being "unfortunately typical of the irresponsible, inflammatory and untrue statements for which the Capital Citizens Council is noted." He also praised the police, saying:

> The people of Little Rock are sick of such utterances. Everyone knows who did the attacking at Central High School. An unruly mob bent on violence charged the police after being advised to stay away from the school. Police Chief Gene Smith resisted the attack and efficiently dispersed the mob with the

minimum force required. For doing his duty and upholding law and order, Chief Smith has been slandered by the rabble rousers. The vast majority of the citizens of Little Rock are deeply grateful to Chief Smith and his men.[59]

A *Gazette* editorial the same day questioned the governor's sincerity in his public appeals against new violence and said: "The fact is that Governor Faubus was there in front of Central High, in spirit, if not in presence." It also quoted an anonymous member of the state police as saying that "two-thirds of those who elected to play Black Shirt to Orval's Benito . . . were from out in the state. Wednesday's message to members of this group, which we do not believe is at all representative of the rest of the state, is that the City of Little Rock, at long last, is prepared to order its own affairs without their assistance."[60]

News reports over the next few days indicated that things were progressing smoothly as evidenced by local headlines: "Integrated High Schools Called Entirely Normal, Orderly in Classrooms" on August 13; "Hall and Central Both Calm on Second Day of Integration" on August 14; "First Week of Integration Ends With All Quiet" on Sunday, August 16; and "Little Rock High Schools Proceeding Quietly" on August 18.[61]

On August 19, the Little Rock City Board of Directors met and issued a statement denying there was a basis for any of the segregationist charges, saying that police "had acted in a completely legal manner in maintaining order and protecting life and property." The board also invited the Justice Department to make "a complete investigation" of complaints that civil rights had been violated.[62] A stream of mail to the Little Rock Police Department ran two to one in favor of its handling of the August 12 incident at Central High. Most of the support came from within Arkansas; of those from out of state, most came from Louisiana.[63]

On August 15, John McLeod Jr., a Little Rock attorney whose daughter attended Hall High, had informed the school board he was invoking Act 7, a 1958 state law with the provision that no student attending an integrated school can be forced to sit in the same classroom with students of another or a different race. The school board agreed to abide by the request, which was widely reported, and later 9 other students made similar requests. Eventually 68 students out of the 2,241 white students enrolled at Central and Hall High Schools requested that they not be assigned to any class with a black student, which, according to Superintendent Terrell Powell, was fewer than had been expected.[64]

■    ■    ■

During the summer, the WEC completed and widely circulated an economic study that documented the dire consequences of having no schools for a year. Grace Malakoff and Anne Helvenston edited the *Little Rock Report—The City, Its People, Its Business 1957–1959,* which drew conclusions from a broad survey of industry and skilled personnel and included responses from 68 local plant officials and 101 professional people in the community. The WEC issued preliminary results in early August, according to the *Gazette,* which said "the Women's Emergency Committee survey is the latest of several warnings that the integration strife and the closed public high schools are damaging the Little Rock economy."[65] The full report appeared on September 6 and included many sobering findings: no new industries had settled in Little Rock since September 1957, while the number of families moving into the city had declined by one-third; the sale of homes was down 20 to 25 percent, new building had dropped 10 percent, and retail sales were only half of those in several surrounding states. The report said one out of five professionals planned to relocate outside Little Rock, and declared, "new people will not come in because of the unsettled school situation."[66]

Initially the WEC board was divided about the wisdom of publishing the report. Brewer noted that the schools were open and "some women felt the truth of our findings might antagonize some of the power structure toward our future program." She later termed the report the "outstanding production of the WEC," and reported that it was widely disseminated both in the state and throughout the South. Due to overwhelming response, the report was soon released in a second, and then a third edition "with the hope that the lesson would not be forgotten and that our dark days would further the determination of other cities not to emulate Little Rock." The official release of the report on September 6 also marked an important milestone for the WEC, as our executive board announced a change in the name of the organization to the Women's Emergency Committee for Public Schools. The statement stressed the WEC's commitment to a "positive program in support of public education— to preserve public education and to encourage improvement of the schools."[67]

■   ▓   ▓

On Friday evening, August 28, two unidentified women threw two tear-gas bombs inside the front door of the school administration building while the board was meeting upstairs. The five members in attendance safely left the building and within thirty minutes had resumed their meeting in the boardroom of the Chamber of Commerce. Brewer reported that "little damage had been done except to the nervous systems of our already up-tight citizens." Neither this episode nor the August 12 incident at the segregationist rally on the capitol grounds was solved by police.[68]

On Labor Day evening, September 7, the second anniversary of the appearance of National Guardsmen at Central High, three charges of dynamite again shattered the calm in the city. The first, at 10:20 P.M., demolished a city-owned station wagon parked in the driveway of Fire Chief Gann Nalley's southwest Little Rock suburban home. The second blast smashed the front of a two-story building housing the Baldwin Company, a local construction firm of which Mayor Werner Knoop was vice-president and cofounder, and tore out a wall of an insurance company office next door. (For my family, this attack hit close to home, also blowing windows out of the Second Presbyterian Church across the street, where we were members.) At 10:58 P.M., the third bomb hit the school administration building, wrecking an empty office that was being remodeled. Three days later, police disclosed a botched fourth attempt where a man had tried to cut through a window of the Prudential Insurance Company building where Letcher Langford, the WEC's nemesis on the city board, had his offices. According to police reports, the attempt was aborted because of the traffic volume, partly due to the blast at Mayor Knoop's office three blocks away.[69]

Community reaction was immediate as thirty-one directors and former presidents of the Little Rock Chamber of Commerce met and quickly posted a twenty-five-thousand-dollar reward for the dynamiters. The Committee for the Peaceful Operation of Our Free Public Schools labelled the bombings "cowardly" and "tactics of terror and anarchy" and declared they were "deliberate invitations to violence . . . by irresponsible spokesmen for extremist groups." Governor Faubus deplored the bombings and suggested that "my enemies will do anything to discredit me." Attorney General Bruce Bennett laid the blame on the Communist Party.[70] Chamber of Commerce president Grainger Williams received personal threats after he and Billy Rector went on television to announce the reward. After the broadcast, a caller to the KTHV switchboard threatened to blow up Williams's home. Later that same evening, Williams received another call at home, telling him "we're on our way, get ready," forcing him to hire guards to watch his house at night.[71]

Response from law enforcement was also swift as Little Rock police and FBI investigators (under a special order from the president covering the use of explosives against public buildings) went into action. Within seventy-two hours, five suspects, all Little Rock residents, were apprehended and charged with the bombings. Within eleven days, one of the five (J. D. Sims, a local truck driver) had pleaded guilty and was in the state penitentiary starting a five-year prison term. The other defendants were: E. A. Lauderdale, the owner of a lumber and roofing company, who was active in the Capital Citizens Council and had twice been defeated for the city manager board; Jesse Raymond Perry, a truck driver; John Taylor Coggins, a used car salesman; and Samuel Graydon Beavers, a carpenter employed by the state.

Eventually all five men were convicted of the bombings, fined five hundred dollars and sentenced from three to five years in prison. According to testimony at the November trial of one defendant, who implicated Lauderdale as the mastermind, the attacks were apparently planned at a Ku Klux Klan meeting three days before

Labor Day. Sims, the first convicted, served approximately twenty-one months of his five-year sentence. Three others completed only a little over five months each, while a fifth defendant's sentence was later suspended. Brewer found this interesting "especially when compared with the relatively more harsh sentences allotted to sit-inners in 1960."[72]

Except for the three Labor Day bombings of the school board office, the mayor's office, and the fire chief's home in which fortunately no one was injured, the schools experienced no additional trouble in staying both open and barely integrated. Although the high schools were at last reopened, as the eve of our first anniversary approached on September 16, not one of us in the WEC felt that our job was finished.

# ▪ 10 ▪

# To the Ladies, God Bless 'Em

The women continued to receive favorable national publicity, including an article in the magazine section of the Sunday *New York Times* on September 13, 1959, that told of their work and included a photo of Mrs. Terry with the caption "First Lady of Little Rock." In late September, Vivion Brewer was surprised by a telegram from Ruth Roberts, story editor for the Loretta Young television program, requesting background material on the WEC to depict the work of the committee in a screenplay. The WEC board met in early October and eagerly discussed the potential benefits of a national broadcast for public schools, and the vast audience that such a program would reach.

Brewer proudly shared the exciting news at an open meeting on November 3, "hoping to cheer and stimulate our membership," and again in a December 1959 newsletter that announced "the Loretta Young Show has sent us a check for $300 for the story of our Committee." She later surmised that a spy may have been in attendance at the membership meeting when she learned that the *States Rights Digest* had carried a lengthy diatribe entitled "Women's Emergency Committee to Race-Mix Our Public Schools." The article included an account of the proposed television program, Brewer's picture, and the caption "for 300 pieces of silver."[1]

The *Gazette* picked up the story on December 13, reporting that the show "will dramatize the history of the Little Rock W.E.C. on NBC television in February." Within days, Dr. Malcolm Taylor of the Capital Citizens Council directed a letter to Miss Loretta Young, with a copy to the president of NBC, objecting to the proposed portrayal of Mrs. Brewer and the WEC, and indicated that copies of the statement were being sent to "the Association of

Citizens Councils of America, newspapers all over the South and to other publications with nation-wide circulation." In his attack, Taylor described the WEC as a "motley crowd of clandestine frustrated women," chided Brewer as "not a resident of Little Rock," and said Little Rock had been "cursed with a steady stream of One-World, One-Race visitors." The letter demanded that plans for the story be cancelled, adding, "I suspect that you have flounced into many living rooms, with your wide-eyed innocence and swirling skirts, for the last time."[2]

The WEC quickly responded and composed another letter asking our friends to show their support for the *Loretta Young Show* and the threatened boycott of her sponsors, adding "we are convinced that our fight to preserve public education in our state is not just a Little Rock problem." Loretta Young released a statement saying that the demands of local segregationists would have no impact on the decision to develop the program, although she called reports that the show would be televised early in 1960 "premature." In her statement she continued, "if that story like any other story we consider, develops into a script—unanimously acceptable to the producers, network and sponsors of the Loretta Young Show—it will be scheduled for production during the 1960–61 season."[3]

Although the program was unfortunately never completed, Brewer found it ironic that there was one positive side to the episode with her sudden popularity as a television celebrity. "Many once-upon-a-time near and dear friends had disappeared," she said. "With the publicity about the Loretta Young Show, all of a sudden I was respectable. Both men and women who had not seen me for sixteen months now spoke with smiles and eager questions. 'Tell us about Loretta Young. Will you go to Hollywood? When will your story be on?' I smiled back and was carefully non-committal."[4]

■   ■   ■

A more immediate concern for the WEC in the fall of 1959 was the upcoming school board election, which posed a number of questions. No one knew if the board members appointed after the STOP election would serve completed terms or only until the next election.

We also were unsure if two or three positions on the board would be contested. Alice Glover, president of the Little Rock Classroom Teachers Association, filed suit in Pulaski County Chancery Court to clarify Act 248 of 1959 on school board elections. On September 17, Chancellor Murray Reed ruled that "an appointed member shall serve only until the next school election, rather than completing the unexpired term if it extends beyond the election." Upon appeal, the state supreme court overruled the lower court and held that two of the appointed members should serve out the terms to which they were appointed instead of having to run in the next election.

The election was set for the first Tuesday in December. Everett Tucker and Frank Mackey were opposed at the last minute by Margaret Morrison and Mrs. H. H. Ray, who maintained they were running as housewives and were not members of any segregationist organization, although both were supported by the Mothers League and the Capital Citizens Council.

We became aware of a potential problem in late September, when four blacks headed by Rev. James McCullum of the Steele Memorial Baptist Church attended the school board meeting to advocate the need for a biracial committee and were soundly rebuffed by Tucker. As school board president, he said the board was already accessible and declared "we are not maintaining communications with any one group more than we are with another." Rumors began to surface that some in the black community believed the WEC was against them, perhaps because of our support for Tucker or our policy not to accept black members.[5]

Many of us grew through our experiences with the WEC into confirmed integrationists, although ironically, the WEC, for most of its existence, was not integrated. Early on, Terry and other WEC leaders, despite their personal interest in seeing integration succeed, felt that in order to expand the base of white support, their public declarations should stress getting the schools open rather than focus on the emotionally charged integration issue. In the fall of 1959, however, the executive committee remained convinced that the WEC as a biracial organization could have no hope of influencing the results of elections in favor of integrated schools. The WEC board finally voted in May 1963 to integrate its membership, and Blanche Evans, a black woman who ran unsuccessfully for the school board, became a member of the WEC board.[6]

Russell Matson, vice-president of the school board, attended a WEC meeting in early November 1959 to discuss the board's application of pupil placement laws, and he encountered sharp questions from our members. Brewer remembered that some women "suspected the tactics of the school board to be less than just," and described some of the questions as "little short of rude." Matson made it clear that he did not favor immediate and indiscriminate integration and defended the pupil placement laws as the "salvation of the Little Rock schools," adding, "we treated all students and parents alike in the assignment hearings."[7]

On November 24, the Committee for the Peaceful Operation of Our Free Public Schools met, and Gaston Williamson praised the WEC before a large crowd that included many of our members and their husbands, declaring the committee was "all honed and polished up again" to work in the election. The committee also installed four unlisted phone lines, which the women manned the week before the election to contact every friendly qualified voter. We also mimeographed and distributed several informational flyers, called GOLIGHTS, to our campaign workers during the busy week preceding the election.

With the election at hand, the women of the WEC again swung into action, setting up card files on qualified voters and checking the STOP and CROSS petitions from the previous spring to determine probable friendly and unfriendly voters. We had carefully examined the results of the May vote in the STOP campaign and had thoroughly reviewed our strengths and weaknesses, and we were prepared to put this knowledge to the test.

On election night, December 1, Tucker defeated Morrison by 8,878 to 4,165, and Mackey defeated Mrs. Ray by 8,882 to 4,082. A related proposal to reduce the Little Rock school millage was also defeated 8,593 to 4,354. Voters had again rejected the segregationist candidates in favor of the two moderate incumbents, but this time it had been by a two-to-one margin.

While the campaign itself was relatively quiet and without the bitterness of recent elections, on election night the two women candidates threatened to protest the outcome to the Pulaski County Election Commission, saying it had replaced "capable and loyal election officials, clerks and judges with people connected with the Women's Emergency Committee for Public Schools." In fact, no protest was filed, and a subsequent request for a federal grand jury investigation was also rejected. The Committee for the Peaceful Operation of Our Free Public Schools called the results a vote of confidence in the entire school board and a "restatement of the fact that our community is in favor of law, order and a free public school system."[8]

Immediately after the election, at the December meeting, Brewer shared two wonderful letters complimenting our members' hard work. Successful candidate Everett Tucker praised the WEC for "having succeeded so magnificently in what it set out to do," and said, "Because of circumstances, it is quite probable that the WEC will never be accorded a fraction of the credit to which it should be entitled, but I certainly want you to know that I am aware of the many contributions to the cause which your group has made." Tucker described himself as "a complete amateur in the world of politics," but added that he had learned one thing: "I don't believe I would ever espouse any cause which the WEC was opposing."

In another letter, our friend Henry Woods expressed his admiration for the "executive ability and organizational talents" of the WEC and credited the victory of Tucker and Mackey in the recent election to the success "in getting our supporters out to the polls." "Apathy is always the greatest obstacle in a political campaign," he continued. "I have never seen a more apathetic electorate; that your organization was able to turn out almost 9,000 votes in the face of such apathy is a little short of miraculous."[9]

We received more good news on December 14 when the U.S. Supreme Court upheld a lower court decision by an 8 to 1 vote nullifying the school closing laws, Acts 4 and 5 of 1958. I helped write a December 1959 "Letter from Little Rock" that stressed the WEC's accomplishments during the past year and urged our members to prepare for the impending fight against Amendment 52, which would abolish the guarantee for free public schools and make tuition grants possible. The newsletter declared, "Little Rock is a different city this Christmas," and "1960 will be a very busy year," adding, "In November we must defeat a proposed constitutional amendment which could bring about the destruction of the public school system throughout the state, district by district."[10]

■    ■    ■

In January 1959, in his inaugural message, Faubus promised further legislation to avoid desegregation. One of his proposals was for a constitutional amendment providing for local option elections to decide how to use local and state education funds. The legislature quickly passed Senate Joint Resolution No. 5, which would have embedded Faubus's school-closing authority in the state constitution. They slated the proposed amendment to appear on the ballot in the general election of November 1960. Brewer labeled Amendment 52 "the most frightening for us" of the anti-integration measures passed during the 1959 legislative session, writing later that "the fight to defeat this amendment was to absorb most of our time and energies throughout 1960."[11]

WEC members sent out over three thousand Christmas letters in December to our friends and supporters, and only fifteen copies remained from a third printing of the Little Rock Report, so Brewer was discouraged when only eight women showed up for the February WEC meeting. Although she acknowledged the WEC's "inescapable involvement" in the Democratic primary that summer, she believed her immediate responsibility was to pull the women together to focus on the defeat of the proposed "school destruction" amendment.

In late February, the WEC became the first group to oppose publicly the so-called "public school amendment" and drafted immediately a three-page study on the consequences, warning people of the dangers—"Some Implications of Proposed Amendment No. 52." Over fifty-five study groups in Little Rock alone were set up for WEC members, and the WEC board assigned selected individuals the task of taking the message to others throughout the state. As Brewer recalled, "we resolved to quit talking to each other and to try to inform the grocer, the mailman, the plumber, the milkman, the laundryman, everyone with whom we had contact."[12]

The WEC was also instrumental in mustering the opposition and encouraging other groups to speak out. While a team of women was busy behind the scenes distributing thousands of pieces of literature, I served on a speaker's bureau that filled numerous requests from clubs and civic groups. Vivion Brewer attended regional meetings of the Arkansas branch of the AAUP in Arkadelphia and Harrison, and Billie Wilson accepted invitations to speak in Stuttgart and eastern Arkansas where resistance to desegregation was high.

Gradually other groups did step forward. In late August, the Arkansas Education Association issued a four-page statement declaring that organization's opposition to Amendment 52, and the Little Rock chapter of AAUW called the amendment a disaster. The Little Rock School Board, with only J. H. Cottrell dissenting, came out against the amendment, and the Pulaski County Bar Association rejected No. 52 by a vote of 65 to 4. Brewer, Irene Samuel, and Pat House of the WEC were later publicly listed among the forty-eight names on a statewide steering committee—the Committee Against Amendment No. 52. This latter fact did not escape the governor's attention, and he appeared on television on October 28 in a last-gasp attempt before the election and attacked Brewer as the "leader of the Women's Emergency Committee of Little Rock, the most ardent integration organization in the state."[13]

In the 1960 general election, Amendment 52 was defeated by a three-to-one margin—247,804 to 83,900. In December 1960, the WEC boasted a growing membership of over two thousand. Another "Letter From Little Rock" news release noted our recent success against Amendment 52: "On November 8 the amendment was *defeated* 3 to 1 in spite of a telecast by the Governor urging the people to vote for the Amendment. PEOPLE OF ARKANSAS WANT NO MORE TAMPERING WITH THEIR PUBLIC SCHOOLS. . . . In Arkansas some of those who do the most talking about state's rights show the least concern about local rights."[14]

One month later, in a January 1961 letter to supporters, new WEC chair Pat House recognized the coalition of groups that joined the WEC to defeat Amendment 52. Among the groups she cited "which worked actively toward the smashing defeat" were: the Arkansas Association of University Women, League of Women Voters, Arkansas Education Association, Presbyterian Synod of Arkansas, North Arkansas Methodist Conference, Little Rock Methodist Conference, Pulaski County Council of Church Women, State Committee on Political Education, AFLCIO, Arkansas Farmer's Union, Education Committee of Masonic Order, the Little Rock PTA Council, and the Little Rock Chamber of Commerce.[15]

■　■　■

During the Democratic primary in July and the runoff elections in August, Brewer had persuaded the WEC board to decline to sanction publicly any particular candidates. Instead, we provided bulletins listing the candidates for various offices and left space for each individual member to fill in her own choices. Members were encouraged to advise friends personally of their positions using sheets that included this declaration: "Because of our concern for public education, I have investigated the voting records, the public statements and the reputations of the various candidates, and I have come to these conclusions. . . . I urge you to vote on July 26 and in the run-off; and I hope you will want to choose these same candidates."[16]

Although Faubus easily won a fourth term against four opponents and Dale Alford was returned to Congress as U.S. Representative from the fifth district, in seven contested races for the state legislature, four candidates we supported were victorious—Ellis Fagan in the Senate; and Harry Carter, Jim Brandon, and Sterling Cockrill in the House. Brewer later reported that "Mr. Carter was the one candidate to call me to express his thanks for the help of the WEC." Fagan, who was running against our old nemesis Letcher Langford, bravely referred to the WEC in a campaign ad, criticizing the city director for his use of Little Rock policemen to deliver letters "when a postman would have done it for four cents." He asked Langford, "Do you believe in a police state?" and added, "Were you trying to make this fine group of women feel like criminals? Or is this your idea of economy in government?"[17]

While Sterling Cockrill expressed a desire to be ignored, Jim Brandon had approached the WEC executive board early on and asked for our help in his race against the incumbent, Willie Oates. In the July primary, Brandon won by 193 votes, which prompted Oates's request for a recount. WEC members served as observers while election crews checked results from ninety-one disputed boxes. The final tally showed Brandon still ahead by 25,920 to Oates's 25,429, with Brandon gaining an additional 298 votes. A *Gazette* editorial at the time noted that although the recount had not changed the outcome of the election, "it had served the public interest in turning up new evidence to support the need for voting machines." Brewer later wrote that Oates's contention of a discrepancy in the counting was certainly borne out, "even if the discrepancies worked against her." She also stressed the impact of this race in retrospect on the eventual adoption of voting machines in state elections two years later: "That there was no secret ballot in Arkansas had long been one of the concerns of the WEC," she said. "The need for voting machines became increasingly imperative. We were pleased to have had a small role in stressing this need."[18]

■   ■   ■

In the midst of the campaign, after the "calm, completely peaceful opening of the schools" on September 6, with five black students at Hall and seven at Central, Brewer decided to resign as chair of the Women's Emergency Committee. This decision was partly the result of her apprehension that the WEC might become only a political pressure group. Another factor was her displeasure that the organization had backed Tommy Russell, a former aide to Governor Faubus, in a race for the Arkansas Senate.

After conferring with Brewer and Terry, Pat House, who had served so capably as WEC legislative leader during the 1959 session, agreed to replace Brewer as chair. At the September 1960 board meeting, as Pat House took over the reins of the WEC, Brewer cautioned the group about complacency, saying "let us not for one moment believe that our task is done." She warned against a sense of "false security" and urged members to remain vigilant against "future trouble—even tragedy in our state by facing up to our problems realistically."[19]

In developing a new slate of officers to work with Pat House, Brewer contacted Jo Jackson, who promised to be an active vice-chair, and asked who the new chair would be. According to Brewer, when she answered Pat House, Jackson declared, "I thought she was already chairman." "Meekly I explained that I had been chairman, but was resigning. 'Oh,' she said again. 'I thought you were like Mrs. Terry—just there!' I could not claim to be like Mrs. Terry—but I was there!"[20]

Jackson remembered that the WEC became increasingly involved in politics over the next few years, despite the fears of some on the board, and stressed the significance of the coalition-building that occurred with other special interest groups. She said men in the Little Rock power structure respected that coalition and wanted its support, "but they didn't want to meet with you." She now believes that many women never recognized how influential the WEC was because the men were afraid of the women's groups. "I think they had a very healthy respect for us, for the women," she said. "They were just not far enough along to sit down at the council table with the women there making decisions."[21]

■   ■   ■

A number of WEC members, including Billie Wilson and Gwen Booe, participated in the Community Unity Conference in early 1960. Wilson, who had worked as a secretary, transcribed all the proceedings of both that conference and a later one. Booe said she gave a disappointing answer when she was asked if she would invite a black person to have coffee with her at Woolworth's lunch counter, which was still segregated at the time. Booe worked at Worthen Bank across the street, and she said, "No, because I never go to Woolworth's on a break and have coffee and that would not be a natural thing for me to do." She also admitted she would have been embarrassed if someone had gotten up and left.[22]

In September 1959, a personable Quaker named Thelma Babbitt arrived in town following the crisis of closed schools to try to get blacks and whites talking to each other. Babbitt came to Little Rock through the American Friends Service Committee in Philadelphia and began to organize a proposed race relations forum. The first Conference on Community Unity was held the following February at Aldersgate, a Methodist camp, to bring blacks and whites together so that they could talk about what was going on in Little Rock. Among the expressed purposes of the conference were "to provide an opportunity to learn what some of the barriers are that separate us and create misunderstanding and tension," and "to seek ways in which we can work together to remove them."[23]

Frances Williams continued her own education through the first conference on February 20 at Camp Aldersgate. It was a first for many of the people on both sides of the racial line. Williams recalled group discussions with younger black participants who "were so aware of how their elderly people were all called by their first names and not given any credit for anything." She said these sessions made her more aware of the problem, and she soon resolved to help change things through her work as a Red Cross volunteer. "I don't know what I did," she said. "But I can tell you right to this day I get mad when they call all these women by their first name or when they call me by my first name. I decided I'm going to fight the battle too."[24]

Vivion Brewer, Irene Samuel, and Dottie Morris from the WEC were also among the ninety-eight participants, two-thirds of whom were white and one-third of whom were African Americans. They also recalled the strong influence it had on their thinking. Billie Wilson and her sister, Gwen Booe, were also there, and Wilson kept notes on the conference. The speakers were identified only by their last initials in her report of the meeting. One, who was identified only as Mrs. T but who identified herself as "the oldest living inhabitant here," when she asked a question and who was called "a leader in cultural and civic affairs" was unmistakably Adolphine Terry.[25] A black Episcopal priest said he did not mind being called "Nigra" instead of "Negro" but found it really offensive when it came out "nigger." Terry remembered that as a child she had been taught always to use the term "colored people" rather than "Negro" or "nigger," and asked, "It has only been in the last twenty years that I have heard the word 'Negro' used. What do colored people like to be called?"

The priest, who did not claim to be an authority, said he accepted Negro personally. Many prominent businessmen in Little Rock, even when they were interviewed years later, were still using the term "niggers" and even "darkies" when they referred to African Americans. No woman who attended that conference ever used terms like that again. Those at the conference also decided the word integration had become "loaded with ugly connotations" after the Supreme Court decision in 1954 and perhaps desegregation had less negative implications, at least at that time.

Mrs. Terry, who gave the final speech at the conference, declared that "we are being desperately hurt all over the world by the things that are happening and have happened here in Little Rock. We are being terribly hurt financially and economically. Don't think, after the things that have happened here in the last few . . . months, that people are going to rush in, no matter what the president of the Chamber of Commerce says on the subject. People are not going to forget it, they are not going to move in here with their businesses and help build up this town. And a lot of people are going to move out, white and colored, because they don't want to live in a town where things like this happen."[26]

Terry suggested that pressure be put on the Chamber of Commerce and on the Urban Renewal movement. She said letters should be sent to Raymond Rebsamen, the Urban Renewal president who had just returned from a trip around the world and should know "what our reputation is," to help work out a gradual course of desegregation. She told a story about a friend who had been to the Congo and was standing on the banks of a river watching some alligators when a young boy asked her, "What about Little Rock?" "In the Congo we are widely and unfavorably known," she said.

Terry also told how the library board on which she served had been desegregated without "the least particle of trouble." When the Children's Hospital had been built three years before, the superintendent decided it would be desegregated and "by heavens, it is desegregated." She said the hospital superintendent first thought she would have different visiting days for the families of black and white children, but decided that was too much trouble and made up her mind they could all either come on Sunday or stay home. It worked. Terry continued:

> Now I talked to a couple of men down at the Chamber of Commerce a few days ago, about an interracial committee and they said "blood will flow in the streets." Well, we have two examples here of the Little Rock Public Library and the Children's Hospital, and blood has never flowed in the streets from them. I think that Little Rock should not sit back and wait for Nemesis to overtake us because we all know, everyone of us knows that segregation is on the way out. No matter how long it takes, segregation is of the past; desegregation is the future. I'm not trying to say integration. But I think the South is acting a hundred years late, just as we did in 1860. We just can't see the future.[27]

Invitations went out to 323 persons for a follow-up conference, and this time 147 persons met at Camp Aldersgate on April 19. A report on the second Conference on Community Unity indicated that enthusiasm for the forums seemed to be building as "virtually 100 percent indicated future conferences should be planned," and "about two-thirds indicated they should be held quarterly." The evaluation also reflected the increased exchange of ideas between the black and white communities. One suggestion was to "explore ways of focusing more sharply and explicitly on similarities of aspirations and somehow bring out more clearly the implications of sit-in demonstrations and motivations behind them."[28]

Brewer described the sessions at Camp Aldersgate as "a wonderful outlet for me," and added, "Here I could think and hear and talk race relations—I learned much, and made many new friends." When Babbitt later was forced to leave Little Rock following a siege of infectious hepatitis, Brewer remembered searching for a new chairman for the Community Unity group "to assure continuance of this movement."

It was the same old story, even among those now dedicated to our program. Businessmen, professional men, representatives of labor, retired and independent men—each had some excuse. . . . After months, many months of earnest hope, this group which Mrs. Babbitt had fostered, disintegrated. It was with wry amusement that I read in 1966, in our local papers, that a series of meetings of very similar pattern was the "first one" ever developed in Little Rock.[29]

Subsequent conferences convened later that year in June and again in November. Babbitt met regularly with an ad hoc planning committee for the conferences, which included several local ministers and other residents who were interested in opening up more effective channels of communication and developing an ongoing group focused on creating greater unity and understanding in the community. Pat Youngdahl, whose husband Jim had helped compose the *STOPLIGHTS* newsletter during the STOP campaign the previous spring, recalled going to planning meetings at Babbitt's house and how scared people were. "Everybody thought Faubus was spying on us," she said. "People were just so frightened. It was a very scary time then—that's where I remember the fear people had in coming."[30]

Youngdahl suggested that the fears that people expressed then appear to have been justified. "People need to be reminded how far that type of thing can go," she said. "When you get repressive you start doing things all out of reason." A review of state police reports obtained from the Faubus papers at the University of Arkansas provides a chilling glimpse of the times. According to a *Gazette* story in 1979, when the Faubus papers were first made available, the governor had used the state police initially during the school crisis to investigate "subversive organizations" such as the WEC and the Arkansas Council on Human Relations, and the practice continued through the early 1960s. The files contained reports on private individuals known to be "integrationists" or who were associated with groups as diverse as the NAACP, the Congress on Racial Equality, the Council on Foreign Relations, and the YWCA. The reports also indicate that state police investigators routinely recorded automobile license numbers of participants at meetings of target groups and conducted background checks on the persons who owned the cars.[31]

A report listing the license plates from cars parked in the vicinity of Mrs. Terry's house on May 9, 1960, records the identity of one owner as Dr. John Samuel, Physician, and includes this information *(Jew)*. Another state police investigator reporting on an "integrated" meeting at Aldersgate on June 2 offered this observation: "The speaker, in my estimation, was here for no purpose but to incite riot, challenge everyone who was present to boycott the moderates, urge to open all facilities to the negro, and congratulated everyone on the part they have played in the token integration movement. . . . By the way, the commies came out in two and threes, which lasted for over an hour."[32]

■　■　■

As one of the first major groups of white women in the South to organize around the issue of building support for integrated public education, the WEC became a model for women in other Southern cities. The WEC sent its envoys to Atlanta, Mobile, New Orleans, and elsewhere to help both men and women put together similar groups. In a January 1962 article on the growth of women as a political force, Roy Reed pointed to the beginning of the movement in 1958 "during the dark days of the Little Rock desegregation trouble." Reed declared that the WEC "has fought Governor Faubus at every turn" and "has grown and prospered until it is one of the capital's truly potent political organizations." He also saw "clear indications that its influence has spread" to other women's organizations like the American Association of University Women and the League of Women Voters.[33]

Over the years, the women and their allies did better on statewide issues than on candidates. In the fall of 1961, they defeated a $60 million bond issue that would have affected public school financing in Arkansas and would have allowed Faubus to share the wealth with his rich supporters at taxpayers' expense. During the 1962 summer primary elections, nine of ten legislative candidates preferred by the WEC were elected. Their most significant achievement came in the fall of 1962 when voters approved the use of voting machines in a statewide election. This was the result of hard work on the part of the League of Women Voters and other women's groups including the WEC. Also in November 1962, proposed Amendment 51, which would guarantee segregated education for students who declined to attend desegregated schools, was defeated by sixteen thousand votes.

By 1963, Pulaski County had a predominantly moderate delegation of eleven representatives and three senators in the state legislature. The Little Rock School Board was also comparatively moderate in its makeup, lacking the extreme segregationists such as those who had served during the crisis. Governor Faubus had shown enough indifference toward racial matters to alienate many of the extreme racists who had once placed him on a pedestal. In a 1963 essay, I gave credit for what I termed this "semi-enlightened leadership" to the Women's Emergency Committee, "whose members spearheaded the reopening of the high schools and whose influence has been directed toward raising the caliber of people in public office." I acknowledged that the group had occasionally discussed disbanding, but noted the remarks of one board member who said, "If we have learned anything in Little Rock, it should be that if we put out little fires as they develop maybe there will not be another big one." I continued:

> Instead of attempting to change the surface image of Little Rock, these women have tried to get at the hard core of what pulled Little Rock into two years of infamy. Their solution is to encourage and develop leadership which can stand firm even in crisis. Little Rock could have used that type of leadership in 1957–59. The Women's Emergency Committee has not always been able to muster public opinion behind its endeavors and, like every organization, it has made mistakes, but it has been a decided force in getting Little Rock soundly on its feet again.[34]

On the third anniversary of the founding of the WEC, the *Gazette* editorialized that nothing could "make the travail of the last few years worthwhile," but said the existence of the organization "is one of the principal means by which we can try at least to rationalize some purifying and strengthening values out of that community-wide submission to the Bessemer process."

> Looking back now, it is still faintly terrifying to speculate on what Little Rock would have done without that first small gathering together of women who were determined that the schools would be saved, and who, by the strength of their example, did more than any other group to create the wave of public opinion that finally saw to it that the schools were saved.
>
> "To the Ladies, God bless 'em."[35]

# ▪ 11 ▪

# They Would Bow Their Heads

In August 1962, Orval Eugene Faubus stood genial and smiling on election night as he cut his victory cake with hundreds of supporters thronging around. This is the man who sent out press releases describing himself as "one of the ten most admired men in the world."[1] He was home free in the Democratic primary without a runoff, and the opposition was to continue for another two years as the political "outs" of Arkansas. I was one of those "outs" who had worked hard for Faubus's opponent, Sid McMath, a former governor responsible for bringing Faubus to state-level visibility as highway commissioner. McMath was running at least partly out of guilt for this, but also because he wanted to be governor again.

McMath had been a gallant and persistent campaigner, but here we were once more on the losing side. It was getting to be a familiar experience. After the 1957 Central High School crisis, the WEC had supported two other unsuccessful Faubus challengers—Lee Ward in 1958 and Joe Hardin in 1960. McMath was the first big name who had been willing to run against Faubus. We were full of hope that, with McMath's charisma and name recognition, coupled with a fifth-term try for Faubus, we would make it this time. We did get a great deal closer, and we measured our success by Faubus's falling percentage points. Although Faubus got 68.8 percent of the vote in 1958, and 58.3 percent in 1960, he got only 51.6 percent against McMath. We had built a whole political subculture of "outs" during these years, analyzing and reanalyzing how Faubus could be defeated.

We knew that Faubus continued to have an apparently unbeatable combination of support from some of the state's richest men and from the great mass of poor whites. We also knew that some of his most tenacious opposition came from women and from blacks because of his barring the black students at Central High and then closing the high schools. The women could not forgive him for closing the schools, and each time he ran, they were back for another round of trying to defeat him. There were also other allies among the "outs" who stayed bonded together through many fruitless campaigns.

Ed Lester was an irrepressible optimist who supplied the campaign with boundless energy and imagination and who almost kept enough money coming in for the McMath campaign to pay the bills. Henry Woods managed the campaign for his law partner, McMath. Woods trusted and accepted everyone, including women, as equal partners in a way we were not used to experiencing.

Both Lester and Woods were involved in the production of a film, *A Man for Arkansas,* for which I did the research and legwork—Lester in raising the money and Woods in approving the content. It was our costliest campaign project, and in it we attempted to show the Faubus tie-ins to the rich, especially Witt Stephens who then owned the Arkansas Louisiana Gas Company. There was much debate about whether we should use that part, but in the end it was included. It effectively demonstrated Faubus's helping the rich get richer while manipulating poor whites to hate blacks rather than to demand a better life for themselves. After the election, one of our supporters ran as a joke a want ad that said: "For sale cheap. 30 min. 35 mm. film *A Man for Arkansas*." There were no takers.

■   ■   ■

One morning in the fall of 1962, I received a call from Irene Samuel who asked, "How would you like to run for the School Board?" I took a deep breath. I had been helping to recruit a candidate for the WEC to support, but I had not thought of myself as doing it.

"I'm asking you to think about it," Irene said. "Talk it over with Pat and let me know. You know a lot about education and you could do some really good things."

I was well aware that the WEC was displeased with Everett Tucker's performance on the school board and wanted to see him replaced. They were hoping against hope, in fact, that he would not run again. Everett Tucker, scion of an old family and an official of the Chamber of Commerce, was a self-proclaimed segregationist, albeit a moderate one. He was in charge of attracting new industries for the Chamber of Commerce, and he had been quite successful until the school crisis. Then he saw company after company on which he had spent many months of work turn away, and he knew we were paying a price we could not afford. One industry, which employed several thousand people, was on the verge of coming, but its officials changed their minds and frankly stated that the racial crisis was the reason. Tucker was closely associated with Billy Rector, a real estate executive, who also was experiencing a depressed market.

After the schools reopened, Tucker and his friends, including Rector, were determined to keep integration at a minimum. The downtown power structure influenced the school board to choose new school sites that would make real estate development around them attractive far to the west of the all-white suburbs. At the same time, other new schools were built far to the east near all-black housing developments to keep the blacks in those schools in the hope of keeping the community permanently segregated.

The school board was also using the Smith Law Firm to uncover every conceivable way to drag its feet in slowing down the entry of black students into what were still mostly all-white classrooms. The head of the law firm, Bill Smith, was a close personal adviser of Governor Faubus, and WEC members were indignant that the governor was able, through the firm, to continue to accomplish his original purpose of keeping black children out of formerly all-white classrooms. The firm was to become immensely wealthy advising Little Rock and other school districts across southern and eastern Arkansas on how to delay desegregation by using repeated obstacles that had to be litigated. The barriers would eventually be overturned in the courts, but in the meantime, the Smith firm (which later became the Friday Law Firm in honor of Hershel Friday, who represented most of those districts) prospered. It was not until the early 1970s that many of those districts actually merged their black and white schools. So Governor Faubus, who remained in office until 1966 when Winthrop Rockefeller was elected, prevailed indirectly through the tactics of his friends long after he had first been defeated at the polls in the STOP campaign.

In 1962, the WEC board felt the school district needed to move in a more straightforward direction toward the planning necessary for successful integration in Little Rock. Although I was not a segregationist, I did not identify myself then as an integrationist. The word "integration" evoked images of intermarriage and Communism in the still-emotional climate in Little Rock. And at that time, I was not so much for speeding up the process of integration as I was for setting it as the community's goal to work toward. Attempting to obstruct the intent of the law seemed to me an ultimately destructive way for a school board to proceed.

There was, in fact, little difference between Everett Tucker and me except in our final goals. He was working as a moderate to maintain the status quo in the comfortably segregated white South, while recognizing that some change was inevitable. On the other hand, I was working, also as a moderate, to move toward that change and to educate myself and others for effective participation in it. Tucker and I represented what one account of the election termed the "same segment of the community"—the "open schools" or "moderate" group. In earlier elections the WEC had even endorsed Tucker, but on those occasions he was opposed by outright segregationists.[2]

I fully understood that the election would be a major contest between the women in the WEC and the downtown power structure. Tucker was powerfully connected, and I had two strikes against me: I was unknown and a woman. There was also the distinct possibility that Tucker was tired of the controversy and would retire from the board as the WEC hoped. A couple of days later, I told Irene I would do it.

I was a young and unknown housewife with three small children, teaching part time at the local university and therefore suspect. Why would I have the nerve to challenge Billy Rector's candidate? Several members of my own church, where I had taught Sunday school, supported my move, but there were others who did not. One pillar of the Second Presbyterian Church became alarmed when I called him to say I was serious about running; he urged me not to do it. Another powerful member of the church took me aside in the vestibule one Sunday and said: "Sara, don't do it. After all, you are a *newcomer* to Little Rock." I had only lived here thirteen years at that time. "How long do I have to live here to not be a newcomer?" I asked. I have now lived here forty-four years and my newcomer status has not yet been removed.

■    ■    ■

Before I announced my candidacy, I called Tucker to see if he might be leaving the board, and I got the distinct impression that if someone he supported offered to run, he would. That was good news because, while I knew his group would probably put up opposition to me, it would be easier if it were someone less well known than Tucker. I announced early, hoping it would encourage Tucker to leave the race to someone else from downtown as he had indicated he would like to do.

In a September 1962 board meeting, the WEC was seeking suitable candidates for both the city council and the Little Rock School Board. In the city manager races, some of our board members felt that "king makers" in the industrial community should not be permitted to make selections for the entire city and that the WEC should consider running a slate of candidates. After a discussion of possible candidates—Gaston Williamson, Bob Downie, Warren Bass, Sam Laser, and Grainger Williams were mentioned—the talk turned to the approaching school board election. At the time Dr. John Allen Harrel, who was our children's pediatrician, and I were both considering running for the school board.

The consensus was that Everett Tucker's actions "had not been in accord with the general thinking of our [WEC] board for a peaceful and progressing school system," although a motion passed that we ought to wait to see if Tucker might be eased out before we made a commitment. After visiting with Tucker at his office, I had returned to the WEC board meeting in progress and reported that he had not committed himself on whether he was going to run, but that he gave the impression he might step down if an acceptable candidate could be found.

WEC minutes indicate that I also reported on a recent meeting with Ted Lamb, who asked if I was elected would I be for the complete and immediate integration of the Little Rock School Board. This was a loaded question in my opinion because, although I believed integration of the board was morally right, I did not think it could be accomplished overnight without a great deal of turmoil. I responded that we should be moving in that direction, but that in the current climate the resulting upheaval might not be desirable. Irene Samuel then mentioned the possibility that blacks in the community might be running their own candidate and suggested that Dr. Harrel and I "meet with a Negro group, and see whether they would be willing to support them."[3]

Tucker did announce later himself, and it was clear where his major support was. One ad with three hundred signatures supporting Tucker included, among the first fifty on the list, fourteen insurance people and seventeen real estate people, with ten of the seventeen from the real estate company belonging to Rector. Not only were they people who profited from what the school board did, they also sent out the word that they would show the women where the power structure in Little Rock was. At one meeting held by businessmen in support of Tucker, one of them said, "We've got a fire and we've got to put it out." Rector declared that "Mrs. Murphy was a woman whose views don't coincide with ours."

I did not know about the fire part, but the latter was certainly true. I did not believe that going through the motions of obeying the law while keeping the schools ostensibly segregated was an honest stance. Besides, I had worked hard in the Women's Emergency Committee's effort to reopen the high schools the year Governor Faubus closed them to keep them segregated. Rector and his friends, the downtown people in power, had remained silent throughout that year, while we had struggled to get public education reinstituted in the community. Rector's later contribution was to start a private academy for whites in the western end of town.

On the Sunday before the Tuesday election, the power structure showed its muscle in all segments of the community. An ad signed by a woman who had supported CROSS said I wanted to speed integration and that I was ultra-liberal. By then I was getting hate telephone calls labelling me as a Communist. I was also a volunteer babysitter during church in the two-year-olds' nursery that Sunday. At least seven or eight young fathers who had signed the Tucker ad looked at the floor as they deposited their offspring with me.

At the same time, the Tucker forces circulated handbills opposing me signed by nineteen blacks, headed by a Rev. F. T. Evans, saying that the WEC had not supported a black candidate, Dr. M. A. Jackson; the handbills stated that blacks should not support me because I had not done anything for them anyway. Although the WEC did have ties in the black community, the businessmen had stronger ones and more money. The custom then in Arkansas politics was to pay black leaders to circulate fliers in black churches the Sunday before an election and then to have them hire black drivers to get voters to the polls on election day. Dr. Jackson was a candidate against Dr. Harrel, a liberal the WEC had asked to run prior to Dr. Jackson's entry into the race. I remember one moment of truth for me when, as Irene Samuel had earlier suggested, I appeared before the black leadership of the Council on Community Affairs (COCA) and had to explain why, if I was asking for their support, the WEC was not willing to support Jackson.

We knew we were dependent on getting all the black vote in my election to win, and it was becoming more and more apparent that the Harrel-Jackson race was going to spill over adversely into mine. Although the Council on Community Affairs asked blacks to vote for Jackson and me, the Tucker fliers told them to vote for Tucker and Jackson. On election day, the Tucker campaign went a step further. They used students in white uniforms from a black beauty school to stand at the polls and tell people they were Dr. Jackson's nurses and they wanted them to vote for Jackson and Tucker. It worked. When the count was in, I got seventy-five hundred votes to Tucker's twelve thousand. The split of the black vote made the crucial difference for me. Harrel also defeated Jackson who, of course, got all the black vote, but only that.

Although we lost, that election opened the door for both liberal and black membership on the school board. We learned to build effective coalitions of women, blacks, labor, and education groups that changed not only Little Rock but eventually the state as well. On the down side, after losing that election, I watched an appallingly large amount of money channeled into legal fees to try and circumvent the inevitable integration. The chief recipient of those fees was the Smith firm.

I had feelings of guilt when I worked day and night in the school board campaign and wondered if my children knew why it was important for me to do this thing. It is hard to explain to children that when you commit yourself to the things you believe in, it is their world as well as yours that you are trying to improve. The test came when I lost. I knew it would be tough going to school, and the next day when I picked up my son, who was then in his first year of junior high school, I asked him how it went. He said two or three of his friends said they were sorry that his mother lost. One boy who had spent the night at our house many times, however, said:

"Yah, yah, yah, your mother lost."

"And what did you say?" I asked.

"I said your mother didn't have the courage to run." All the hours away from home, the meetings, the handshaking, the envelope-addressing, the telephoning, suddenly seemed worth it.

■    ■    ■

In May 1963, the WEC board met to discuss the future direction of the organization "with the purpose of broadening the base of its operation to make it into a political action group." One proposal from a previous meeting was to cover the operations of the John Birch Society, which I felt was too far afield for a group like ours. I proposed setting up ongoing legislative committees to handle work with legislators; I also suggested more public meetings to give the membership a chance to participate more actively in the work of the organization, and to give them an opportunity to ask questions concerning our activities. Martha Bass and Jo Jackson both suggested that we tie in with other groups interested in education. At this same meeting we decided to become integrated, and we voted to issue a statement in our newsletter that "our membership is open to all women interested in public education."[4]

The minutes from that meeting also reflect the first talk of dissolving the group. Adolphine Terry praised the marvelous work we had done in the community, but she felt now that the "emergency" was over we ought to "close with a flourish." She suggested that if a new emergency arose we could open up again. Pat Youngdahl said the WEC had provided leadership for many other groups working in the fields of education, human relations, and politics, and that we ought not to disband because of the influence we could have. After a prolonged discussion, a motion passed to continue the WEC on a broader basis than in the past, and "to concentrate on public education and issues related to it, including the election of candidates dedicated to these principles."[5]

Pat Youngdahl grew up in southeastern Missouri in a small town where her father operated a dry goods store and her mother was a teacher. She later attended Stevens College and Washington University where she remembered being "part of a group that did one of the first sit-ins in Saint Louis in an ice cream parlor" in the late 1940s. It was here that she met her husband, Jim, where both were active in youth groups and the campus YMCA. After Jim finished law school at the University of Arkansas in Fayetteville, they moved to Little Rock in early 1959 while the high schools were still closed. Like many other young mothers who became involved with the WEC, her family was not directly affected, because one child was in elementary school and the others were in preschool at the time.

Youngdahl said her attitudes on racial issues probably came from two places. "Even though it was the South, my family were more hill people," she said. "They had come from around Poplar Bluff and Cape Girardeau, and hill people and delta people were different. Also from my father who was an open-minded person. He was one of the few people in our town who called blacks 'mister.' He felt very strongly about respect for everybody."[6] Another influence that helped shape her convictions was the fact that her family was very active in the Methodist Church. "Growing up, the Methodist Church had very far-sighted literature," she said. "Now the people in the Women's Society that read that literature and talked about it, I'm sure many of them didn't share those attitudes. But in terms of human rights and racial issues the literature was very compelling to me. I think probably those two things—having the reinforcing attitudes. Like many towns, we had a white school and a black school, but I know that my parents thought it was unfair the black school was so poorly equipped."

In the fall of 1963, Youngdahl served as chair of the committee that decided to dissolve the WEC. She maintained that tension had grown over time and recalled that Irene Samuel and Pat House "had gone off into a more political vein and backed a couple of questionable candidates." While they emphasized the big picture, other members were not interested in broad-based political activities, and were unwilling to get down into the rough and tumble part of politics to support candidates who were not so pure in order to get other things done. According to Youngdahl, that was when the group began coming apart. Many WEC members were "single issue" conservative women from the community who had originally lined up for one cause—to open the schools. "At the beginning there was such a clear goal with the schools being closed," Youngdahl said. "One thing is right and one thing is wrong. We don't get that very often. So many people could commit to that goal—they weren't interested in doing other things. And then to have it be successful was remarkable."[7]

■　　■　　■

About seven years is the normal cycle of effectiveness for an organization; too many outlast their original purpose, that is how bureaucracies begin. Self-perpetuation becomes more important than the task at hand. When the WEC finally disbanded, however, it did not actually stop. It had empowered women to know that they could have an impact; it gave us the realization that we could change things.

Although the women were now more civically aware and active in other organizations, according to Vivion Brewer the organization was doomed to splinter. Without a unifying goal and often divided in support of candidates, the membership gradually declined and weakened. Brewer's favorite quote from Governor Faubus was his comment, during his fifth term on learning of the demise of his relentless antagonist, that the WEC members probably "will try to infiltrate other organizations. It might have been better to have them all in one group."[8]

The WEC did have strong leadership, but it also had a lot of ordinary women who believed what was happening was wrong—some out of religious conviction, some out of social conviction. It was an interesting time for women to learn how to work together and to discover what would work and what would not. Here, it really was a little group of women who turned things around.

Mamie Ruth Williams agreed with Brewer and Youngdahl about the conflict that had developed on the board. She said that what the WEC had done and what it stood for was absolutely incredible, but she feared the increasing involvement in politics "would destroy everything that Mrs. Terry had wanted and built." Williams called Adolphine Terry "the most amazing woman that ever lived" and said Terry shared her concerns about the group becoming a political power base. Williams also recalled making the motion to disband the organization after contacting other members. "I began to realize everyone had their own agenda," she said. "Irene was going to take the WEC people and put them into the election for whoever her candidate was. As far as I could tell, that was wrong. . . . I felt like we stood for everybody and I didn't want us to become the vehicle for this or that candidate."[9]

■   ■   ■

After a quiet summer, the WEC finally voted to disband in a November 1963 gathering at Mrs. Terry's home, where we had all gone through so much together in the past five years. I presented Pat House a charm for her service as chair of the organization, and the group presented a plaque to Mrs. Terry with these words: "In deep appreciation for your unique, selfless and unremitting contribution to humanity and for your inspiration and guidance to the Women's Emergency Committee." Many of us remembered how Terry had called the first meeting in September 1958 with Velma Powell and Vivion Brewer to see what could be done about reopening the schools. Pat House said that Mrs. Terry had been "the shoulder we've cried on," and added, "She would listen to our varying opinions and come up with what should be done. Without her there would not have been a WEC in the sometimes mighty troubled waters."

House stressed that the group had accomplished its goals not only for reopening the schools but in serving as a catalyst to awaken interest in public education and government. She noted that members were active in numerous other community groups and concluded that the work of the WEC would be carried on by various other organizations. "There are new organizations such as the Interfaith Conference of which we are hearing so much and the Arkansas Committee on Civil Rights," she said. "Problems can be solved through these channels."[10]

Forrest Rozzell, executive secretary of the Arkansas Education Association, outlined a blueprint to raise an additional $57.5 million a year for education, and Joe Stroud of the *Gazette* editorial staff advocated increased consolidation of school districts. Jim Youngdahl discussed the gap in education opportunity for black and white students and called for greater speed in desegregation. Jo Jackson, who had coordinated the workshop on public education with the theme: "Women in Action—What Women Can Do," urged the women to become more involved in government and civic interests, and to stay informed. During a box luncheon, Dr. Richard Yates, Pat House's former history professor at Hendrix College, pointed out that a smaller percentage of women voted than men. He said that he once believed that women's role in politics was "a light and trifling one," but he had since changed his mind. "The critical point in politics is the making of public policy and not the mere holding of public office," he said. "Your most important role is to influence elections and ride herd on the men who hold office."[11]

In an article the next day, *Arkansas Gazette* staffer Bill Lewis reported that the WEC met its initial objective of bringing about the reopening of the four Little Rock public high schools, and that it figured prominently in local school-related elections in 1958–59. He recalled when the WEC and other women's groups helped defeat Faubus's school-board packing bill and how the sponsor, Rep. T. E. Tyler, was "involuntarily retired." During the battle between STOP and CROSS forces in the 1959 school board election, he said Faubus frequently singled out the WEC for scorn, as the women "kept up a constant barrage of studies, statistics and statements with which it answered errors of fact by its opponents, from Governor Faubus down."[12]

Upon learning that the WEC had voted itself out of existence, the *Pine Bluff Commercial* declared, "If the men of Arkansas had more self respect, they would bow their heads at the demise of the Women's Emergency Committee of Little Rock." The editorial, with the title "Taps," also offered this admonition:

> The ladies now disband, and thus signal the end of an era in which they were one of the few things to be remembered with pride. . . . In essence, the committee took the lead after this state's so-called leadership had either gone over to the side of retrogression and racism or had fled through the nearest available exit. The ladies now pass the seals of leadership back to their conventional custodians. These custodians ought to be on notice, however, that the committee could be put together again in an afternoon, and doubtless will be should the need arise.[13]

Another editorial appeared in the *Arkansas Gazette* that said the most common misconception surrounding the WEC during its existence was that it was concerned only with the "preservation of the Little Rock public school system," rather than "the continuance of the public school concept in Little Rock, in Arkansas, and in the South and the country as a whole." It pointed out how the WEC's influence had spread to other cities in Arkansas and throughout the South, and had served as a model for other groups with its "techniques of direct political action that came to be widely copied at other critical points in the Southern School Crisis."

> Little Rock was where the first shock of major battle was felt, but it was also the place where the tide first began to turn. Those of us who shared the same command post under fire have never doubted that the outcome would have been somewhat different, had it not been for the selfless volunteers of the Women's Emergency Committee.[14]

■    ■    ■

Before it disbanded in 1963, the WEC began working closely with a new group of black leaders, mostly men, through the Council on

Community Affairs (COCA). The WEC and COCA were able to put together a loosely knit coalition with labor and educational interests that began to put better Little Rock people, including one former WEC member (Jean Gordon) and a black COCA leader (T. E. Patterson), on the Little Rock School Board. The women continued in post-WEC days to help build the coalition of liberal whites and blacks into a statewide network. They were an important force in eventually ending the Faubus and segregationist political reign by helping get out the votes that elected a racially liberal Winthrop Rockefeller in the mid-1960s.

Although the WEC never got around to addressing the problem of race relations directly, the Panel of American Women did. The panel was an important successor to the WEC in 1963, as an interracial, interfaith group that presented programs about the problem of prejudice. Some of us were WEC veterans who knew that successful school integration hinged on a change in community attitudes.

The Panel of American Women, so named because it "looked like America" thirty years before the Clinton cabinet, deliberately mixed a Catholic, a Jew, an African American, sometimes an Asian American, and a white Protestant for its presentations. We recruited young women who had warmth and commitment but who also had solid standing in the community. Many mainstream whites who still clung to stereotypes about groups different from their own came out of curiosity to hear what these women they knew were talking about. Patterned after a similar group in Kansas City, the panel was able to get these discussions about prejudice into the mainstream of Little Rock civic clubs, church groups, and women's organizations. Most restaurants, motels, and filling-station restrooms were still tightly segregated across Arkansas in 1963. Those who invited us out of town were often faced with the dilemma of where we could stay or eat together. The invitations poured in, however, as the word spread that the panel was made up of a group of mothers who talked in a comfortable, nonlegalistic way about a situation that troubled the whole South. As the first positive public voice for integration in Little Rock, the panel gave its members confidence to participate in many other community change efforts.

# ▪ 12 ▪

# Panel of American Women

I emerged from my experiences in opposing Faubus and in being a candidate myself with the strong feeling that work needed to be done in changing attitudes—my own as well as others. The state could not make a successful transition from a segregated to an integrated society without more education to change the way whites felt about blacks. It was as simple as that.

I had no idea how this new kind of education of hearts as well as minds could proceed, but it stayed in the back of my mind. Most human relations efforts I had seen were fringe efforts that seemed to attract only a small number of people whose hearts were already in the right place. We needed to get to mainstream people who set mores and controlled power in their community.

I was attending a national committee to support public schools in Washington in 1963 when I met Homer Wadsworth, who was then president of the Kansas City School Board. When Wadsworth found out I was from Little Rock, he invited me for coffee and said he wanted more information about what happened to cause the 1957 school crisis at Little Rock. "I've never been able to understand why it happened at Little Rock," he said. "Little Rock was far ahead of Kansas City in the mid-1950s in planning for integration."[1]

▪ ▪ ▪

Kansas City had desegregated its schools in 1956 with a minimum of difficulty, while the following year in Little Rock, the entrance of nine black students at Central High School caused a major community explosion. I explained that Governor Faubus had largely incited the resistance by playing on the fears and prejudice he knew existed against blacks. But I was curious to know what they had done at Kansas City to mobilize public opinion along healthier lines. His response was immediate.

"The most effective thing that has been done by far are programs put on by a volunteer group known as the Panel of Americans," he said. "It's primarily women, although an occasional man participates. And the idea is a very simple one. Panelists from different racial and religious backgrounds tell on a personal, straightforward level what their experiences with prejudice have been."

He got my attention. Maybe this would work at Little Rock. I learned that a woman named Esther Brown had started the Kansas City panel, and I knew that I wanted to meet her. A few weeks later, I set up a meeting of community leaders in Little Rock and invited Brown to come tell about the Kansas City panel, which was then in its eighth year.

Esther Brown was a dynamo of a person who talked in superlatives, and if she had been selling hair spray or perfume, I would have bought it by the carload. She wore her brown hair in a short, bouffant style that framed her face, and she had on a bright red suit the first time I saw her. Her eyes sparkled with enthusiasm. When I expressed misgivings about how the panel might be received in Little Rock, where mobs had been in the street three years ago, she dismissed my concern. "They'll love you," she declared. "You'll be so attractive and do such a wonderful job that the governor will be inviting you to speak before the legislature."

Brown made the panel sound so appealing and plausible that it seemed certain the panel could work as well here as anywhere. Brown was no neophyte in human relations. Back in 1948, while living in Topeka, she had helped create some of the tumult that led to the *Brown* (no relation) *v. Topeka* case. Her housekeeper complained to her that she was concerned about being asked to pay higher taxes for a new white school. She said the school her children attended was badly in need of repairs and located in an area that turned into a virtual swamp when it rained. Brown went to inspect the school on a rainy day and found water standing all around. She helped organize the blacks in the school to protest and subsequently became acquainted with officials in the NAACP. One thing led to another and Brown's efforts, plus that of others, eventually culminated in the landmark case that went to the Supreme Court and established the need for desegregation of the schools as the law of the land.

Brown's original training was in social work, in which she worked briefly before marrying and becoming the mother of four children. Her husband, Paul, lost his job because of her activities in Topeka, but the irrepressible Brown turned that into a positive when she told about it later. "No one would hire him because of all I had done and so he had to go in business for himself," she said. "Now we're rich, so it worked out fine. Actually we aren't, but it makes a better story that way."

On Brown's first visit to Little Rock, I set up a meeting of twenty-five people, consisting of a few civic leaders and many women who might be interested in participating in the panel. When Brown arrived, I cautioned her to proceed carefully because Little Rock was not as enlightened as Kansas City. "Now stop worrying," she said. "I know what to say to them. I'll emphasize the low-key middle-class appeal of the Panel and how much fun it is."

All of the women who agreed to come to that first meeting were enthusiastic about the panel and could see its possibilities for Little Rock. The most enthusiastic of all was Brownie Ledbetter, an energetic and well-connected woman who had grown up in Little Rock but who had only a couple of years before returned from Germany where her husband had served in the army. She helped recruit panelists and moderated the first few panels because she had Little Rock roots, and we felt the panel should have as indigenous an appearance as possible.

A few people that I called for that first meeting, however, pointed out that I might stir things up by opening up talk about prejudice, and they refused to come. "How would you like to have rocks thrown through your window and crosses burned in your yard?" one friend said. "Think about Pat and the children." Another friend told a hair-raising tale about how the Ku Klux Klan had intimidated an integrated camp group some years before. I discussed my starting the panel with Pat, omitting the crosses, the rocks, and the KKK, and he endorsed the idea. It did not seem particularly risky to him.

Brown described for us how the Kansas City panel worked. Each panel had a Catholic, a Jew, a black, a Hispanic or an Asian, and a white Protestant, each of whom spoke for five minutes from written talks. Each told how prejudice had affected her life and the lives of her family. A moderator opened and closed the program and conducted a question period. The vulnerability of the minority panelists in revealing the hurts they had experienced made it difficult for people in audiences to attack them. Their use of humor also broke down the tenseness of discussing an emotionally loaded subject. Brown assured us that the reaction would be overwhelmingly positive.

Adolphine Terry was among those who attended the first luncheon with Brown. She surveyed the crowd and with her usual candor declared: "I'm delighted to see so many people here. This is a highly controversial program you're discussing, you know." That was Terry's way of giving it her stamp of approval. No potential black panelists were at that first meeting because I did not know any black women outside those who worked in my home and a few teachers I had met working in political campaigns. I did invite Rev. Negail Riley, a young black minister whom I had met at a political meeting and liked.

Brown pointed out that we needed charming, intelligent, and attractive young women from diverse backgrounds, knowledgeable about issues and willing to talk about them. She said it was important for the panel to portray a different and more current image of minorities than the one most white audiences then held. Riley rose from his seat and declared: "I have just the charming, articulate and attractive woman you need. I'm married to her!"

Before Brown's plane left that day, we went by the Riley residence to meet Gwen Riley. She was certainly the most stunning black woman I had ever met. Gwen Riley was the first black reservations clerk for Trans World Airlines at Los Angeles. She probably would have been the first black stewardess for TWA had she not married Negail Riley, who was the first black graduate of Perkins Theological Seminary at Southern Methodist University in Dallas, Texas. They had a two-year-old daughter named Beryl. Negail Riley was the campus minister at Wesley Chapel at Philander Smith College.

The Riley's home was gracious and appealing. There was a portrait of somebody's grandfather in the hall and a silver tea service on the dining-room table. Several good, modern paintings hung on the living-room walls. Riley was a handsome woman with large brown eyes and high cheek bones, and she made us feel instantly at home. She had the kind of star quality that gets your attention when she enters a room. We knew we had to have her on the panel.

"Negail has just sprung this on me," said Gwen, who hesitated only briefly. "I don't know whether I can do this or not. I don't have a speech or anything."

"Don't worry," I said quickly. "I'll write you a speech. I mean, we'll write it together." I did not know anything about panel speech-writing or about Gwen, but I knew we could make the Little Rock panel fly if we got Gwen to be a part of it.

Gwen, who was articulate, funny, and honest, taught me as we began to work together on her speech that when you lived the down side of prejudice, you had to laugh at what you heard out there, not because it was funny but because you knew what contorted, wild images of blacks were stored away in those minds. I also learned from her that it felt really good to talk about prejudice when you had for so long had to greet bigoted remarks with silence.

The speech that Gwen finally settled on told about her exclusion as a child from the city park, the zoo, the library, the museum, and from first-rate schools. Then Gwen moved into the heart of her speech, where she talked about the fact that her own two-year-old Beryl did not know that there are those who would look down on her because of the color of her skin. "When I look at her with those bright eyes shining I can't bring myself to tell her," Gwen would say. After a pause, she would ask almost in a whisper, "Do you think she should be told?"

The handkerchiefs would come out and Katy Lambright, a white Protestant panelist, would wait for the noses to be blown and the sniffling to cease. She would say she had never had to face telling her children anything like that nor did she want it to happen to other children. And we as majority members of society had a responsibility in that, she would say. "One of the most tragic things we do is to teach our children to hate, and I have long been convinced that this is the way they learn it," Lambright would add.

On one panel on which Riley and Lambright appeared, an Asian woman, Pat Jang, had told how it felt as a child to have a teacher reject her because she was Chinese. The first question was for Jang because no one wanted to begin with dealing with the black panelist. After all, this was the unmentionable subject brought out in the open and discussed. Some of the things touched at the roots of what a person was. The questioner doubted that a child of eight could know that a teacher disliked her on the grounds of prejudice rather than for some other reason. Perhaps she was imagining this? Jang replied that the same sort of treatment had been accorded her brother and cousins by the same teacher. The woman, rebuffed at that point, decided to try another tack.

"But all of us have been rejected for something at some time," she said. "I have been, you have been. Why make so much of it?" A man in the audience agreed. "I was singled out at school because I had buck teeth." We explained that buck teeth did not determine the area of town he could live in or whether he could attend that school or not. "I don't have one bit of prejudice and I don't think most of the people in this room do," said a woman at the rear. "I don't feel any prejudice toward Jews, toward Catholics, toward anyone on the panel but Gwen Riley and I can't understand why you are talking to us. Why don't you go to the groups where there is prejudice?" "However far you've come, we have someone to answer your problem," Gwen said, smiling. "If it's the Jew, we can help you there. If it's everyone but Gwen—if I'm your problem—we're here for that too." The audience howled. After the program a little middle-aged woman came up and shook Gwen's hand vigorously. "There were people in this church who thought the roof would fall in if a Negro were ever allowed to come in," she said. "I'm glad they can see it's still standing."

I met civil rights leaders from across the South in Gwen's kitchen who were working with Negail to plan sit-in strategies for college students at the lunch counters in Kress and McClellan's downtown. From them I learned more about the civil rights movement and how important it was to have a bridge like the panel to interpret it back to the community at large.

A *Gazette* editorial in 1963 welcomed the arrival of the panel to Little Rock, declaring, "the 'testimony' of these courageous women offers a revealing commentary on the universality of prejudice—and on its nuances. . . . This problem cries out for attention, and in handing out credits to people who are working on remedies, Little Rock's 'Panel of Americans' must be high on anybody's list."[2]

Starting out as a white Presbyterian who grew up in a small Tennessee town, the closest thing I knew to religious prejudice was the way my father felt about Methodists, Baptists, and Church of Christ members whom he called Campbellites. (The latter referred to a person named Campbell who organized the denomination.) There were no Jews or Catholics in my hometown of Wartrace. Daddy felt superior to but tolerated Methodists and Baptists, but he was certain the Campbellites were dead wrong in their religion. Our house was next door to the Church of Christ, and at night he would stand in the althea bushes that separated our property and listen to their preachers. He would later march up and down the house refuting what they had said. It also irritated him that they did not use instrumental music, which they said was not sanctioned by the Bible. They sang a cappella and often off-key, unaided by the upright piano in the church and the pump organ in the Sunday school rooms we had at the Presbyterian church. My father believed that congregations should be accompanied. He also believed that you sprinkled for baptizing, and the Campbellites were dead wrong on that score for dunking new converts under, like the Baptists did. We felt the closest to the Methodists because they sprinkled too, and in addition, my mother had been one before she married.

My closest friend was a Church of Christ member, and I spent a lot of time with her on the front row of those nightly evangelistic services while I knew Daddy was in the althea bushes shaking his head in strong disagreement with everything that was said. It made the plea to come up front and accept Jesus at the end of each service like sweet, forbidden fruit that especially tempted me because I knew what it would do to my father just outside the open window of the church.

The black churches were on the other side of town, as were the black homes and a one-room elementary school. When we discussed who we agreed and disagreed with in the community, we meant the white community. We only had direct contact with those blacks who worked for us. When the woman who did our washing got sick, I went with my mother to visit her. I often went with her to take food or Christmas gifts to some of the blacks she knew. But as far as knowing any blacks as equals or knowing any Jews or Catholics at all, I did not as a child. Although my horizons were broadened in graduate school in New York, I still had a lot to learn when I started the panel. I had no idea the profound effect the panel would have on my life.

Change came fast in the South in the 1960s. The metamorphosis of a society cracking out of its carefully constructed two-race class system was something to behold. It took a while for community leaders to realize that all the money that had been spent on building two of everything from schools to drinking fountains and restrooms had been a bad investment. *Brown v. Topeka* had brought a flurry of black school construction in the 1950s by school boards who thought that belatedly obeying the earlier "separate but equal" mandate might ward off any serious integration. By the 1960s, more court decisions and the Civil Rights Act of 1964 made it clear that the clock would not turn back. And there we were, with such glaring mistakes as costly school buildings schizophrenically placed as far away from each other as they could be on either end of each Southern town. Busing children long distances could not be avoided, considering how short-sighted school boards had placed the schools.

The panel appealed to me at the outset because it was a means of presenting facts about social change to audiences of the unconverted. Little Rock was split into two communities that did not communicate or know enough about each other to solve problems together. Whites, in fact, did not believe blacks could or should be participants in decision-making because they did not accord full human status to blacks. White males generally felt the same way about women. Another reason for my interest in the panel was that it was something women could do to change the unreasonably hierarchical structure in which they, like blacks, were caught.

■　　■　　■

Although we occasionally spoke to black audiences, the panel was mainly directed toward reaching and changing those whites who were not likely to receive human rights education of other kinds. Since open discussion of the problems of prejudice, particularly as they affected blacks, was considered controversial and dangerous, many white Southerners had never had an opportunity to hear, on a person-to-person basis, how their own prejudice affected others. The women on the panel were able to overcome this taboo and bring those problems into focus as a first step toward solving them.

As I began searching for panelists, I got to know a side of Little Rock I had never known before. We could not just blame Governor Faubus for what happened at Central High School. Those prejudices he played upon ran deep in the grain of the community. Interviewing panelists, I heard about that bigotry firsthand. A black panelist told me about her father being beaten and jailed to make him confess to a crime he was unaware had been committed. I heard another black woman tell about her husband sitting all night with a shotgun across his lap at a picture window to protect a neighbor who had helped the nine black students enroll at Central High School. Her window had been shattered by gunshots fired from cars driving up and down the street. A Jewish panelist showed me a vicious anti-Semitic paper published in Little Rock. She also had me tune in on a radio program featuring the same preacher who edited the paper denouncing Jews. A Catholic friend told me how her children had been taunted by neighborhood children who told them that the Catholic Church was evil and persecuted people. I also heard about a neighborhood that circulated a petition to get rid of an Asian couple who had moved in. All of this had happened not somewhere else but here in Little Rock where I lived and was rearing my children.

As we wrote speeches, I learned what an uphill battle it had been for some blacks to get where they were. I had worked at three jobs and borrowed money to get through college, but Faustenia Bomar, the registrar at Philander Smith College, had persevered through worse. She remembered existing on a diet of cornbread and molasses so that she could stay in school. The day we put the final touches on her speech we were sitting in her office watching the civil rights march on Washington. "It will be different for my grand-children," Bomar said. And we believed with all our hearts that it would be.

Later, the sedate, reserved Bomar appeared on a panel before a church audience one evening when, during the question period, a teenager stood and looked directly at her. "You're different, but most Negroes get drunk on Saturday night, are dirty, and have low morals. If they were all like you it would be all right but they aren't." Bomar looked back at him with a disarming smile. "The only Negroes you probably know are those you have seen mowing lawns and working in white homes. Nearly all of them would choose a better lifestyle if they could. I'm sorry you don't know more blacks because I'm not that unusual. There are many, many more like me and I wish you could know some of them."

A woman in the audience, obviously irritated by the boy's question, proceeded to squelch him with: "Isn't it a shame that some of us with no more than a high school education feel that a black must have a Ph.D. before he's good enough to associate with us?" Later, the church formed a committee to call Bomar and express regret about the incident.

The idea that all blacks carouse on Saturday night was brought up on another panel of which Mildred Terry, an elementary school teacher, happened to be a member. "I can't answer for all blacks but I can tell you about my family," said Terry, laughing. "We spend Saturday evening polishing shoes and studying Sunday school lessons in preparation for going to church the next morning." In her panel speech, Terry told about how her son, Alvin, was punched in the back, knocked down the steps, and repeatedly called "nigger" at the West Side Junior High School where he was one of the first black students to attend. After one panel program, a white student came up and offered to carry the sound equipment to the car. When he and Terry were alone, he said: "You don't know me but you would if I told you my name. I was one of those boys who harassed Alvin. I hadn't thought about how it made him feel until I heard you talking today. Please tell him I'm sorry I did it." "I certainly did remember his name when he gave it," Terry said later, laughing. "He made

Alvin's life miserable but I can't get over what he said today. I was really moved to know he finally understood what he had done."

Benton, twenty miles south of Little Rock, was a town that blacks knew to pass through quickly because it had a reputation for being a bad place for them. The local Rotary Club worked for two months prior to the panel's appearance getting the restaurant in which they met to agree to serve blacks so Bomar could come. "I have always been afraid to drive through this town," Bomar said triumphantly on the panel that night. "Blacks have always been made to feel unwelcome here. Yet here I am seated in this lovely restaurant having dinner with you tonight." The Rotarians interrupted her with applause, and two more invitations to appear in Benton were received.

But not all of our bookings turned out so well. A man who had invited us to speak at the Presbyterian Church in Conway called to uninvite us. An interracial meeting had been held at the church a few nights before at which the inadequacies of a Negro school were discussed, and the meeting was covered in the local paper. The ensuing furor caused him to call the minister about the panel appearance. The minister called a meeting of the church session and they decided that, since there was some unrest in the church about the previous meeting, they simply would not have the panel at that time. I was annoyed at the fear projected by the ruling body of this church and said so. "Your church has a chance to make a real witness to its commitment to what it stands for," I said. "I am saddened by the fact that it does not feel it can openly discuss a topic that involves no more than learning to live with and love one's neighbor."

After the Women's City Club booked us, the program chairman called and inquired: "Is there a Negro [whispered] on the panel?" When I said yes, she went on: "We really want to hear the panel, but would it be possible for you to come without the Negro? It's in our constitution that we can't let Negroes join, and we also don't allow them on programs, because if you let the barriers down one place, you let them down everywhere else. I'm not prejudiced, but the other members are."

In addition to losing that one, the Business and Professional Women's Club at Hot Springs voted against having the panel after the program chairman had invited us. "I was appalled by the prejudice shown when the program came up for discussion," she later reported. Program chairmen became crusaders in their own right as they took up the cause of getting us past reluctant boards and committees. They often had to cajole and reassure boards that the panel would not "stir up trouble" but would offer a chance for low-key, reasonable dialogue about a problem they were not accustomed to discussing.

■   ■   ■

It was dusk when we rolled into Stuttgart, the center for the state in rice production and duck hunting. We could see the sun setting over the vast, flat fields that surrounded the town. Most of us had been busy at other things all day before we headed out to do the panel at the Methodist Church there, and we were tired and hungry. We looked around for a place to eat on the town's main street, and the best prospect seemed to be the Esquire Cafe. We parked the car and went in.

There were only a few people scattered around, one of them a thin, blonde man on a counter stool. We seated ourselves on other counter stools and waited for someone to serve us. The waitress behind the counter nodded toward us and looked questioningly at the blonde man, who turned around and eyed us with hostility. He got up slowly and came toward us. "If you want to eat here, there's a place for you out back," he said, glaring at me, whom he had already identified as the leader of the group. "You're saying we can't be served here?" I asked. "That's correct," he said. "Not unless you go out to the other room." We knew what "the other room" was. Lots of restaurants in Southern towns had white sections in front and black sections in the back. I arose with all the dignity I could muster, followed by Gwen Riley and the others. "Then we do not wish to eat here," I said.

Later, as we presented the panel at the church, the words had special meaning as we thought about the hate on the man's face back in the restaurant. While I listened to the other women speak, I wondered uneasily if he might be calling some of his buddies. I could imagine that, after a few bottles of beer, they might be waiting for us on that deserted stretch of road that we would have to cover before we got to the main highway. I decided I must be crazy to have brought the mothers of fourteen children into this town seething with irrational hatred. I thought about how nice and safe it was at home, with all the children bedded down, but I did not want to be there at all. I wanted to be right here. I remembered what Martin Luther King had said that something in a person dies when she fails to stand up for what she knows is right. I would not have traded all the security in the world for getting to say what we said in Stuttgart that night.

After we finished the speeches, we got some innocuous questions about religion. Then a whiny-voiced woman said she guessed all the prejudice was in the big cities. They certainly did not have any against Catholics or Jews because it was such a nice, friendly little town. "Yes, I'm sure this is normally a nice, hospitable town," I said. "But we are also a nice bunch of ladies, and we were not able to get our supper here because a restaurant owner refused to let us sit down at his counter and eat." Connie Obsitnik, the Catholic on the panel, said, "It's not just Gwen's freedom that was at stake. It was all of ours too. We couldn't get a sandwich either."

"We don't want a Selma here," said the minister, Reverend Golden. "We're afraid. Outside agitators can come in and stir things up. We don't want them—we have to move slowly to keep from having trouble." (I like to remember what President Roosevelt said, "The only thing we have to fear is fear itself.") "How slowly do you think we should go?" asked Riley sweetly, "We've been waiting a hundred years to be treated like other Americans." "You all don't understand the other side," said a man from DeWitt. "I run a drugstore and I have to make money. If I serve Negroes I'll lose my business. But if you all had come in my drugstore, I'd have seen that you were served if I had to do it myself. I'd have surely been glad when you left though!"

"I understand the importance of money, but I wonder if you realize [what] you're losing when you refuse to take mine," said Riley. "It's green, like everyone else's. If all the businessmen in town got together and agreed to obey the law, as they have done in many towns, then you wouldn't have to worry about other customers going down the street to another place." Jean Gordon, the white Protestant added, "If we showed concern and tried to solve our own problems, there wouldn't be any fear of outside agitators."

The "outside agitators" theme recurred all evening. One woman talked at length about how they had gotten along well for so long side by side in Stuttgart. Other white people told her it would continue that way if outside agitators would stay away because "we treat our Negroes so well." "Excuse me, but they are not our Negroes," said Obsitnik. She also suggested jokingly that maybe *we* were outside agitators, but they protested strongly that no, they had invited us there. And then they started speaking up. A man said he guessed the black problem was their real problem of prejudice, and a woman said something about man's inhumanity to man. The others were not through though. One asked about the African's treatment of whites and another asked about demonstrations in northern cities. Raida Snyderman, the Jewish panelist, explained that there had to be demonstrations to let people know how they felt and that fights started only when someone tried to block them. Snyderman had been quite shaken by the restaurant experience.

After the meeting, we were swamped with people who stayed to talk. One man told me he had never known that you could discuss such things out in the open, and he was amazed it could be done with such poise as we had demonstrated. A woman wanted to know how Riley could be so intelligent and beautiful. Two teenagers, who had heard us at Camp Tanakoe the summer before, came up to tell what happened afterward. "Later, at a regional camp, I was seated at a table with a black girl and I started to get up. Then I remembered what you said on the panel and I didn't leave. I sat and ate with her every day and I wouldn't have done that if I hadn't heard the panel." The other girl also had made a black friend at the regional camp on the strength of our panel exposure.

After the meeting, before refreshments, we stood in a circle with Riley included, crossed, and held each others' hands and sang the "Doxology." Later, some of the attendees formed a committee and went to visit the restaurant owner and express their disapproval of what happened.

Since it was only a few months after the passage of the Civil Rights Act, Gwen and I decided to test its effectiveness. When we got back to Little Rock, we went to the FBI and related our experience with the restaurant. It was apparent they were not anxious to enforce this law, but our complaint put them on the spot. They promised to call on the restaurant owner, and we promised to send a panel back to the same restaurant later to see if anything had changed. We called on a six-foot-six priest named Father David Boileau to accompany the next panel going in that direction and to lunch at the Esquire Cafe. The bishop had exiled Boileau to Slovaktown in nearby rural Prairie County because of his activities in civil rights at Little Rock. The integrated group of women, with Boileau looming above them, triumphantly entered the restaurant and, without incident, ate and departed. "Why did we work so hard to integrate that place?" asked one of them afterward. "It was lousy food."

On another occasion, as we were leaving for a country church many miles from Little Rock, Pat suggested that I keep my motor running while we presented our program. I told the panel that as we drove up and Gwen giggled. "Your motor may not be running, but I notice you parked on a corner with plenty of space for a quick getaway." When we went inside the church, I rounded up the program chair who hesitantly showed us to the restroom. Her attitude implied that this was not part of the bargain. We returned to the front row of the church sanctuary where we sang two hymns, uncomfortably conscious of the steely stares in our direction throughout the songs. When we were seated before the audience and I looked them directly in the eye for the first time, my heart began pounding hard. They looked for all the world like the grim faces in the well-known Grant Wood painting. Only the pitchfork was missing.

In the middle of Sissy Griffin's Catholic speech, police calls began to come in over our public address system. We learned later that two teenagers had tuned in police calls on a car radio just outside the church window for that reason. It occurred to me that we might be greeted with a mob at the back of the church because I had no idea how many were outside. I went over, calmly turned off the public address system, and told the women to continue. I was no longer afraid. "Do you feel that more educated people have less prejudice?" a hesitant questioner asked when we got to the question period. Ruth Kretchmar, a Jewish panelist, shook her head and smiled. "It's a matter of the heart, not of the mind."

Someone asked if the problem could not be better solved by the church than by law. Gwen answered that the fact that she would like to stop for a cup of coffee with the rest of the panel had nothing to do with religion. She also pointed out that eleven o'clock Sunday morning in churches was the most segregated place anywhere. Afterward, every single member of the church filed by to tell us it was the best program they had ever had. One old farmer, whose weather-beaten face reflected years of hard work, squeezed Gwen's hand and said in a low voice: "Forgive us our trespasses." We will never forget that night.

■   ■   ■

Not very many years ago, although there were plenty of people who did not like liberals, liberalism had not become the unmentionable "L" word that it is today. At the height of the Cold War, when we were told the Soviet Union was the evil empire and all Russians were the enemy, anyone who called for progressive change in our system was labeled a Communist. "Liberal" was not strong enough. In the South especially, the uses for Communist labelling included keeping women in their place and the blacks in their own schools.

When I was working on an early childhood project at the Arkansas State Department of Education in the early 1970s, women were expected to put either "Miss" or "Mrs." in front of their names when signing letters. Buried in the bureaucracy and with no outlet for expressing my burgeoning interest in the women's movement, I decided to sign my letters "Ms." It was a small, token gesture that no doubt left many school administrators thinking a typographical error had been made. None of them ever challenged it.

Then one day, I had to appear before a legislative committee to request funds for early childhood education. The program was under fire because sentiment was at that time strongly against offering public education to children under five or six. A short, rotund doctor, whose last name was Royal and who was serving in the legislature from Royal, Arkansas, peered at me over his glasses and asked:

"Don't you sign your name as 'Ms. Sara Murphy'?" he asked.

I admitted that I did, wondering what that had to do with early childhood education.

"Do you know what that means?" his voice took on a sinister tone as he pursued the questioning.

"Yes, I do," I replied. "It means that I believe it is irrelevant at work whether I am "Miss" or "Mrs." I prefer not to be classified in that way."

"But do you know what it *really* means?" he asked again.

I looked at him blankly. He leaned across the table conspiratorially so that we were almost eyeball to eyeball.

"What it really means is 'Marxist sister.'" He almost spit out the words.

Funding for the program was handily defeated for which I was sorry, but I was pleasantly surprised to find that the "Ms." had made such an impact. As I arrived at higher levels of feminist enlightenment, I, of course, dropped the "Ms." because titles before names on letters and in newspaper stories were used only for women and the practice was sexist in itself.

This was not the first—or last—time that I was called a Communist. The first was a decade or so before when Billy Rector and his friends became upset when I had the audacity to run for the Little Rock School Board. Other times were when we were doing the Panel of American Women and a member of the audience, hoping to discredit us because we were an integrated group of women, would ask:

"Aren't you all Communists?"

We had a wonderful answer that we delivered with a smile.

"No, we aren't." That was all. No explanation, no defensiveness, no attempt to let him know we thought there was something good inside him too. It usually rendered the questioner, who had hoped to gain the floor for further questioning, as silent as the power structure had been when Faubus closed the schools.

# Epilogue

*July 6, 1992*

I visited the Terry mansion today. It is now the Decorative Arts Museum, a part of the Arkansas Arts Center. I went in through the front gate and up the long brick walk to the columned porch, where, on a sunny October day back in 1958, we had placed tables to sign up for committee tasks in the Women's Emergency Committee to Open Our Schools. It was also where we had stood when we announced the end of the WEC in 1963.

Inside, I was greeted by a young black guard in uniform at a desk. The rooms were full of boxes that contained the most recent museum exhibit being taken down. I went into the two front parlors, where the fireplaces were just as I remembered them, except that Mrs. Terry's father, in his Confederate uniform, was no longer over the mantelpiece. I missed him. When we gathered at that first WEC meeting at Mrs. Terry's, his presence seemed to furnish us the credibility we needed. His portrait established that we were not outsiders plotting against the South, but indigenous women who knew it was time to change. There was something reassuring and solid about having him there, but something even more solid and reassuring about his white-haired, gracious descendant, whose sparkling eyes and slight smile told us that she was already chuckling inwardly about what she knew we could do together.

I wandered back to the dining room where expensive, stylish antique furnishings had replaced the heavy old buffet, the sturdy, upholstered chairs, and the much used dining-room table of Mrs. Terry's time. We used to sit around that massive dark oak table and make monumental decisions as the WEC board. Mrs. Terry, at the end of the table, reading the *New York Times* while directing the work of the cook in the kitchen and the gardener outside, would follow our lengthy discussions and sometimes arguments, never missing a beat. A single word from her as she peered through her glasses would settle the debate and the meeting would move on. Outside in the atrium that adjoined the dining room, Mrs. Terry's parrot would squawk in assent. A great wave of homesickness for Mrs. Terry and the parrot and the comfortable old table came over me. I realized what an anchor she had been for me and many other young Little Rock women through a time of terrible transition from the past to what was then a still uncertain future. I wanted the old table back, and I wanted Mrs. Terry back to tell us we would still make it through.

I told the young guard about our gathering there to get the schools open and integrated. I also told him about the house's ghost. I climbed the wide steps that I remembered sitting on when, at later WEC meetings, so many women came that there were not enough chairs. At the top of the steps were more boxes and a bright, modern vase not yet packed. Plaques and pictures on the wall recorded the history of the house from the time it was built in 1840 by Albert Pike. The plaques seemed woefully incomplete in capturing the spirit of the house's early use.

Nowhere was there a mention of its use as the headquarters for the rebellion of a large group of Little Rock women who protested in 1958 the closing of their high schools by Gov. Orval Faubus to avoid integration. Nowhere was it mentioned that Mrs. Terry had served as the general who guided that rebellion to its successful conclusion. If it had been a men's war, you can bet it would be recorded on those plaques. The WEC is no more than a footnote or a paragraph, if mentioned at all, in the published accounts of the Central High School crisis at Little Rock. Yet, as finally noted modestly on a plaque at a branch library named in Terry's honor in 1990, "The Women's Emergency Committee to Open Our Schools, under Mrs. Terry's leadership, became a rallying point for citizens who succeeded in reopening the city's high schools which had been closed by the governor to prevent integration."[1]

A young woman who had recently moved from Kansas to Little Rock stopped me outside the Terry mansion as I was leaving and asked where she could see a house furnished as it used to be. She was disappointed to learn that the Terry home was now a museum for decorative arts instead of a restoration of what it had been in earlier times. Mrs. Terry was not into interior decorating and seeing it as it once was might not have been what the young woman expected either. It had been filled with an odd assortment of furniture the Terry and Fletcher families had used for many years, some of it quite old and interesting but not the elegant period pieces the newcomer no doubt hoped to see.

Mrs. Terry and her sister, when they had deeded the home to the city of Little Rock upon their deaths, wanted the place to be "alive and enjoyed by the people of Arkansas." A former WEC member, after visiting one exhibit, said she had a hard time associating Mrs. Terry with all those little "tinkly glass things," but Mrs. Terry would not particularly mind. She would be glad that lots of people visit the house now to see the exhibits, whatever they are. And if she were here, she would be engaging them in spirited debates about politics and philosophy, glancing only peripherally at the material things on display.

# Notes

## Introduction

1. Gunnar Myrdal, *An American Dilemma* (New York: Harper & Row, 1944), 1073–78.
2. Lillian Smith, *Killers of the Dream* (1949; reprint, New York: W. W. Norton, 1978), 144–45.
3. Ibid., 146–47.
4. Anne C. Loveland, *Lillian Smith, A Southerner Confronting the South* (Baton Rouge: Louisiana State University Press, 1986), 118.

## Chapter 1 / Adolphine Fletcher Terry

1. John Gould Fletcher, *Arkansas* (1947; reprint, Fayetteville: University of Arkansas Press, 1989), ix, 96–98. Fletcher called Pike a great orator, a prominent lawyer, a poet, and "the most eminent man in Arkansas" in the 1830s.
2. Mike Trimble, "A Portrait of Albert Pike: Surviving a Tortured Existence," *Arkansas Times,* 15 September 1994.
3. John Gould Fletcher, *The Autobiography of John Gould Fletcher* (1937; reprint, Fayetteville: University of Arkansas Press, 1988), 10.
4. Adolphine Fletcher Terry, *Cordelia: Member of the Household* (Fort Smith: South and West Press, 1967), 5–6.
5. Fletcher, *Arkansas,* 100.
6. Terry, *Cordelia,* 6. In *The Ghosts of an Old House,* John Gould Fletcher does not allude to Mary Pike's ghost other than to refer to hearing "dull dragging feet go fumbling down those dark back stairs."
7. Terry, *Cordelia,* 6; Adolphine Terry, "Life Is My Song, Too," Fletcher-Terry Papers, Archives and Special Collections, University of Arkansas at Little Rock Library, 20. Mrs. Terry writes that Albert Pike and his wife "weren't suited to each other."
8. Terry, *Cordelia,* 6–7; additional accounts of the ghost and the children's deaths appear in Terry, "Life Is My Song, Too," 20–21.

9. Fletcher, *Arkansas,* 97. Fletcher writes that by 1851 Pike was considering settling in New Orleans, and by 1852–53, he was already visiting Washington.

10. Terry, *Cordelia,* 7.

11. Betty Fulkerson, "The Albert Pike House . . . the House that Kept Up," *Delta Review* 4, no. 1, (January–February 1967): 29, 58.

12. Terry, *Cordelia,* 6–7. The Mary Pike stories also appear in Terry, "Life Is My Song, Too," 20–22.

13. Fletcher, *Arkansas,* 96.

14. Ibid., 100; Terry, *Cordelia,* 6.

15. Terry, *Cordelia,* 6.

16. Terry, "Life Is My Song, Too," 4.

17. Ibid., 21–22.

18. Ibid., 22–23. Also, brochure prepared by the Decorative Arts Museum, The Arkansas Arts Center, Little Rock.

19. Terry, "Life Is My Song, Too," 1–2, 6–9.

20. Terry, *Cordelia,* 4, 8–12; the "black sister" reference came from an interview with Terry's son, Bill Terry, by the author, 13 August 1992; Terry, "Life Is My Song, Too," 41–42, points out that Mary Durham became very close to Adolphine's mother when Mrs. Fletcher lost her first child, and she took in Cordelia in part because of their close friendship. Terry noted, however, that she seemed to be less anxious about them, mentioning kidnapping as a possibility that seemed to be of concern, "after Cordelia came to live with us."

21. Terry, *Cordelia,* 26.

22. Adolphine Fletcher Terry, *Charlotte Stephens: Little Rock's First Black Teacher* (Little Rock: Academic Press of Arkansas, 1973), 21–23. This same account is also in Terry, *Cordelia,* 47–48.

23. Terry, "Life Is My Song, Too," 38–39.

24. Ibid., 60–61.

25. Interview with Edwin Dunaway by the author, 18 August 1992.

26. Terry, "Life Is My Song, Too," 85–88.

27. Ibid., 82–83; Sara Murphy, "Education," in *Arkansas: State of Transition,* ed. Louis Guida (Legal Services Corporation, 1981), 46.

28. Terry, "Life Is My Song,Too," 93–98. "More blacks than whites at wedding," from interview with daughter-in-law Betty Terry by author, August 13, 1992.

29. Terry, "Life Is My Song, Too," 102–9.

30. Adolphine Terry [Mary Lindsey, pseud.], *Courage* (New York: E. P. Dutton, 1938), 175.

31. Carolyn Auge, "Adolphine Fletcher Terry, 1882–1976," *Quapaw Chronicle* (August/September, 1976), Fletcher-Terry Papers.

32. *Arkansas Gazette,* 10 November 1917.

33. Kay Koehler, "Woman Suffrage Pioneers Recall the Early Days— and Look Ahead," *Arkansas Gazette,* 22 June 1969.

34. Adolphine Fletcher Terry calendar-diary, 4 January 1958, Fletcher-Terry Papers, Archives and Special Collections, University of Arkansas at Little Rock Library.

35. James Reed Eison, "Dead But She Was in a Good Place," *Pulaski County Historical Review* (summer 1982): 30–33. Eison's account relies on news stories that appeared in the *Arkansas Gazette* at the time. Peggy Harris, "We Would Be Building" (master's thesis, University of Arkansas at Little Rock, 1992); Marcet Haldeman-Julius, *The Story of a Lynching* (Girard, Kans.: Haldeman-Julius Publications, Little Blue Book No. 1260, n.d.).

36. Harry Ashmore, *Hearts and Minds: The Anatomy of Racism from Roosevelt to Reagan* (New York: McGraw Hill, 1982), 119.

37. Ibid.; "Feeling Is Tense," *Report of Association of Southern Women for the Prevention of Lynching* (Atlanta, Ga., 1938), Archives and Special Collections, University of Arkansas at Little Rock Library, 10–13.

38. From transcribed interview with Adolphine Terry by John Pagan, January 1973.

39. Dunaway interview, 18 August 1992.

40. Ibid.

41. Terry, "Life Is My Song, Too," 139–42.

42. Dunaway interview, 18 August 1992.

43. Terry, "Life Is My Song, Too," 158–64, 171–72.

44. Dunaway interview, 18 August 1992.

45. Terry, "Life Is My Song, Too," 154.

46. "Reminiscences of Jessie Daniel Ames: 'I Really Do Like a Good Fight,'" 1964 interview with Pat Watters, transcribed and edited by Jacqueline Hall, *New South* (spring 1972): 31.

47. *Report of Association of Southern Women for the Prevention of Lynching* (1937), Archives and Special Collections, University of Arkansas at Little Rock Library, 8, 17.

48. Ibid., 8.

49. "Reminiscences of Jessie Daniel Ames," 34.

50. "With Quietness They Work," *Report of Association of Southern Women for the Prevention of Lynching* (1937).

51. "Reminiscences of Jessie Daniel Ames," 36.

52. Jacqueline Hall, *Revolt Against Chivalry, Jessie Daniel Ames and the Women's Campaign Against Lynching* (New York: Columbia University Press, 1979), 99–100.

53. Terry calendar-diary, 13 June 1938.

54. Interview with Edwin Dunaway by author, 22 June 1993; B–12, Guide to Little Rock Housing Authority Scrapbooks, 1, Archives and Special Collections, University of Arkansas at Little Rock Library.

55. Dunaway interview, 18 August 1992.

56. *Arkansas Gazette,* 3 June 1951. Ives was later to have the Tuxedo Courts housing project renamed for her.

57. Griffin Smith, "Localism and Segregation, Racial Patterns in Little Rock, Arkansas, 1945–1954," (master's thesis, Columbia University, 1965), 42.

58. Ibid., 46.

59. Ibid., 45–50.

60. *Arkansas Gazette,* 3 June 1951.

61. Smith, "Localism and Segregation," 58.

62. Ibid., 59.

63. Interview with Harry Ashmore by author, 13 June 1994.

64. *Arkansas Democrat,* 27 April 1950, B12.

65. *Arkansas Gazette,* 11 May 1950.

66. Smith, "Localism and Segregation," 64. Blacks had originally spoken out for a park near Philander Smith College when the original discussion of spending money on Gillam Park was pursued, but the 1949 bond issue was only for Gillam.

67. *Arkansas Gazette,* 21 February 1953.

68. Interviews with Charles Bussey by author, 30 August 1993, and Vircie Winstead, who worked for the Housing Authority for many years, by author, 7 September 1993.

69. "Housewives Appeal to Little Rock School Board Not to Take Their Homes," *Arkansas Gazette,* August 1952.

70. *Arkansas Gazette,* 18 July 1952.

71. Bussey interview, 30 August 1993. Bussey added that I. S. McClinton, a black political leader, and Harry Bass of the Urban League were Little Rock Housing Authority liaisons for vote-getting in the black community. This was a role Bussey himself was to assume with prominent whites later on. Bussey later became the first black mayor of Little Rock.

72. *Arkansas Gazette,* 1 April 1952.

73. *State Press,* 30 January 1953.

74. Interview with Annie Abrams by author, 19 May 1993.

75. Story about Urban League, *Arkansas Gazette,* 3 June 1951, and petition story, *State Press,* 23 May 1952, both in Little Rock Housing Authority Scrapbooks; interviews with Charles Bussey, 19 May 1993, with Fred Darragh, 27 May 1993, and with Dunaway, all by author.

76. Adolphine F. Terry to Lester B. Granger, executive secretary, National Urban League, 5 January 1954, Urban League File, series I, box 103, Library of Congress, Washington, D.C.

77. *Arkansas Gazette,* 21 September 1952.

78. *Arkansas Gazette,* 27–31 July 1952.

79. Terry calendar-diary, 14 September 1958.

80. Ashmore interview; Ashmore speech, 14 June 1966, at Arkansas Council on Human Relations dinner honoring Terry.

# Chapter 2 / Little Rock in the 1950s

1. Betty Friedan, *The Feminine Mystique* (New York: Dell Publishing Company, 1963), 15.

2. A few black families moved many miles into the country farther west where, by the 1990s, white developers were making an attempt to push them out once again to make way for the ever-expanding, still mostly white, suburbs. An example is the black community of Pankey on the western edge of Little Rock. The residents of Pankey, some of whom moved from West Rock seven or eight miles to the west, are now under pressure, as white suburban expansion continues westward, to move again. It has a striking similarity to what happened to the Indians in this country a century or so ago.

3. Wilson Record and Jane Cassels Record, *Little Rock, U.S.A.* (San Francisco: Chandler Publishing Company, 1960), 18, quotes *Southern School News* as saying buses were desegregated in Little Rock and North Little Rock on April 25, 1956.

4. Smith, "Localism and Segregation," 43; interviews with Sanford Tollette, 13 August 1993, and with James Humphrey, 16 August 1993, both by author. Tollette said he was taken to the pool by his mother the first day where he said he and other black children were made to shower twice before being allowed in the pool. The author's children were also present that day.

5. The objecting board member could have been J. N. Heiskell, although Terry does not identify him as such. Fred Darragh recalled that

when Booker Worthen asked him to go on the Library Board some time after the Little Rock crisis, Darragh told him they needed a black on the board. Worthen told him that Mr. Heiskell would not have a black at that time. Darragh interview.

6. Terry, "Life Is My Song, Too," 228; Smith, "Localism and Segregation," 80; minutes of the Little Rock Library Board of Trustees, January 10, 1951.

7. Interview with Evangeline Upshur by the author, 23 July 1992. While Dr. Upshur was a "first" in Little Rock, she pointed out that a black female dentist had come to North Little Rock in the 1930s but stayed only a short time.

8. Smith, "Localism and Segregation," 81; Record, *Little Rock, U.S.A.,* 18. This coincided with the Montgomery, Alabama, bus boycott that occurred after Rosa Parks refused to move to the back of the bus in that city in late 1955.

9. Women were prominent in the Montgomery bus struggle, including the indomitable Rosa Parks, who started the boycott when she refused to move to the back of the bus. A black college professor named Jo Ann Robinson and her Women's Political Council ran mimeograph machines all night so people could get the word to stay off the Montgomery buses the next morning. A handful of white women, including a librarian named Juliette Morgan, wrote letters to the editor defending the action of the blacks and drove their cars to pick up their black maids, who were shunning the buses. Taylor Branch, *Parting the Waters: America in the King Years, 1954–63* (New York: Simon & Schuster, 1988), 129, 145, 164, 193.

10. Numan V. Bartley, *The Rise of Massive Resistance: Race and Politics in the South During the 1950s* (Baton Rouge: Louisiana State University Press, 1969), 253.

11. Record, *Little Rock, U.S.A.,* 13.

12. Ashmore, *Hearts and Minds,* 216–19; Harry S. Ashmore, *Civil Rights and Wrongs* (New York: Pantheon Books, 1994), 105.

13. This is taken from an account the author wrote in 1965 of the event.

14. Bartley, *Rise of Massive Resistance,* 254.

15. Ibid., 255.

16. John Pagan, "Orval Eugene Faubus and the Politics of Racism," (unpublished essay, Oxford University, 1974), 6–7.

17. Virgil Blossom, *It Has Happened Here* (New York: Harper Brothers, 1959), 15–16.

18. Daisy Bates, *The Long Shadow of Little Rock* (1962; reprint, Fayetteville: University of Arkansas Press, 1987), 51–52.

19. Orval Faubus, *Down From the Hills* (Little Rock: Pioneer Press, 1980), 200–204; Blossom, *It Has Happened Here*, 58–66; Numan V. Bartley, "Looking Back at Little Rock," *Arkansas Historical Quarterly* 25 (summer 1966): 110.

20. Interview with Orval Faubus by author, 19 August 1992.

21. Neil R. McMillen, "White Citizens' Council and Resistance to School Desegregation in Arkansas," *Arkansas Historical Quarterly* 30 (summer 1971): 95–99.

22. Blossom, *It Has Happened Here*, 27–28.

23. *Arkansas Gazette, Crisis in the South, The Little Rock Story* (*Arkansas Gazette*, 1958), 94; Bates, *Long Shadow of Little Rock*, 53.

24. Blossom, *It Has Happened Here*, 37.

25. McMillen, "White Citizens' Council," 101.

26. *Arkansas Gazette*, 22–23 August 1957.

27. Faubus is quoted in the *Southern School News*, September 1957, 6–7, as saying, "People are coming to me and saying if Georgia doesn't have integration why does Arkansas have it?"

28. Interview with Ruth Arnold Ray by author, 12 June 1992; Vivion Brewer, "The Embattled Ladies of Little Rock," Vivion Brewer Papers, Sophia Smith Collection, Smith College, Northampton, Massachusetts, 4. Brewer mentions that Mrs. Faubus told Mrs. Terry when the latter gave a tea for her that, because of the treatment Farrell had received at Central, "her husband was only too glad to have the chance to bring disgrace on Central High School."

29. Roy Reed, who was aware of the story circulated by the women and who spent many hours interviewing Faubus in the 1980s while preparing a Faubus biography, was convinced that it was not a factor in Faubus's decision to bar the black students from Central in 1957.

30. Faubus interview. Farrell later took his own life.

31. Ibid. The Cherrys were originally from Jonesboro in northeastern Arkansas.

32. Sam Faubus quoted in news article in *Time*, 23 September 1957, 13.

33. Ashmore, *Hearts and Minds*, 260.

34. Bartley, *Rise of Massive Resistance*, 263–65.

35. Blossom, *It Has Happened Here*, 47–48. The Mothers League speaker was identified in this account as W. R. Hughes of Dallas, executive committee chair of the Association of Citizens Councils of Texas.

# Chapter 3 / Crisis at Central High

1. Blossom, *It Has Happened Here,* 59–60, gives an account of the Thomason lawsuit.

2. *Arkansas Gazette, Crisis in the South,* 94. Thomason filed the suit on August 27. Chancellor Murray O. Reed granted the temporary injunction she asked for because of the governor's testimony on August 29, and Federal District Judge Ronald N. Davies, brought down from North Dakota on temporary assignment, threw out the injunction on August 30.

3. Interview with Bill Shelton by author, 1 December 1993.

4. Interview with Gaston Williamson by author, 10 December 1993.

5. Blossom, *It Has Happened Here,* 74.

6. The Federal Bureau of Investigation did extensive interviews on the reported weapon sales and on other segregationist activities during September 1957 at Little Rock. Their findings are in an FBI file as part of the Little Rock Crisis Papers, Archives and Special Collections, University of Arkansas at Little Rock Library.

7. FBI reports for 8 September 1957, Little Rock Crisis Papers. Interviews with individual women documented that calls were made to get Mothers League members and others to come to Central High School at 6 P.M. September 3, 1957. Among the callers interviewed were Anita Sedberry, Mrs. O. R. Aaron, and Margaret Jackson.

8. Branch, *Parting the Waters,* 223.

9. Terry calendar-diary, 4 January 1958.

10. Ernest Q. Campbell and Thomas F. Pettigrew, *Christians in Racial Crisis: A Study of Little Rock's Ministry* (Washington, D.C.: Public Affairs Press, 1959), 21.

11. Jean Gordon was the other circulator of the petition supporting Virgil Blossom and his plan.

12. Interview with Daisy Bates by author, 16 April 1992.

13. Blossom, *It Has Happened Here,* 94–98.

14. Ibid., 102.

15. Interview with Henry Woods by author, 30 August 1992.

16. *Life Magazine,* 7 October 1957, 38–39.

17. Blossom, *It Has Happened Here,* 104–7; Record, *Little Rock, U.S.A.,* 59–63; Relman Morin story, *Sacramento Bee,* 23 September 1957.

18. Woods interview.

19. Ashmore, *Civil Rights and Wrongs,* 130.

20. *Arkansas Gazette,* 25 September 1958.

21. Blossom, *It Has Happened Here,* 133; *Arkansas Gazette, Crisis in the South,* 95.

22. *Arkansas Gazette, Crisis in the South,* 95–96; Melba Patillo Beals, *Warriors Don't Cry* (New York: Simon & Schuster, 1994), 195. Beals quotes from "Army Has Orders to Remove Troops of 101st at School,"*Arkansas Gazette,* 29 November 1957.

23. Beals, *Warriors Don't Cry,* 133–34.

24. Elizabeth Huckaby, *Crisis at Central High: Little Rock 1957–58* (Baton Rouge: Louisiana State University Press, 1980), 102.

25. Blossom, *It Has Happened Here,* 152–55; Huckaby, *Crisis at Central High,* 130.

26. Huckaby, *Crisis at Central High,* 111; Blossom, *It Has Happened Here,* 146.

27. Interview with Grainger Williams by author, 29 July 1992.

28. Terry calendar-diary, 28 January 1958.

29. Terry calendar-diary, 18 February 1958.

30. Bates, *Long Shadow of Little Rock,* 116; "Little Rock Today—The 42 Incidents," *New York Post,* 8 April 1958.

31. Bates, *Long Shadow of Little Rock,* 120–22.

32. Although not identified by name, Sammie Dean is the "blond with a pony-tail" in Huckaby, *Crisis at Central High,* 109, 135, 171.

33. Interview with Hazel Bryan Massery by author, 27 July 1992.

34. Interview with Sammie Dean Parker Hulett by author, Dallas, Texas, 9 December 1992.

35. Jerry Hulett, "Sammie's Story, A Biography of Sammie Parker Hulett," unpublished paper, University of Texas at Dallas, n.d.

36. Terry calendar-diary, 19 February 1958. This could have been entered later despite the date on the calendar because Terry would write over dates in occasional long stretches.

37. Terry calendar-diary, 27 February 1958.

38. Terry calendar-diary, 11 April 1958.

39. *Arkansas Gazette, Crisis in the South,* 97; Terry calendar-diary, 18 April 1958.

40. *Arkansas Gazette, Crisis in the South,* 98.

41. Adolphine Terry, "Life Is My Song, Too," 234.

42. Interview with Ernest Green by author, Washington, D.C., 7 December 1992.

43. Hulett interview. Hulett still thought that the black students had been recruited from New York, Minnesota, and other places outside Little Rock.

44. Green interview; interview with Mildred Terry (Green's cousin) by author, 17 November 1993.

45. *The Ernest Green Story,* a made-for-TV movie by Disney Productions; Beals, *Warriors Don't Cry.*

46. Hulett interview.

47. Massery interview.

48. Irving Spitzberg, *Racial Politics in Little Rock 1954–1964* (New York: Garland Publishing Company, 1987), 38–40; Elizabeth Jacoway, "Taken by Surprise," in *Southern Businessmen and Desegregation,* ed. by Elizabeth Jacoway and David R. Colburn (Baton Rouge: Louisiana State University Press, 1982), 19.

49. Spitzberg, *Racial Politics,* 70.

50. Jacoway, "Taken by Surprise," 28.

51. Ashmore interview; Ashmore, *Civil Rights and Wrongs,* 128.

52. Ashmore interview.

53. Spitzberg, *Racial Politics,* 39.

54. Paula Barnes, "The Junior League Eleven: Elite Women of the Little Rock Struggle for Social Justice," Sara Murphy Papers, Special Collections Division, University of Arkansas Libraries, Fayetteville.

55. Richard Martin, "Country Club of Little Rock: Still for Whites Only," *Arkansas Times,* 16–17. According to Martin, the first three Jews were admitted in the 1970s.

56. Ashmore interview.

57. J. N. Heiskell also received the medal for distinguished service to journalism from Syracuse (New York) School of Journalism and the first Columbia University Graduate School of Journalism Award, and he was made a 1958 Lovejoy Fellow of Colby College. *Southern Education News Report* copy, March 1958, May 1958, and July 1958.

58. Terry calendar-diary, 8 May 1958.

59. Terry calendar-diary, 14 May 1958. 9 May–3 June entries deal with details of the plans for the dinner and the dinner itself which are the basis of the account that follows.

60. Ashmore interview.

61. Upshur interview.

62. Ashmore interview.

63. Terry calendar-diary, 22 May–2 June 1958.

64. Capital Citizens Council rallies at Little Rock had been attracting two hundred–four hundred people that spring. One held after the dinner on July 19 attracted one thousand. The speaker was Dr. Henry Lyon of Montgomery, Alabama, who spoke on "Why Racial Integration is Un-Christian." *Southern Education News Report* copy, April 1958 and July

1958. But at the time of the *Arkansas Gazette* dinner, the Marion Hotel manager said this was its largest crowd ever. See *Arkansas Gazette, Crisis in the South*, 98.

65. Terry, "Life Is My Song, Too," 236.

66. Terry calendar-diary, 4 June 1958.

67. Terry calendar-diary, 29 April, 2 August 1958.

68. Woods interview.

69. Terry calendar-diary, 16 June, 23, 27 July 1958.

70. Terry calendar-diary, 6–30 July 1958.

71. Terry calendar-diary, 15 August 1958.

72. Terry calendar-diary, 31 August 1958.

73. Terry calendar-diary, 5–6 September 1958.


# Chapter 4 / Call Out the Women

1. Ashmore interview, in which he confirmed the hat and white gloves. Ashmore also told this story in his June 14, 1966, speech at a dinner honoring Adolphine Terry: "We came, finally, to the foreordained day when the governor padlocked the city's high schools and turned away all of Little Rock's children, white and colored alike. It was then that Miss Adolphine sighed and said, 'I see. The men have failed again. I'll have to send for the young ladies.'" Fletcher-Terry Papers.

2. John Pagan, "Orval Eugene Faubus," 72.

3. Brewer, "Embattled Ladies," 5; Terry calendar-diary, 12 September 1958.

4. Pagan, "Orval Eugene Faubus," 75, quoting from the *Arkansas Gazette*, 12 September 1958, 14A.

5. Terry calendar-diary, 12 September 1958.

6. *Arkansas Gazette*, 13 September 1958. Faubus has liked to argue that he did not close the high schools, the people did, when they voted, but his proclamation closed them for the interim period until the election. He argued, as he had done in 1957, that "domestic violence was impending."

7. Terry calendar-diary, 15 September 1958.

8. "Reprisal on School Board Pledged by Mothers League," *Arkansas Gazette*, 3 September 1958; "Mothers Group Condemns Use of Marshals," *Arkansas Gazette*, 3 September 1958; "Reactions Range from Sobs to Hope, From Defiance to Calm in Little Rock," *Arkansas Gazette*, 13 September 1958.

9. *Arkansas Gazette, Crisis in the South,* 100; interview with Frank Lambright by author, 18 August 1992.

10. *Arkansas Gazette,* "Mothers Say Recall Petitions Still Not Ready," 25 September 1958, 13A.

11. Terry calendar-diary, 18 September 1958.

12. Pagan, "Orval Eugene Faubus," 75, quoting the *Memphis Commercial Appeal,* 2 September 1958.

13. *Arkansas Gazette,* 4, 6 September 1958.

14. Pagan, "Orval Eugene Faubus," 75; Paul Mertz, "'Mind Changing Time All Over Georgia': HOPE, Inc. and School Desegregation, 1958–1961," *Georgia Historical Quarterly* 77 (spring 1993): 42.

15. Brewer, "Embattled Ladies," 5.

16. Ibid., 6.

17. Ibid., 7.

18. Interview with Frances Williams by author, 5 August 1992.

19. Bates interview. Bates told about her meeting with Terry, although it is not mentioned in the Terry accounts. Vivion Brewer reported in "Embattled Ladies" that "years later, Mrs. Daisy Bates told me that she had written a long article blasting our committee because we were working *for* the Negroes, not *with* them, but she put it away without publishing it in deference to Mrs. Terry whom she admired wholeheartedly."

20. Brewer, "Embattled Ladies," 7. The summary of the first meeting in the WEC minutes says, "the group numbered about 60," which is the figure Terry used in her diary.

21. Ashmore speech, 14 June 1966, Arkansas Council on Human Relations dinner honoring Terry.

22. Brewer, "Embattled Ladies," 11.

23. Ibid., 8.

24. Interview with Barbara Shults by author, 9 October 1992.

25. Brewer, "Embattled Ladies," 9.

26. Ibid., 10.

27. Terry calendar-diary, 12 September 1958.

28. Brewer, "Embattled Ladies," 9.

29. Terry calendar-diary, 16 September 1958.

30. The summary of the first meeting in the WEC minutes also said she had in mind an organization similar to the ASWPL. "This group played a major role in reducing the number of lynchings in the South to a fraction of what they had previously been."

31. Terry calendar-diary, 19 September 1958. Terry sometimes started writing on one date and continued on another, so exact dates in the diary do not always correspond with those on which she was writing.

32. Anonymous to A. Terry, 18 September 1958, Fletcher-Terry Papers.

33. Faubus interview.

34. Ibid.

35. *Arkansas Gazette, Crisis in the South,* 100.

36. Interview with Irene Samuel by author, 14 August 1993.

37. Brewer, "Embattled Ladies," 13–14.

38. Ibid., 9.

39. Ibid.

40. *Arkansas Gazette,* 17 September 1958, 2A.

41. Brewer, "Embattled Ladies," 10–11.

42. Ibid., 13.

43. Ibid., 33.

44. Interview with Charles Johnston by author, 4 November 1994.

45. Brewer, "Embattled Ladies," 25–26. The Ninth Street reference was to the 1927 lynching when the body of a black man was dragged along there.

46. Ibid., 10.

47. Ibid., 12.

48. "A Statement from Lawyers" (advertisement), *Arkansas Gazette,* 22 September 1958.

49. Interview with Bob Shults by author, 9 October 1992. The senior partner who changed his mind about signing, too late, was Will Mitchell, who later headed the decisive STOP campaign.

50. Ibid. The Friday firm, after several years of not representing the school board, was rehired in the 1990s and was still legal counsel to the board at the time this book was written.

51. *Arkansas Gazette,* 22 September 1958. Bob Shults was on the St. Paul board and Gordon Wilson, husband of Billie Wilson, a WEC steering committee member, was on the Westover Hills board. Frank Gordon, whose wife, Jean, was working in the WEC, was president of the latter.

52. Terry calendar-diary, 23 September 1958.

53. Ibid.; interview with Gwen Booe by author, 3 June 1992.

54. Booe interview.

55. *Arkansas Gazette,* 24 September 1958; Brewer, "Embattled Ladies," 13. (Brewer erroneously identifies Mrs. Sam Cottrell as also

being in the picture); Elise Cottrell to Ada May Smith, 6 January 1959, Box I, File 7, WEC Files, Arkansas History Commission. The letter, with "Mrs. Samuel Cottrell" as the letterhead, described Cottrell's fund-raising from two friends in Fayetteville, Mrs. LeMon Clark and Mrs. Delbert Swartz, and suggested that Brewer contact Mrs. Guerdon Nichols about starting a group there.

56. Brewer, "Embattled Ladies," 19.

57. Minutes of the September 23, 1958, WEC meeting, File 1, Box 2 and File 5, Box 1, WEC Files. Wixom's husband was on the faculty at the medical school and had tutored one of the Little Rock Nine, Ernest Green, in physics the year before.

58. Brewer, "Embattled Ladies," 19.

59. Ibid., 23–24.

60. Terry calendar-diary, 17 September 1958.

61. Brewer, "Embattled Ladies," 17.

62. Ibid., 16–17. "Governor Tells Plan for Private Schools," *Arkansas Gazette,* 19 September 1958.

63. Brewer, "Embattled Ladies," 20.

64. Ibid., 20–21; *Arkansas Gazette,* 26 September 1958. Although Brewer's account lists Maurice Mitchell as one of the lawyers who appeared, the *Arkansas Gazette* account identifies Lester as being on the program instead. Daisy Bates, in *The Long Shadow of Little Rock,* calls Bill Hadley one of the "white casualties" of the first year of integration. He later moved to Washington, D.C.

65. Terry calendar-diary, 25 September 1958.

66. Brewer, "Embattled Ladies," 20–21.

67. Bob Shults interview.

68. Terry calendar-diary, 26 September 1958.

69. Brewer, "Embattled Ladies," 22.

70. Terry calendar-diary, 30 September 1958.

71. *Arkansas Gazette, Crisis in the South,* 100; Bates interview.

72. *Arkansas Gazette, Crisis in the South,* 100; "U.S. Court Extends School Leasing Ban to Oct. 15 Hearing," *Arkansas Gazette,* 7 October 1958.

73. "Private School May Get Start by Next Week," *Arkansas Gazette,* 17 October 1958; "Private Firm Says Senior Registration to Start Monday," *Arkansas Gazette,* 18 October 1958.

74. *Arkansas Gazette, Crisis in the South,* 102; 4 February 1959 testimony in federal court by Superintendent Terrell E. Powell.

# Chapter 5 / Breaking the Silence

1. Brewer, "Embattled Ladies," 40.
2. Ibid.
3. Interview with Irene Samuel by author, 21 July 1992.
4. Interview with Jane Mendel by author, 10 June 1992. The club referred to was the Jewish Westwood Country Club.
5. Mendel interview.
6. Samuel interview, 21 July 1992.
7. Pat House made this point in a joint interview with Irene Samuel by author, 4 June 1992.
8. Interview with Parma Basham by author, 24 September 1992.
9. Mendel interview.
10. Ibid.
11. Interview with Pat House by author, 7 July 1992.
12. Interview with Margaret Kolb by author, 13 June 1992.
13. Ibid.
14. Ibid.; telephone interview with Irene Samuel by author, 21 October 1994.
15. Kolb interview.
16. Ibid.
17. Interview with Mamie Ruth Williams by author, 3 July 1992.
18. Ibid.
19. Interview with Mamie Ruth Williams by author, 16 August 1993.
20. Williams interviews.
21. Brewer, "Embattled Ladies," 41.
22. Ibid., 51.
23. Ibid., 41–43.
24. Blossom, *It Has Happened Here,* 185.
25. Ibid.
26. Interview with Frank Lambright by author, 21 August 1992.
27. *Arkansas Gazette, Crisis in the South,* 101; Brewer, "Embattled Ladies," 37–38.
28. *Life,* 7 October 1957, 38–48.
29. *Arkansas Gazette,* 19 October 1958.
30. Interview with William F. Rector by John Pagan, 2 January 1973.
31. Rector interview by Pagan.
32. Grainger Williams interview.
33. Brewer, "Embattled Ladies," 44–45; Rector interview by Pagan.

34. Brewer, "Embattled Ladies," 45.

35. Ibid., 46.

36. Ibid., 47.

37. Interview with Adolphine Terry by John Pagan, 2 January 1973; Brewer, "Embattled Ladies," 47; Grainger Williams interview.

38. Brewer, "Embattled Ladies," 48.

39. Dunaway interview, 18 August 1992.

40. Samuel/House interview, 4 June 1992; Brewer, "Embattled Ladies," 50.

41. Brewer, "Embattled Ladies," 54–57.

42. Interview with Irene Samuel and Pat House by author, 21 May 1992; Brewer, "Embattled Ladies," 84–85.

43. Billie Wilson Papers, Special Collections Division, University of Arkansas Libraries, Fayetteville.

44. Grainger Williams interview.

45. E. Grainger Williams Papers, A–33, Box 1, Archives and Special Collections, University of Arkansas at Little Rock Library.

46. Grainger Williams interview.

47. Copy "A"–"C," E. Grainger Williams Papers; *Arkansas Gazette,* 3 March 1959; Grainger Williams interview.

48. Letter to the *(Arkansas Gazette)* editor, undated, E. Grainger Williams Papers.

49. Frances Williams interview.

50. Terry calendar-diary, undated clipping from a publication that notes that "she formed the Women's Emergency Committee, with 48 members, to fight the rabble rousers on radio and television, with fliers and house-to-house survey. Today the WEC has 1,600 members."

## Chapter 6 / Barefooted and Pregnant

1. Eleanor Reid to Adolphine Terry, 17 December 1958, Adolphine Terry letters, Fletcher-Terry Papers.

2. Interview with Eleanor Reid by author, 11 June 1992; interview with Eleanor Reid by Charlotte Gadberry, 19 April 1978, Arkansas Women's Oral History Project, Archives and Special Collections, University of Arkansas at Little Rock Library.

3. Reid to Terry, 17 December 1958.

4. "How Faubus Used State Police," *Arkansas Gazette,* 3 June 1979.

5. Samuel/House interview, 4 June 1992; Spitzberg, *Racial Politics,* 87.

6. Samuel/House interview, 4 June 1992.

7. Roy Reed,"Crisis Created Female Political Force," *Arkansas Gazette,* 7 January 1962, E1.

8. *Arkansas Gazette,* 28 August 1963.

9. *Arkansas Gazette,* 30 August 1963.

10. Reid interview by Gadberry.

11. Pat House, Legislative Notes, WEC Files.

12. Ibid.

13. House interview.

14. Interview with Pat House, B9, Arkansas Women's Oral History Project, 1973, Archives and Special Collections, University of Arkansas at Little Rock Library.

15. Ibid.

16. Brewer, "Embattled Ladies," 76.

17. Ibid.

18. "Tyler's Bill Derailed," *Arkansas Gazette,* 3 March 1959. The subsequent account is taken from this news story.

19. Ibid.

20. Brewer, "Embattled Ladies, 78; Spitzberg, *Racial Politics,* 106–7.

21. Interview with Willie Oates by author, 24 August 1992.

22. Ibid.

23. Ibid.

24. Brewer, "Embattled Ladies," Appendix 31, "Why We Are Opposed to Another Term for Willie Oates."

25. Oates interview.

26. "Effect of the Little Rock School Situation on Local Business," survey conducted by Social and Economic Issues Committee of the American Association of University Women (Little Rock Branch), 24 January 1959, Box 5, File 3, Fletcher-Terry Papers.

27. "Letter from Little Rock," WEC Files.

28. "Coffelt Files Suit to Stop CHS Closing," *Arkansas Gazette,* 13 September 1958; Brewer, "Embattled Ladies," 87.

29. "Women Reply to Second Request from Langford," *Arkansas Gazette,* 24 April 1958.

30. WEC Files.

31. Brewer, "Embattled Ladies," 88–90.

32. Ibid., 92.

33. Ibid., 99.

34. Ibid., 103. Copy of the entire correspondence between Langford and the WEC is included in "Embattled Ladies."

35. Ibid., 93.

36. Ibid., 104–7.

## Chapter 7 / A Question of Conscience

1. Paul Mertz, "'Mind Changing Time All Over Georgia': HOPE, Inc. and School Desegregation, 1958–1961," *Georgia Historical Quarterly* 77 (spring 1993).

2. "Virginia Integration Woes Said Unlike Little Rock's," *Arkansas Gazette,* clipping (no date), Billie Wilson Papers. WEC minutes for 3 March 1959, say that Lightsey spoke to the WEC board the week before.

3. Mertz, "Mind Changing Time All Over Georgia," 49.

4. Billie Wilson, "Report to the W.E.C. on the Atlanta Trip," Billie Wilson Papers.

5. Billie Wilson to Fran Breeden, 23 February 1959, Billie Wilson Papers.

6. Billie Wilson to Fran Breeden, 26 February 1959, Billie Wilson Papers.

7. Ibid.

8. Original "Talk at Atlanta" speech written by Billie Wilson, Billie Wilson Papers.

9. "Effects on School Closing," speech by Mrs. Gordon N. Wilson, Women's Emergency Committee to Open Our Schools, Little Rock, Ark., 4 March 1959, Billie Wilson Papers.

10. Speech actually given in Atlanta after being edited by HOPE, Billie Wilson Papers.

11. Wilson, "Report to W.E.C."

12. Mertz, "Mind Changing Time," 52–60.

13 Ralph McGill to Sharon Wilson, 5 March 1959, Billie Wilson Papers.

14. *Atlanta Constitution,* 3 March 1958, Billie Wilson Papers.

15. Letter to the Editor, "Little Rock Doing Well, He Contends," *Atlanta Journal,* 10 March 1959.

16. "Report from Atlanta," *Arkansas Democrat,* undated news clipping, Billie Wilson Papers.

17. Anonymous letter, Billie Wilson Papers.

18. Mrs. D. W. Holland to Billie Wilson, 1 April 1959, Billie Wilson Papers.

19. *Arkansas Gazette, Crisis in the South*, 25.

20. Interview with Billie Wilson and Gwen Booe by author, 3 June 1992.

21. Ibid.

22. Undated copy of advertisement, Billie Wilson Papers.

23. *Memphis Commercial Appeal*, Arkansas edition, 6 December 1958.

24. Interview with Sharon Wilson Adair by author, 9 December 1992.

25. Ibid.

26. Mimi Dortch, *1993 Arkansas Interfaith Conference* (summer 1993), videotape.

27. Interview with Dick Hardie by Mimi Dortch, *1993 Arkansas Interfaith Conference*.

28. "History of the Presbytery of Arkansas," (Little Rock, Ark.: Presbytery Office, 1994).

29. Ernest Trice Thompson, *Through the Ages, A History of the Christian Church* (Richmond, Va.: Covenant Life Curriculum, 1965).

30. "History of the Presbytery of Arkansas."

31. Notes on Murphy family members made by Mary Bailey Alderman, the author's aunt, now in the possession of the Murphy family.

32. *Arkansas Gazette, Crisis in the South;* Bates, *Long Shadow of Little Rock*, 190–95.

33. Campbell and Pettigrew, *Christians in Racial Crisis*, 112–13.

34. "'Courage' Poke Draws Replies from Pastors," *Arkansas Gazette,* 3 September 1958.

35. Campbell and Pettigrew, *Christians in Racial Crisis*, 32.

36. Aldersgate meeting, Box 15:3, File 540:5, Orval Faubus Papers, Special Collection Division, University of Arkansas Libraries, Fayetteville.

37. "Segregation Group Formed by Methodists," *Arkansas Gazette,* 14 October 1958, 1B.

38. Interview with Colbert Cartwright by Mimi Dortch, *1993 Arkansas Interfaith Conference*.

39. Ibid.

40. Interview with Rev. Dale Cowling by Mimi Dortch, *1993 Arkansas Interfaith Conference*.

41. "Negro Plans Another Try at Attending White Church," *Arkansas Gazette,* 15 October 1958.

42. "Two Ministers, Board of Church Urge Vote for Reopening Schools," *Arkansas Gazette,* 22 September 1958.

43. Telephone interview with Margaret Morrison by author, 19 June 1992.

44. Greater Atlanta, Georgia, Council of Churches, "Out of Conviction: A Second Statement on the South's Racial Crisis," signed by 312 ministers, November 1958 brochure, Billie Wilson Papers.

45. Henry Alexander, *Little Rock Recall Election* (New Brunswick, N.J.: Eagleton Institute of Politics, Rutgers University, 1960), 7.

# Chapter 8 / Stop This Outrageous Purge

1. *Arkansas Gazette,* 8 February 1959; Brewer, "Embattled Ladies," 112.

2. *Arkansas Gazette,* 9 February 1959.

3. "Faubus Would Fire Trio on Purge List; Plans New Aid Bill," *Arkansas Gazette,* 10 February 1959.

4. "Rowland Says He's for Purge of 3, or More," *Arkansas Gazette,* 10 February 1959, 1–2.

5. Huckaby, *Crisis at Central High,* 157–58.

6. Ibid., 157.

7. *Arkansas Gazette,* 10 December 1958.

8. *Arkansas Gazette, Crisis in the South,* 9.

9. *Arkansas Gazette,* 25 April 1959, 6.

10. "Teachers Turn in Affidavits; Officials Plan Check Later," *Arkansas Gazette,* 15 April 1959; Brewer, "Embattled Ladies," 119.

11. Bobbie Forster, "Ways to Community Acceptance of Integration Weighed by Panel," *Arkansas Democrat,* 4 February 1959.

12. Brewer, "Embattled Ladies," 110; Interview with Carroll Holcomb by author, August 24, 1994. Holcomb suggested that the Longs did not contest the dismissal for personal reasons, preferring simply to leave.

13. "Minimum Plan Approved by 819–245 Vote," *Arkansas Gazette,* 3 March 1959.

14. Copy "A"–"C," a summary of action by the Chamber of Commerce, A–33, Box 1–1, E. Grainger Williams Papers; "Minimum Plan Approved by 819–245 Vote," *Arkansas Gazette;* Alexander, *Recall Election,* 10.

15. Earlier larger estimates of WEC participants included those who had attended meetings and worked in some capacity, some of whom had not paid dues.

16. WEC minutes, 5 May 1959.

17. Brewer, "Embattled Ladies," 123; interview with Billie Wilson by author, 3 June 1992; Samuel/House interview.

18. "Teacher Purge Begun by Three Board Members," *Arkansas Gazette,* 6 May 1959.

19. Brewer, "Embattled Ladies," 124.

20. "Teacher Organizations Call Action Illegal; Suit Planned," *Arkansas Gazette,* 6 May 1959.

21. "Here's List of Teachers Under Fire," *Arkansas Gazette,* 6 May 1959.

22. "ALC's Probe May be Source of Purge List," *Arkansas Gazette,* 8 May 1959, 2A.

23. Wilson interview.

24. Alexander, *Recall Election,* 14.

25. "Teacher Purge Begun by Three Board Members," *Arkansas Gazette;* "Group Shows Teacher Trust," *Arkansas Gazette,* 6 May 1959, 2.

26. "Teacher Organizations Call Action Illegal; Suit Planned," *Arkansas Gazette.*

27. "PTA Council, Irked by 'Purge,' Pushes Recall," *Arkansas Democrat,* 6 May 1959; "School, Civic Groups Assail Purge Attempt," *Arkansas Gazette,* 7 May 1959.

28. Alexander, *Recall Election,* 14.

29. Ibid., 6.

30. "School, Civil Groups Assail Purge Attempt," *Arkansas Gazette.*

31. *Arkansas Gazette,* 6 May 1959.

32. "Some Teachers Talk Walkout," *Arkansas Gazette,* 6 May 1959.

33. Wilson interview.

34. Alexander, *Recall Election,* 15.

35. Wilson interview.

36. Alexander, *Recall Election,* 15–16; *Arkansas Gazette,* 7 May 1959.

37. Alexander, *Recall Election,* 17.

38. "Petitions Circulate to Recall Purgers as Protests Swell," *Arkansas Gazette,* 8 May 1959.

39. Alexander, *Recall Election,* 17–18.

40. Ibid., 18.

41. Ibid.

42. "Foes of Recall Proposal Get Brushoff at Forest Heights," *Arkansas Gazette,* 8 May 1959.

43. "75 Walk Out on McKinley at Angry School Ceremony," *Arkansas Gazette,* 8 May 1959.

44. Billie Wilson to Mrs. Prater, principal at Hardin Bale, 19 May 1959, Billie Wilson Papers. Wilson also wrote letters of apology to John and Mary Ella Bale (the school was named for his father) and to "Connie," who apparently was the PTA president.

45. "Bale," *Arkansas Gazette,* 8 May 1959, 5A.

46. "Tucker Asks Three to Offer Plan," *Arkansas Gazette,* 9 May 1959.

47. "Chronology of WEC part in STOP," WEC Files.

48. Alexander, *Recall Election,* 18.

49. "Leading Citizens Organize 'STOP' to Combat Purge," *Arkansas Gazette,* 9 May 1959.

50. Samuel/House interview, 4 June 1992.

51. Brewer, "Embattled Ladies," 126.

52. Shults interviews.

53. "Leading Citizens Organize 'STOP' to Combat Purge," *Arkansas Gazette;* "Recall Picks Up Momentum as 'STOP' Opens It's [*sic*] Office, Starts Signature Campaign," *Arkansas Democrat,* 9 May 1959.

54. "Recall Vote Backers May File Tomorrow New Petitions Show," *Arkansas Gazette,* 10 May 1959; "Mothers League Seeks Recall of Matson, Lamb, Tucker; 2 on Board Explain Firings," *Arkansas Democrat,* 10 May 1959.

55. Alexander, *Recall Election,* 22.

56. Ibid., 21.

57. "Signers Hit 8,000 Mark as STOP Pushes Drive," *Arkansas Democrat,* 11 May 1959.

58. "Chronology of WEC effort in STOP," Irene Samuel account, WEC Files.

59. Alexander, *Recall Election,* 21.

60. Ibid., 24.

61. "McKinley Says Purge Victims 'Integrationists,'" *Arkansas Gazette,* 10 May 1959; "Attorney Defends Teachers," *Arkansas Democrat,* 21 May 1959; CROSS advertisement, *Arkansas Democrat,* 21 May 1959; "Purged Teachers Threaten Lawsuit," *Arkansas Gazette,* 22 May 1959; editorial entitled "Reasons for Firing Teachers," *Arkansas Gazette,* 22 May 1959; Brewer, "Embattled Ladies," 128.

62. "CHS Mothers Aim at Matson, Tucker, Lamb," *Arkansas Gazette,* 10 May 1959.

63. "STOP list," Billie Wilson Papers.

64. Samuel/House interview, 4 June 1992; Alexander, *Recall Election,* 19, 24.

65. Samuel/House interview, 4 June 1992; Alexander, *Recall Election,* 23–26.

66. "Effort to Disrupt STOP Rally Foiled"and "Negro Teachers Honored at Rally Attended by 500," *Arkansas Gazette,* 20 May 1959; Alexander, *Recall Election,* 27–28.

67. *Arkansas Gazette,* 25 May 1959.

68. Interview with Jo Jackson by author, 3 June 1992.

69. Ibid.

70. "Governor Comes Out for McKinley Slate," *Arkansas Gazette,* 23 May 1959.

71. Brewer, "Embattled Ladies," 132. She quotes a letter from Ralph Gray, Winston C. Beard, and William T. Greenwood to the editor of the *Arkansas Gazette.*

72. Ibid.

## Chapter 9 / A Community Divided

1. *Arkansas Gazette,* 26 May 1959.

2. Samuel/House interview, 4 June 1992.

3. Alexander, *Recall Election,* 30.

4. Ibid., 30–31.

5. Woods interview.

6. Spitzberg, *Racial Politics,* 18.

7. Alexander, *Recall Election,* 26.

8. Ibid., 29.

9. Ibid.; House interview.

10. Spitzberg, *Racial Politics,* 29.

11. Woods interview.

12. Author's conversation with Marilyn Criner, summer 1992.

13. *Arkansas Gazette,* 27 May 1959.

14. *Arkansas Gazette,* 25 June 1959.

15. Brewer, "Embattled Ladies," 134–35; Spitzberg, *Racial Politics,* 111.

16. Brewer, "Embattled Ladies," 135.

17. *Arkansas Gazette,* 16 June 1959. Henry L. Hubbard was appointed but ineligible to serve.

18. *Arkansas Gazette,* 8 July 1959.

19. "Board Takes Steps to Reopen Schools as Vacancy Filled," *Arkansas Gazette,* 10 July 1959; Brewer, "Embattled Ladies," 135.

20. "Teacher Purge Expunged; New Board Keeps Powell, Hubbard Gives up Post," *Arkansas Gazette,* 16 June 1959.

21. "School Officials Study Norfolk Plan, Tucker Says Little Rock Has Choice," *Arkansas Gazette,* 17 July 1959, 1B.

22. "Pupil Assignment Has Met the Test," *Arkansas Gazette,* 21 June 1959.

23. Brewer, "Embattled Ladies," 136–39. The notes on the meeting were made and then typed up by a WEC member, but Brewer did not recall who it was.

24. Brewer, "Embattled Ladies," 136–39.

25. Ibid., 139.

26. Ibid., 142–43.

27. Ibid., 144.

28. Ibid., 147.

29. Ibid., 148.

30. Ibid., 151–52.

31. Ibid., 150.

32. Ibid., 150.

33. Ibid., 151

34. *Arkansas Gazette, Crisis in the South,* 54.

35. Williamson interview.

36. Ibid.

37. Ibid.

38. "The Peaceful Operation of Our Free Schools," *Arkansas Gazette,* 19 July 1959.

39. "Civic Leaders Stress Stand for Schools," *Arkansas Gazette,* 30 July 1959.

40. Gaston Williamson, "Committee for the Peaceful Operation of Our Free Public Schools, Statement by Chairman." The statement is dated July 30, 1959, in ink, but the meeting where it was given actually occurred July 29 and was covered by the *Arkansas Gazette* in the story "Civic Leaders Stress Stand for Schools"; all in Sara Murphy Papers.

41. Gaston Williamson, "The Reopening of Little Rock's High Schools," Statement for Commission on Civil Rights, Gatlinburg, North Carolina. Again, the date was wrong on the paper because it cites events up through December 1959. The date given is March 21, 1959, but it appears to have been March 21, 1960; all in Sara Murphy Papers.

42. "Segregationist Leader Vows All-out Fight," *Arkansas Gazette,* 15 July 1959.

43. "From the People," *Arkansas Gazette,* 9 June 1959.

44. Billie Wilson to the Editor of the *Arkansas Gazette,* 16 June 1959, Billie Wilson Papers.

45. *Arkansas Gazette,* 23 July 1959.

46. *Southern School News,* September 1959, 1.

47. Brewer, "Embattled Ladies," 155–56.

48. *Southern School News,* September 1959, 1; Brewer, "Embattled Ladies," 164.

49. Brewer, "Embattled Ladies," 162–64.

50. *Arkansas Gazette, Crisis in the South,* 56.

51. *Southern School News,* September 1959, 2; *Arkansas Gazette, Crisis in the South,* 57.

52. *Southern School News,* September 1959, 2; *Arkansas Gazette,* 7 August 1959.

53. "Faubus Discourages Violence; Struggle Was Lost at Polls," *Arkansas Gazette,* 12 August 1959; *Southern School News,* September 1959, 2.

54. Brewer, "Embattled Ladies," 165–66.

55. *Arkansas Gazette,* 12 August 1959.

56. *Arkansas Democrat,* 12 August 1959. *Southern School News,* September 1959, 2.

57. Brewer, "Embattled Ladies," 166.

58. Spitzberg, *Racial Politics,* 111–19; "Police Arrest 24 in Wake of Rally, Fight Near Central," *Arkansas Gazette,* 13 August 1959, 1B.

59. "Segregationist Duo Seeks Funds, Deplores Brutality," *Arkansas Gazette,* 14 August 1959, 3A; *Southern School News,* September 1959, 2.

60. *Arkansas Gazette,* 14 August 1959.

61. *Arkansas Gazette, Crisis in the South,* 58–59.

62. "City Board Backs Police, Asks Probe of Criticisms," *Arkansas Democrat,* 19 August 1959, 15; *Southern School News,* September 1959, 15.

63. "Little Rock Police Department Gets Much Mail, Runs About 2 to 1 in Favor of the Way the Police Handled the Mob," *Arkansas Gazette,* 19 August 1959; *Southern School News,* September 1959, 15.

64. "Parent Says Integration in Class Not Required," *Arkansas Gazette,* 16 August 1959; Brewer, "Embattled Ladies," Appendix 9.

65. *Arkansas Gazette,* 2 August 1959.

66. *The Progressive,* December 1959, 7.

67. Brewer, "Embattled Ladies," 180–84, 193.

68. Ibid., 194; *Southern School News,* October 1959, 2.

69. "Dynamite Tossers Damage Three Little Rock Targets," *Arkansas Gazette,* 8 September 1959; Brewer, "Embattled Ladies," 194–97; *Southern School News,* October 1959, 2.

70. "Bombings Bring Irate Response at Little Rock," *Arkansas Gazette,* 9 September 1959.

71. Grainger Williams interview.

72. *Southern School News,* October 1959, 2; Brewer, "Embattled Ladies," 195–97.

## Chapter 10 / To the Ladies, God Bless 'Em

1. WEC board minutes, 8 October 1959; Brewer, "Embattled Ladies," 215–26.

2. Dr. Malcolm G. Taylor, president, Capital Citizens Council, to Miss Loretta Young, NBC TV, 18 December 1959 , WEC Files.

3. *Arkansas Gazette,* 20 December 1959.

4. Brewer, "Embattled Ladies," 222.

5. Brewer, "Embattled Ladies," 201–3.

6. WEC board minutes, 1963, Box 2, File 1, WEC files.

7. Brewer, "Embattled Ladies," 208–9; *Southern School News,* December 1959, 3.

8. *Southern School News,* January 1960, 5.

9. Brewer, "Embattled Ladies," 210–12; Everett Tucker to Vivion Brewer, 4 December 1959, and Henry Woods to Vivion Brewer, 3 December 1959, WEC Files.

10. WEC "Letter From Little Rock," December 1959, WEC Files.

11. Brewer, "Embattled Ladies," 75–77.

12. Ibid., 228–29.

13. Ibid., 233–35; WEC Minutes, February 1960, WEC Files.

14. WEC newsletter, December 1960, WEC Files.

15. WEC letter, 19 January 1961, WEC Files.

16. Brewer, "Embattled Ladies," Appendix 28.

17. Ibid., 244.

18. Ibid., 245–46.

19. WEC board minutes, 13 September 1960, WEC Files.

20. Brewer, "Embattled Ladies," 272–73.

21. Jackson interview.

22. Wilson/Booe interview.

23. Minutes of planning committee meetings; Conference on Community Unity agenda, 20 February 1960; Box 31, File 319, Arkansas Council on Human Relations Collection, Special Collections Division, University of Arkansas Libraries, Fayetteville.

24. Frances Williams interview.

25. "Conference on Community Unity," Camp Aldersgate, 20 February 1960, Billie Wilson Papers.

26. "Conference on Community Unity" report, 15–16.

27. Ibid.

28. Minutes of evaluation committee meeting, 11 May 1960; Box 31, File 319, Arkansas Council on Human Relations Collection.

29. Brewer, "Embattled Ladies," 81.

30. Interview with Pat Youngdahl by author, 17 November 1994.

31. "How Faubus Used State Police," *Arkansas Gazette,* 3 June 1979.

32. State police reports, Box 14, File 9, Orval Faubus Papers.

33. "Crisis Created Female Political Force," *Arkansas Gazette,* 7 January 1962.

34. This is taken from an account the author wrote in 1963 on the political environment in Little Rock, now in possession of the Murphy family.

35. *Arkansas Gazette,* 7 January 1962.

# Chapter 11 / They Would Bow Their Heads

1. In fact, he had been declared so in a *U.S. News and World Report* survey.

2. *Southern School News,* December 1962, 11.

3. WEC board minutes, 5 September 1962, WEC Files.

4. WEC board minutes, 8 May 1963, WEC Files.

5. Ibid.

6. Interview with Pat Youngdahl by author, 20 November 1994.

7. Ibid.

8. Brewer, "Embattled Ladies," 277; *Southern School News,* December 1963, 7.

9. Mamie Ruth Williams interview, 16 August 1993.

10. "Rozell Blueprint Aims at $57 million," *Arkansas Democrat,* 3 November 1963.

11. *Arkansas Democrat,* 3 November 1963.

12. *Arkansas Gazette,* 3 November 1963, 3A.

13. *Pine Bluff Commercial,* 5 November 1963.

14. *Arkansas Gazette,* 5 November 1963.

## Chapter 12 / Panel of American Women

1. This is taken from an account the author wrote in 1964 on the history of the panel in Little Rock.

2. *Arkansas Gazette,* 10 October 1963, 6A.

## Epilogue

1. These words appear on a plaque at the Adolphine Fletcher Terry Library opened in 1990. The Decorative Arts Museum was opened in 1981.

# Bibliography

## Archives

Archives and Special Collections, University of Arkansas at Little Rock
Library
Arkansas Women's Oral History Project
Fletcher–Terry Papers
Little Rock Crisis Papers
Little Rock Housing Authority Scrapbooks
Reports of the Association of Southern Women for the Prevention
of Lynching
E. Grainger Williams Papers

Arkansas History Commission, Little Rock
WEC Files

Library of Congress, Washington, D.C.
Urban League File

Smith College, Northampton, Massachusetts
Vivion Brewer Papers

Special Collections Division, University of Arkansas Libraries, Fayetteville
Arkansas Council on Human Relations Collection
Orval Faubus Papers
Sara Murphy Papers
Billie Wilson Papers

## Interviews

*The following are personal interviews conducted by the author unless
otherwise indicated.*

Annie Abrams, 19 May 1993.
Sharon Wilson Adair, 9 December 1992.

Harry Ashmore, 13 June 1994.
Parma Basham, 24 September 1992.
Daisy Bates, 16 April 1992.
Gwen Booe, 3 June 1992.
Gwen Booe and Billie Wilson, 3 June 1992.
Charles Bussey, 19 May, 30 August 1993.
Fred Darragh, 27 May 1993.
Edwin Dunaway, 18 August 1992, 22 June 1993.
Orval Faubus, 19 August 1992.
Ernest Green, Washington, D.C., 7 December 1992.
Carroll Holcombe, 24 August 1994.
Pat House, 7 July 1992.
Pat House and Irene Samuel, 21 May, 4 June 1992.
Sammie Dean Parker Hulett, Dallas, Texas, 9 December 1992.
James Humphrey, 16 August 1993.
Jo Jackson, 3 June 1992.
Charles Johnston, 4 November 1994.
Margaret Kolb, 13 June 1992.
Frank Lambright, 18, 21 August 1992.
Hazel Massery, 27 July 1992.
Jane Mendel, 10 June 1992.
Margaret Morrison (telephone), 19 June 1992.
Willie Oates, 24 August 1992.
Ruth Arnold Ray, 12 June 1992.
William F. Rector (by John Pagan), 2 January 1973.
Eleanor Reid, 11 June 1992.
Eleanor Reid (by Charlotte Gadberry), 19 April 1978.
Irene Samuel, 21 July 1992, 14 August 1993, (telephone) 21 October 1994.
Bill Shelton, 1 December 1993.
Barbara Shults, 9 October 1992.
Bob Shults, 9 October 1992.
Adolphine Terry (by John Pagan), January 1973.
Betty Terry, 13 August 1992.
Mildred Terry, 17 November 1993.
Sanford Tollette, 13 August 1993.
Evangeline Upshur, 23 July 1992.
Frances Williams, 5 August 1992.
Grainger Williams, 29 July 1992.
Mamie Ruth Williams, 3 July 1992, 16 August 1993.
Gaston Williamson, 10 December 1993.
Billie Wilson, 3 June 1992.
Vircie Winstead, 7 September 1993.

Henry Woods, 30 August 1992.
Pat Youngdahl, 17, 20 November 1994.

# Newspapers

*Arkansas Democrat*
*Arkansas Gazette*
*Arkansas Times*
*Atlanta Journal*
*Memphis Commercial Appeal*
*Pine Bluff Commercial*
*The Progressive*
*Southern Education News Reports*
*Southern School News*
*The State Press*

# Other Sources

## Books

Alexander, Henry. *Little Rock Recall Election*. New Brunswick, N.J.:
    Rutgers University, Eagleton Institute of Politics, 1960.
*Arkansas Gazette. Crisis in the South, The Little Rock Story. Arkansas
    Gazette,* 1958.
Ashmore, Harry. *Civil Rights and Wrongs*. New York: Pantheon Books,
    1994.
————. *Hearts and Minds: The Anatomy of Racism from Roosevelt to Reagan.*
    New York: McGraw Hill, 1982.
Bartley, Numan V. *The Rise of Massive Resistance: Race and Politics in the
    South During the 1950s*. Baton Rouge: Louisiana State University
    Press, 1969.
Bates, Daisy. *The Long Shadow of Little Rock.* 1962. Reprint, Fayetteville:
    University of Arkansas Press, 1987.
Beals, Melba Patillo. *Warriors Don't Cry*. New York: Simon & Schuster,
    1994.
Blossom, Virgil. *It Has Happened Here*. New York: Harper Brothers,
    1959.
Branch, Taylor. *Parting the Waters: America in the King Years 1954–63.*
    New York: Simon & Schuster, 1988.

Campbell, Ernest Q., and Thomas F. Pettigrew. *Christians in Racial Crisis: A Study of Little Rock's Ministry.* Washington, D.C.: Public Affairs Press, 1959.

Faubus, Orval Eugene. *Down From the Hills.* Little Rock: Pioneer Press, 1980.

Fletcher, John Gould. *Arkansas.* 1947. Reprint, Fayetteville: University of Arkansas Press, 1989.

———. *The Autobiography of John Gould Fletcher.* 1937. Reprint, Fayetteville: University of Arkansas Press, 1988.

Friedan, Betty. *The Feminine Mystique.* New York: Dell Publishing Company, 1963.

Haldeman-Julius, Marcet. *The Story of a Lynching.* Little Blue Book, no. 1260. Girard, Kans.: Haldeman-Julius Publications, no date.

Hall, Jacqueline. *Revolt Against Chivalry, Jessie Daniel Ames and the Women's Campaign Against Lynching.* New York: Columbia University Press, 1979.

Huckaby, Elizabeth. *Crisis at Central High: Little Rock 1957–58.* Baton Rouge: Louisiana State University Press, 1980.

Jacoway, Elizabeth, and David R. Colburn eds.. *Southern Businessmen and Desegregation.* Baton Rouge: Louisiana State University Press, 1982.

Loveland, Anne C. *Lillian Smith, A Southerner Confronting the South.* Baton Rouge: Louisiana State University Press, 1986.

Murphy, Sara. "Education." In *Arkansas: State of Transition,* ed. Louis Guida. N.p.: Legal Services Corporation, 1981.

Myrdal, Gunnar. *An American Dilemma.* New York: Harper & Row, 1944.

Record, Wilson, and Jane Cassels Record. *Little Rock, U.S.A.* San Francisco: Chandler Publishing Company, 1960.

Smith, Lillian. *Killers of the Dream.* New York: W. W. Norton, 1978.

Spitzberg, Irving. *Racial Politics in Little Rock 1954–1964.* New York: Garland Publishing Company, 1987.

Terry, Adolphine Fletcher. *Charlotte Stephens: Little Rock's First Black Teacher.* Litttle Rock: Academic Press of Arkansas, 1973.

———. *Cordelia: Member of the Household.* Fort Smith, Ark.: South and West Press, 1967.

——— [Mary Lindsey, pseud.]. *Courage.* New York: E. P. Dutton, 1938.

Thompson, Ernest Trice. *Through the Ages, A History of the Christian Church.* Richmond, Va.: Covenant Life Curriculum, 1965.

## Articles

Bartley, Numan V. "Looking Back at Little Rock." *Arkansas Historical Quarterly* 25 (summer 1966).

Eison, James Reed. "Dead But She Was in a Good Place." *Pulaski County Historical Review* (summer 1982).

Fulkerson, Betty. "The Albert Pike House . . . the House that Kept Up." *Delta Review*. January–February 1967.

McMillen, Neil R. "White Citizens' Council and Resistance to School Desegregation in Arkansas." *Arkansas Historical Quarterly* 30 (summer 1971).

Mertz, Paul E. "'Mind Changing Time All Over Georgia': HOPE, Inc. and School Desegregation, 198–1961." *Georgia Historical Quarterly* 77 (spring 1993).

"Reminiscences of Jessie Daniel Ames: 'I Really Do Like a Good Fight.'" 1964 interview with Pat Watters, transcribed and edited by Jacqueline Hall. *New South* (spring 1972).

## Theses and Other Academic Papers

Harris, Peggy. "We Would Be Building." Master's thesis, University of Arkansas at Little Rock, 1992.

Hulett, Jerry. "Sammie's Story, A Biography of Sammie Parker Hulett." Unpublished paper, University of Texas at Dallas, n.d.

Pagan, John. "Orval Eugene Faubus and the Politics of Racism." Unpublished essay, Oxford University, 1974.

Smith, Griffin. "Localism and Segregation, Racial Patterns in Little Rock, Arkansas, 1945–1954." Master's thesis, Columbia University, 1965.

## Videotape

Dortch, Mimi. *1993 Arkansas Interfaith Conference* (summer 1993).

# Index

Graham, Mrs. Nathan, 85
Gray, Alice, 73, 85, 169
Gray, Chad, 169
Green, Ernest, 47, 56–57
Griffey, Annie, 14
Griffin, Marvin, 38
Griffin, Sissy, 251
Griswold, Nat, 195
Guthridge, Amis, 38, 170, 193–94, 197–98
Guy, Walter, 58
Guy Committee, 58

Hackett, Mattie, 125
Hadley, W. H., Jr., 87
Hall, Jacqueline, quoted, 19
Hall High School, 34–35, 144, 161, 192–94, 197, 199–200, 213
Hamilton, Katherine, 118
Hammons, O. P., 124
Hardie, Richard B., Jr., 144–47
Hardin, Joe, 190, 223
Harrel, Jennie, 165
Harrel, John Allen, 227–29
Harris, Roy V., 142
Hartsfield, William B., 139
Hawkins, Lefty, 190, 196
Hay, T. B., 89, 147
Hays, Brooks, 14–15, 25, 28, 34, 48, 59, 103, 162
Hays, Steele, 14
Heiskell, J. N., 13, 28, 32, 61, 63
Help Our Public Education (HOPE), 135–41
Helveston, Anne, 190, 200
Henderson, Mrs. Russell, 148
Henry, Jo Ann, 168
Henry, Marguerite, 87
Higgins, Charles A., 134
Hill, Tommy, 144

Hoffman, Jean, 162, 166, 170
Holcomb, Carroll, 119
Horace Mann High School, 34–35, 47, 57, 157, 193
Hotze, Peter, 4
House, Archie, 43, 192
House, Byron, 121
House, Pat, 95–96, 110, 117, 123, 154, 183, 187, 192, 211–14, 231, 233–34; background of, 119–22
Housing Authority Act (1937), 20
Howell, Max, 124
Hoxie, Arkansas, 37
Hubbard, H. L., 186
Huckaby, Elizabeth, 56, 157
Hudson, Albert, 153
Hulett, Jerry, quoted, 54

Interracial Woman's Committee, 19
Ish, G. W. S., 32
Ives, Amelia B., 20

Jackson, Jo, 178–79, 214, 230, 234
Jackson, M. A., 229
Jackson, Margaret, 48, 50–51, 69, 154, 171–72, 198
Jacoway, Elizabeth, quoted, 59
Jang, Pat, 242
John Birch Society, 230
Johnson, Jim, 37–38, 65, 67, 184
Johnston, Charles, 81, 164
Johnston, Janet, 187, 198

Karam, Jimmy, 49, 103–4, 106–7, 133
KARK (Channel 4), 88
KATV (Channel 7), 87, 121

Long, Lewis, 159
*Long Shadow of Little Rock, The,* 52
Lorch, Grace, 151
Lorch, Lee, 150
lynchings, 11–13, 17–19
Lyon, Frank, 105


McClellan, John, 184–85
McClinton, I. S., 21, 177
McCullum, James, 207
McDermott, Mrs. W. P., 17
McDonald, Floella, 12
McDonald, W. C., 186
McGill, Ralph, 62, 140
McKinley, Ed I., 106–7, 150, 157,
    161–62, 164–65, 167–68,
    173–74, 179, 182, 185
McLean, Louise, 24
McLeod, John, Jr., 199
McMath, Sid, 28, 48, 116, 174,
    223–24
McRae Tuberculosis Sanatorium, 32
Mackey, B. Frank, 186, 207–9
Malakoff, Grace, 197, 200
*Man for Arkansas, A,* 224
Mann, Woodrow, 48, 103
Marion Hotel, 62–65
Marshall, Thurgood, 81
Martin, Blanche, 7–9
Martin, Paul E., 91
Matson, Russell, 106–8, 157, 161,
    167, 169, 171–72, 181, 189,
    196, 208
Matthews, Jess, 51, 157
Mehaffey, Pat, 126
*Memphis Commercial Appeal,* 3, 142,
    144
Mendel, Ed, 94
Mendel, Jane, 93–95, 177
Menkus, Jo, 93

Mertz, Paul, quoted, 136
Meyer, Sylvan, 140
Middleton, Opal, 163, 178
Mitchell, Maurice, 188
Mitchell, Will, 166, 171, 174, 184,
    187–88
Morin, Relman, quoted, 68
Morris, Dottie, 76–77, 93, 98, 109,
    130–31, 134, 190, 215
Morrison, Margaret, 106, 153–54,
    167, 207–8
Moser, M. L., Jr., 150, 173–74
Mothers League of Central High
    School, 41, 45–47, 49–51, 69,
    80, 106, 124–25, 129, 154, 161,
    171–72, 207
Murphy, Patrick C., 30, 44, 64,
    169–70, 181, 239, 251
Myrdal, Gunnar, quoted, xiii, 150


Nalley, Gann, 201
*Nashville Tennessean,* 27
*Nation,* 130
National Association for the
    Advancement of Colored
    People (NAACP), 37–38, 41, 55,
    57, 72, 129, 132, 142, 149–51,
    158, 194, 197, 218, 238
National Association for the
    Advancement of White People
    (NAAWP), 106–7, 157, 167
*New South,* 195
*New York Herald Tribune,* 151–52
*New York Post,* 52
*New York Times,* 55, 60, 66, 98, 148,
    205, 256


Oates, Gordon, 126
Oates, Willie, 79, 125–28, 213
Obsitnik, Connie, 249–50

policy and purpose statement
of, 101, 133; and political
action, 209, 212–13, 219–20,
230–33, 236; and public school
television panel, 88–90; and
state legislature, 115–18,
122–25; and STOP campaign,
157–63, 170–83, 187–94; and
1958 school board election,
105–9; and 1958 school
election, 79–82, 84–90; and
1959 school board election,
206–9

Wood, Frances Sue, 162–64, 168

Woods, Henry, 48, 65, 174–76,
182, 184, 190, 209, 224

Woodson, Pauline, 106


Yates, Richard, 121, 234

Young, Loretta, 205–6

Youngdahl, Jim, 179, 218, 231, 234

Youngdahl, Pat, 218, 231–33